Spinner

People And Culture In Southeastern Massachusetts

Volume IV

ISSN 0730-2657
ISBN 0-932027-08-3
0-932027-09-1 paperback

Acknowledgements

Spinner Publications would like to thank the following organizations and individuals whose generous support makes our publication possible.

Grant Support
Massachusetts Council on the Arts and Humanities — Merit Aid Program and Folk Arts Program
Massachusetts Foundation for Humanities and Public Policy — A state-based affiliate of the National Endowment for the Humanities
The Crapo Foundation
The Students of Southeastern Massachusetts University
The Southeastern Massachusetts University Foundation
The Polaroid Foundation
The New Bedford Arts Lottery
The AT & T Foundation
The Dartmouth Arts Lottery
The Westport Arts Lottery

Sustaining Members
Hugh Cameron
Francis Considine
Freestone's Restaurant
Janet Freedman
Jeanne Swiszcz
Long & Parent Insurance Agency

We would like to express a special thanks to Southeastern Massachusetts University. *Through its facilities, its faculty and students, Spinner has benefited greatly. In particular, we are grateful to* Dan Georgianna *and* Donna Huse. *Professor Georgianna has given valuable time in editing, writing, consulting and grant writing. Professor Huse contributed her time in grant writing, editing and consulting. She has also worked with her students in developing subject material for these pages. Jane Strillchuk and David Allen were both students of Professor Huse when they wrote their stories. Also, contract learning students Linda Donaghy and Rachel Barnet have made major contributions to this volume.*

We would also like to thank North American Printing, Inc., United Data of Providence and the New Bedford Five Cents Savings Bank *for their assistance.*

Finally we are grateful to our Subscribing and Supporting Members *for their commitment and financial support.*

Foreword

The bulk of this fourth *Spinner* volume is made up of work from the Federal Writers' Project. In many ways, the work of these Depression-era men and women parallels the work that *Spinner* has produced over the last eight years. Both attempt to record the human condition in Southeastern Massachusetts. The difference is, 50 years have given us more time to consider changes in the workplace, the effects of modern technology on traditional ways, and the impact of immigration on society.

In this volume we hear many voices. Through the Federal Writers we listen to whaler Joe Antone express indignation about his ill-treatment aboard American whaling vessels; and later, we feel his humility at being a WPA worker under investigation! We also talk and fish with Captain Nat, Tiverton Fisherman, and for a day, live a more artisan-like existence in a pre-industrial setting. With hand-line and purse-seine, we tarry off-shore to trap eels and other critters which are dragged ashore and shared with friends and family.

We also meet Captain Manuel Captiva, "The Portuguese Fisherman." With a broken-English dialect familiar to many of us, Captain Captiva speaks with pride and a bit of critical humor about his people's habits and traditions and about Portuguese assimilation in the Provincetown community.

The three captains give oral accounts of their experiences and put us closely in touch with another time and another place. In much the same way, *Spinner* writers listen to and record the stories of people living today, before they are forever lost. In this volume, we have Marsha McCabe's moving biography of Carrie Silveira, David Allen's colorful oral history with Everrett Coggeshall, and Jane Strillchuk's adventure with Ray Connors. Carrie Silveira struggles courageously between the old world of her immigrant parents and the new world of an independent woman with her own business (in the 1920s) and her own ideas. Everrett Coggeshall takes us down home in Westport — smashing stills, fixing wells, harvesting ice and peddling fruits and vegetables during the Depression. Meanwhile, Ray Connors talks of adventure, romance and bittersweet memories aboard the *Commonwealth* on the Fall River Line.

On a more contemporary note, the closing of the Berkshire/Hathaway textile mill has given *Spinner* the opportunity to address the dynamics of social change in our community. We were able to witness the immediate effects of economic decisions on people's lives. We were allowed to document the dying breath of an industry accused of being outdated, out-competed, under protected, and in some cases, milked and neglected. And yet, we heard from a workforce, primarily of immigrant stock, about family, pride in their work and loyalty to the company; we heard working managers talk of superior quality production and the potential to be competitive, given the chance to modernize and develop niches in the marketplace. Still, an industry that so dramatically affected hundreds of thousands of lives in the area closed its doors with no more than a whimper — scrapping its looms and turning manufacturing space into real estate.

Among the workers, there was obvious concern over the loss of jobs and some sadness in the breakup of a "family" of workers. Yet, some expressed relief they would be leaving a dead-end job in a vanishing trade. Said one man in the weave room, "Guess I'll go fishing."

Professor Dan Georgianna contends that the decision to close the mill rested simply with the will of capital to gain ever higher returns through financial investment. Robert Henry, on the other hand, feels that the mill closing is one more chapter in the historical movement of technological determinism, the Protestant ethic and the American aspirations toward youth and mobility. In any event, an era seems to have come to an end, with much less thunder than when it arrived.

My work with *Spinner* has given me a unique education. Recording the stories and images of the lives of people in Southeastern Massachusetts has shown me the importance of creating a "people's history." While it is true that the powerful forces behind technology, economy and the state have shaped what we think and the choices we make, it is also true that people, acting in their own interest, and carrying all their traditional, cultural and familial baggage, have in some way shaped their society to be what they believe it should be.

It is our goal at *Spinner* to continue to discover the people, the land, the sea, the workplace and the family; and to document and illustrate our findings. By learning how people have shaped history, by acting rather than reacting, we might better act upon the present, and prepare a meaningful future.

Joseph D. Thomas

Sculptural relief ornamenting the facade of the Orpheum Theater, New Bedford. Photograph by Joseph D. Thomas.

Credits

Spinner IV Production

Editing: Joseph D. Thomas
Marsha L. McCabe

Assisting Editors: Paul A. Cyr
Dan Georgianna
Donna Huse

Design: Lizanne Jones Croft

Photography: David W. Allen
Rachel Barnet
Joseph D. Thomas

Illustration: Stephen Cook
Clement E. Daley
Diedra Harris-Kelley
Robert A. Henry

Writers: David W. Allen
Paul A. Cyr
Linda Donaghy
Dan Georgianna
Robert A. Henry
Marsha L. McCabe
Jane M. Strillchuk
Joseph D. Thomas
John M. Werly

Contributing Artists and Historians: Ronald Barboza
Gardner Chace
Kenneth Champlin
Terry Deacon
Robert Demanche
Catherine Lugar
John Robson

Contributions: Jean Andrews
Eugene and Jacqueline Baer
Kim Baker
Bill Betts
Florence Brigham
Dan Brule and Associates
Louise Brule
Al Cartier
Mary Collier
Ray Connors
Robert Croft
Carl Cruz
Jack Delano
Mary Ann Gabriel
Alvin Goldwyn
John Gossen
Stacie Hallal
Bertha Hart
T. M. Holcombe
Leo Larue
Sandra Leger
James E. McKenna
Mark Mitchell
Rodman Moeller
Stanley Nowak
Lucia Paull
Anaisa Pereira
Jim Posgay
Louise Rosskam
Rick Rousseau
Veronica Russell
Al Saulnier
Manuel Silva
Frances Silveira
Priscilla Smith
Myrtle Snow

Hooten Squire
Edward Sylvia, C.P.A.
Jane Thomas
Paul Thomas
Eleanor Tripp
Eunice Turgeon
John Webster
Steve Wilson
Michael Zaritt

Berkshire/Hathaway Manufacturing Co.
Casa Da Saudade Library
Dukes County Historical Society
Fall River *Herald News*
Fall River Historical Society
Fairhaven Academy
Library of Congress
Marine Museum of Fall River
Millicent Public Library, Fairhaven
National Archives
New Bedford Free Public Library
New Bedford Whaling Museum
St. Anthony of the Desert Church
St. Lawrence Parish
Satkin Mills/Fred Satkin
Southeastern Massachusetts University
The *Standard-Times*
The *Vineyard Gazette*
Westport Public Library

Making cut glass at Pairpoint Manufacturing Company in New Bedford.

Contents

Legacy of the New Deal

Introduction

by John M. Werly

John Werly is a professor of history at Southeastern Massachusetts University. Though he has published works relating to the New Deal, he identifies himself as a generalist in American History.

The Great Depression looms in stark contrast to the prosperity which preceded it and the terrible war which followed it. Viewed as a national event, the Depression is generally dated from the Wall Street Crash in the fall of 1929, which ended the speculative mania of the Twenties, to the late 1930s. Well-known humorist Will Rogers took a dim view of the stock speculator in noting that "there is nothing that hollers as quick and as loud as a gambler. Now they know what the farmer has been up against for eight years." While the market crash did not cause the worst depression in the nation's history, it illustrated a wider economic collapse which brought the workplace to a near halt from 1929-1933. Over that period the total national income was cut in half, national unemployment rose from 3% to 25%, and an average of

200 banks failed each month, wiping out the life savings of nine million Americans.

To the laboring public, the Depression showed no mercy. Workers were forced to endure the cruel indignities of a collapse they did not create, thus aggravating prejudices they had suffered for decades. The plight of workers and organizers worsened as the years wore on. In 1933 over 200 striking workers were shot by police or by company guards.

Actually, women lost their jobs more quickly than men and were criticized for taking work away from men. One Minneapolis woman described her daily visit to the local unemployment department: "So we sit in this room like cattle, waiting for a nonexistent job, willing to work to the farthest atom of energy, unable to work, unable to get food and lodging,

unable to bear children. Here we must sit in this shame looking at the floor, worse than beasts at a slaughter."

Black workers lost their jobs before whites, in city and country alike. Southern sharecroppers were particularly devastated: infant mortality among black children was double that of whites. In 1933, 24 blacks were lynched around the country. That same year, total farm income was cut in half, surpluses mounted and banks foreclosed on mortgages at unprecedented rates. Throughout the Thirties, disastrous dust storms and drought plagued the nation's midlands.

Herbert Hoover, elected during the prosperity of the Twenties, reacted to the Depression by preaching cooperative individualism. It was his misguided belief that individuals, corporations, local governments and

The photographs on pages 3 through 7 are part of the collection of Farm Security Administraiton (FSA) and U. S. Office of War Information (OWI) photographs made under the tutelage of Roy Stryker between 1937 and 1942. A more extensive photo-essay begins on page 96 of this volume and runs through page 121.
Right: "The small farm of John Collins. He raises about six acres of vegetables and has 11 cows. To supplement his income he rents his truck out to a nearby army camp." Taunton, January 1941. Farm Security Administration photograph and caption by Jack Delano.

the media would cooperate in a selfless manner to temper their crass materialism. He urged labor and business to come together to restore confidence in the economy.

Hoover did, however, establish the setting for the New Deal by initiating legislation such as the 1932 Reconstruction Finance Act. In fact, Rexford Tugwell, braintruster for Roosevelt, later admitted that "practically the whole New Deal was extrapolated from programs that Hoover started." The public perception of their President conflicted with this revisionist interpretation, however, as hungry farmers shot jackrabbits they called "Hoover Dogs" and the urban homeless built makeshift "Hoovervilles," protecting themselves from the cold with newspapers they called "Hoover blankets."

In Southeastern Massachusetts, the Depression started earlier, was more severe and lasted much later than in the nation as a whole. The war years had brought prosperity to Southeastern Massachusetts as wartime demand for cotton, tire yarn and machine tools spurred industrial growth in the factory towns of the region. Ultimately, the great reliance on the production of cotton would bring about the decline of the one-industry economies of New Bedford and Fall River even before the '29 crash.

In Fall River and New Bedford, with a combined population exceeding 250,000, over 60,000 people were employed in the textile mills in the late Twenties. As the exodus of the mills to Southern states became endemic throughout the Thirties, the region's economy collapsed. In Fall River, between 1925 and 1940, 73 mills closed down. With its tax base eroding and thousands of textile

"Fall River, Mass. January 1941." FSA photograph by Jack Delano.

"What we did at FSA constitutes a unique episode in the history of photography. And yet, what was it precisely that we did? Was it art? Was it sociology . . . journalism . . . history? For me, it was the equivalent of two Ph.D.'s and a couple of other degrees thrown in. I know it was an education to every photographer we had, too. If I had to sum it up, I'd say, yes, it was more education than anything else. We succeeded in doing exactly what Rex Tugwell said we should do: We introduced Americans to America." — Roy Stryker, *In This Proud Land*

workers laid off, Fall River in 1931 became one of the first American cities to declare bankruptcy. The city's finances were placed in the hands of the state legislature. Social services were cut, libraries and hospitals closed — all at a time when people were most in need of assistance. Among the casualties were two Fall River cornerstones — the American Printing Company, which moved to Tennessee in 1934, and The Fall River Line, which ceased operations in 1937.

The Depression of the 1930s also humbled the New Bedford cotton textile industry so badly that the city lost nearly two-thirds of its 56 textile mills. Unemployment in New Bedford in 1937, at 32.3%, was the highest of any American city with a population over 100,000, with the exception of Scranton, PA, which was .1% higher. Not only did the Depression hit the region earlier than in most other regions, but the economic deprivation lingered longer here than in the

nation as a whole. In a 1940 survey of 102 cities conducted by the Bureau of Labor Statistics, New Bedford ranked fourth from last in percentage of workers gainfully employed.

On Cape Cod, a tourist industry was providing slight economy; in the rural and coastal areas, farmers and fishermen bartered with doctors, plumbers or anyone else, to derive a subsistence income.

When the nation went to the polls in 1932, the contrast in candidates was not one of ideas or programs but of images: Hoover as the weary, beaten man; FDR as the jaunty man of confidence, action and optimism. A taxi driver remarked, "If we can get rid of Old Gloom and put in a feller that can laugh and act human, the Depression will be half over." The results were a landslide victory for FDR with 57% of the popular and 89% of the electoral votes, setting the

"Children," Fall River, January 1941. FSA photograph by Jack Delano.

"Our goal was to record on film as much of America as we could . . . destitute migrants and average American townspeople, sharecroppers and prosperous farmers, eroded land and fertile land, human misery and human elation. Most of these people were sick, hungry and miserable. The odds were against them. Yet their goodness and strength survived." — Roy Stryker, In This Proud Land.

stage for the New Deal.

The intent of Roosevelt was never revolutionary. He sought to rebuild American corporate capitalism and reaffirm middle class values based on the ideas of the Populist and Progressive reformers of earlier eras. In fact, the New Deal often neglected the marginal and unorganized workers such as sharecroppers, migrants and slum dwellers. Racism was never directly confronted as blacks received relief while whites gained employment.

The famed Hundred Days legislation created the most dramatic impact of the FDR presidency. The new president announced in his March 4th inaugural "The only thing we have to fear is fear itself — nameless, unreasoning, unjustified terror." On the following day he closed all banks in the nation by declaring a banking holiday and called Congress into

emergency session. The pace and scope of the alphabet soup agencies created in the next three months was bewildering: the AAA passed the House in five hours, the CCC was pushed through Congress in ten days by a voice vote and the Tennessee Valley Authority and the National Industrial Recovery Act were each passed within a month. By the time Congress adjourned on June 16th, FDR had delivered 15 major addresses and 15 significant acts of legislation were law.

The Hundred Days was a small part of a long and varied presidency in which FDR responded to changes in public mood and momentum. By 1935 the leaders of the business community turned against the President and he denounced them as selfish and inconsiderate of the nation's economic health. In addition, he received added pressure from a congress elected the previous year by a more liberal constituency, from a growing and more militant union movement and from the rising popularity of demagogues such as Huey Long. The result was the so-called Second New Deal of 1935. The Emergency Relief Appropriation Act of April 1935 permitted the President to initiate enormous public works programs for the jobless such as the Works Progress Administration. The National Labor Relations Act renewed backing of the President for the principle of collective bargaining. The Social Security Act organized a system of unemployment compensation, old age retirement and survivor's insurance.

Above: WPA poster, designed by Federal Arts' Project designers, graphically heralds one tenet of the WPA. From the Library of Congress. *Right:* Boston Writers Project, hard at work, 1937. WPA photograph from the National Archives.

The Works Progress Administration (WPA) was the brainchild of Harry Hopkins who hoped to shape a comprehensive work relief program for manual laborers as well as white collar workers. In the ensuing years, the WPA built or renewed 5,900 schools, 2,500 hospitals, nearly 13,000 playgrounds and 1,000 airport landing fields. As recorded by James McKenna of the New Bedford district office, relief programs funded employment for thousands of New Bedford's unemployed and permitted the construction and improvements to the city's schools, parks, beaches, sewers, cemeteries, police, fire and water departments.

A good portion of WPA expenditures was allocated to Federal Project Number One, establishing programs in art, music, theater and writing. The Treasury Relief Art Program called for the decoration of federal buildings with murals and sculpture. The Federal Music Project was formed under Nikolai Sokoloff with the intent of employing musicians and performing for the public. The Federal Theater Project, under the tutelage of Hallie Flanagan, produced a breadth of live theater ranging from circus and vaudeville to classical, contemporary and experimental drama. The fourth concern was the Federal Writers Project, organized under the direction of journalist Henry Alsberg in the fall of 1935 to utilize the skills of unemployed white collar workers, principally writers, editors, teachers, librarians and office workers.

Originally funded with $4,400,000 and eventually granted a total of $27 million, the Writers Project was established in all 48 states, Alaska, Hawaii, Puerto Rico, New York City and the District of Columbia. Employment levels ranged from an original 2,381 to a peak of 6,686 people in April, 1936. The total, including 40% women, represented two percent of the entire WPA rolls. FWP employees dipped to 1,000 by the late fall of 1941 and the project was finally disbanded in 1943. In addition, more than 12,000 others (mostly journalists, politicians and academics) volunteered their services to the FWP as state advisory groups.

Jobs varied from standard 40 hour week office positions to more flexible research positions allowing workers to check in every couple of weeks. Some were required to produce 750 words a day, others were told to write 2,000 per week, all averaging $20 weekly. Those who gathered factual information at the local level were college students and others of white collar backgrounds, but seldom writers by trade. Some were established writers, others were rising stars. Saul Bellow, Conrad Aiken, Ralph Ellison, Claude McKay, Studs Terkel and Richard Wright were Federal Writers. Wright wrote much of his classic, *Native Son,* while employed by the FWP. Many writers, however, were often ashamed of their dependence on federal employment and sought to get off as quickly as possible.

The Federal Emergency Appropriation Act of 1939, cut off funds for the WPA, renamed that year the Work Projects Administration. The FWP was decentralized. Each state was required to establish its own projects and share the costs with locally recruited co-sponsors. The coordination of the State Writers Projects was provided by a staff in Washington and the overall organization was renamed the WPA

Writers Program. Project Director Henry Alsberg, accused of being soft on communist and other "subversive" elements on the project, was ousted by the new WPA Director, Francis C. Harrington, a former Army colonel.

As the war in Europe drew closer, the FWP shifted its attention to a planned Defense Series, including civilian defense manuals and guides

for servicemen. When the Writers Project was disbanded in 1943, wartime production was limited to a Naval Academy guide, servicemen's guides to New Orleans and Vicksburg, and several health pamphlets.

In its early years, the primary concern of the FWP was the publication of the *American Guide Series,* books focusing on local history and geography. The Guide Series recognized a growing dependence on the automobile and an improved national economy in the mid 1930s. Federal Writers traveled throughout the country to detail the sights and

Norton expresses concern for the erosion of the beautifully colored clay cliffs at Gay Head, "a national asset, as worthy of protection as Niagara and the Grand Canyon of Arizona."

The state and local guides began to appear in print in 1937, beginning with Idaho. Besides the state guides, there were 30 city guides and 20 regional publications such as *U.S. One, Maine to Florida* and *The Oregon Trail.*

Most of the guides were well-received by reviewers who noted consistent themes of optimism, national pride and diversity of people and places throughout the volumes. In part, these themes correspond to the improved domestic mood and increased nationalism resulting from growing aggression of the Germans, Italians and Japanese. In later years, John Steinbeck lauded the series in his *Travels With Charley,* referring to the authors as "the best writers in America, who were, if that is possible, more depressed than any other group while maintaining their inalienable instinct for eating." Proudly citing his ownership of a complete set of the guides, he was sorry he and his dog, Charley, didn't take them along on their tour of the nation.

As the research for the *American Guide Series* neared completion in early 1937, the FWP turned to its other major endeavor, the *American Life Series.* With the able direction of John Lomas and Benjamin Botkin, the FWP began a systematic effort to collect local folklore. Botkin developed guidelines in which he urged that those interviewed tell their stories freely and warned the interviewers to take "down everything you hear, just as you hear it, without adding, taking away or altering a syllable. Your business is to record, not to correct or

pleasures the driver might encounter. Americans began taking to the road again. The plan was to organize the material for each state in three parts: first, a series of short essays covering various aspects of the history, economy, social and cultural life; second, descriptions of most of the important cities and towns with maps of each; and third, a section detailing

road tours throughout the state.

Field workers carefully assembled data gathered from searching through archives or made from local interviews. Writers collated this material and submitted it to the state level where it was edited and revised. The central office in Washington planned to condense the state contributions into a unified national

guide, to be published in five regional volumes of about 600 pages each. Eventually, each state published its own Guide; excess usable material was set aside for local Guides and future projects.

The excerpts printed here by Lucrecia Norton on Gay Head, Nomans Land and Gosnold were planned for the local Guide Series.

improve." Through the personal observations recorded by Cape Cod writer Alice D. Kelley in "Records of Interviews with Portuguese Fisherman," we see how one writer employed those techniques and how she approached her subject.

In all, the *American Life Series* produced 150 volumes, ranging from *Baseball in Old Chicago* and *The Cape Cod Pilot* to the *Italians of New York, The Armenians of Massachusetts* and *The Negro in Virginia*. A wide variety of ethnic experiences from Southeastern Massachusetts are contained in the manuscripts, including those of the Portuguese, Irish, Lebanese, Polish and Scotch. These not only recount the epic struggle of first generation immigrants but also the biases of the authors, ranging from the most objective to the most patronizing. Elsie Moeller, for instance, wrote an appraisal of the "industrious, thrifty, righteous, peaceful and courteous" first generation Portuguese in 19th and early 20th century Cape Cod and New Bedford. She refers to "these people being alien to our English blood" and reports of a graduating class in Falmouth in which "fifty of the children were Portuguese and but ten were American . . . What a change from the old days when a dark-skinned newcomer was a curiosity."

How can the impact of the Federal Writers Project be evaluated? It was such a sweeping effort and yet such a small part of the overall relief programs of the New Deal. The volume of the works alone is impressive: 800 titles including state and regional guides, anthologies of folklore, individual books, pamphlets, leaflets, articles and radio scripts, totaling 3½ million copies. In their immediate goal, the four Arts Projects did provide work to unemployed artists of the Depression decade. In their desire to achieve group goals by collective means, the projects often

tolerated incompetence and discouraged genius. As a 1937 article in *Fortune* noted, too often the Arts Projects serves as an "artistic Old Soldier's Home" for second-rate writers, painters, actors and musicians. Similarly the corporate journalism employed in the writing of the guides too often sacrificed elegance of expression for a consistent style. In a scholarly article written in 1961, the Massachusetts FWP director, Ray Billington, noted that the Arts Projects all suffered from a fear of censorship. The most serious example was the investigation of the Federal

Theater Project by the House Special Committe on Un-American Activities, chaired by Martin Dies of Texas. Reacting to conservative appeals that the theater program was pure "propaganda for communism," the Dies Committee excoriated Hallie Flanagan in a rash of bitter invective and concluded that the Federal Theater Project was riddled with Communists. It was primarily for this purely political reason that the WPA funds were slashed by Congress in 1939.

11

Governor Hurley, Sacco & Vanzetti and the Massachusetts Guide

by Paul A. Cyr

Paul Cyr is Curator of Special Collections at the New Bedford Free Public Library.

When Massachusetts Governor Charles Hurley addressed the State American Legion Convention held in New Bedford in August 1937, he departed from his prepared speech to blast the Massachusetts section of the Roosevelt Administration's Federal Writers' Project. They had put him in a very awkward situation with their new book, *Massachusetts: A Guide To Its People And Places.* The Guide was prefaced with a letter, signed by the Governor and the Secretary of the Commonwealth, which called the book a "major accomplishment" and a "valuable work." Evidently this endorsement had been given before the work was read from cover to cover. Shortly after publication, the

AMERICAN GUIDE SERIES

MASSACHUSETTS

A GUIDE TO ITS PLACES AND PEOPLE

Written and compiled by the Federal Writers' Project of the Works Progress Administration for Massachusetts

FREDERIC W. COOK, SECRETARY OF THE COMMONWEALTH, COOPERATING SPONSOR

Illustrated

HOUGHTON MIFFLIN COMPANY - BOSTON

The Riverside Press Cambridge

All photographs in this essay were taken from the pages of *Massachusetts: A Guide to its Places and People,* the state's contribution to the American Guide Series.

book Hurley had endorsed was criticized for its references to the Sacco and Vanzetti case, the Lawrence Strike and the Boston Police Strike, none of which were complimentary to the Commonwealth of Massachusetts.

The Sacco and Vanzetti references were the biggest problem. The strong feelings the case aroused had not died down. During Harvard's Tercentenary Celebrations the previous year, handbills were passed out criticizing Harvard's President Lowell for his membership on the committee. The committee had reviewed the case against the two anarchists and upheld their conviction for robbery and murder.

To make matters worse, the tenth anniversary of the execution of Sacco and Vanzetti would be commemorated the day after the close of the American Legion Convention in New Bedford.

Sacco and Vanzetti are mentioned in the Massachusetts Guide during a suggested walking tour of downtown Dedham. When the tourist reaches the Norfolk County Courthouse, where the trial took place, the writer digresses on interesting trials in the history of the town. Sacco and Vanzetti are mentioned again in a background chapter on the history of labor in Massachusetts. The reference appears between an explanation of the inequities of the "lay system" of payment used on fishing boats and an account of the Women's Trade Union League — unusual topics to include in a guidebook for tourists, but characteristic concerns for the Federal Writers' Project. Even the section on Boston contains a passage on Sacco and Vanzetti:

Hardly had the excitement of the Police Strike subsided when Boston became the storm center of another crisis, concerning the arrest, trial, conviction, and execution of two obscure Italian laborers. The affair dragged out over seven years and was debated in every civilized quarter of the globe. The entire machinery of justice was smeared with suspicion and petitions flooded the office of Governor Alvan T. Fuller in an effort to stay the execution and obtain a new trial. The men were executed in Boston August 23, 1927. The authorities no doubt breathed easier when the affair was safely over — though, as it turned out, the affair was far from over; Sacco and Vanzetti had become, for a new generation to whom "Haymarket" was scarcely more than a word, the classic example of the administering of justice to members of unpopular political minorities.

Having endorsed the Massachusetts Guide, Governor Hurley released a statement to the press explaining that references to the Sacco-Vanzetti case in the Guide were an expression of facts as interpreted by a group and did

THE OLD STATE HOUSE AND THE 'BLOODY MASSACRE,' 1770

THE OLD STATE HOUSE IN 1801, THE LION AND UNICORN REMOVED

not coincide with his views. After all, he admitted, "the purpose of writing this volume was primarily to give unemployed writers work under the authority of the federal government." Hurley also noted that Sacco and Vanzetti were referred to three times, in a total of 41 lines, "while the famous Tea Party was given nine lines, and the Boston Massacre only five."

Hurley was answered by Dr. Ray A. Billington, the Massachusetts State Director for the Federal Writers' Project, who said that references to Sacco and Vanzetti were "necessary for interpreting contemporary Massachusetts." He went on to say:

These statements on the Sacco-Vanzetti case are simply statements of fact. They are not expressions of editorial comment or of our belief. We do not say it is true or not that the determining factor in the Sacco-Vanzetti case was the affiliation of the two men with an unpopular minority political party. We merely say there was a wide belief that their affiliation was the determining factor.

Governor Hurley asked that further printing of the Massachusetts Guide be held up pending review of the book by "an editorial board, or at least some state official, to approve the manuscript to prevent the injection of propaganda." Former Governor Joseph B. Ely declared, "They ought to take the books to Boston Common, pile them in a heap, set a match and have a bonfire."

The New Bedford *Standard-Times* reported that Governor Hurley's speech at the American Legion

LEYDEN ST., PLYMOUTH, FIRST STREET IN MASSACHUSETTS

SEEDING CLAMS

Convention was very popular with his Legion comrades:

A blistering attack by Massachusetts Legionaire governor, Comrade Charles F. Hurley, on "two or three men who are trying maliciously to besmirch the proud record of Massachusetts by adding prejudicial chapters to the WPA Massachusetts Guide Book," threw the American Legion Convention session into an uproar of applause at noon today . . . "If these men don't like Massachusetts and the United States, they can go where they came from," cried Governor Hurley as the assembled gathering rose enmasse and cheered . . .

"Some time ago the Secretary of State was asked to approve a writers' project and this is no criticism of him. After the guide book was completed, it was sent to Washington, but some good writers had put in a few extra chapters which were not in it when it left here. A guide book should be socially and economically sound, but evidently we have in this state and nation a few people who have made up their minds to run things. Here is one governor who makes up his own mind, as I showed in taking my position on the Child Labor Amendment.

"I have referred this book to the state librarian for a review. When he submits his review to me I will send a copy to the President, not with the thought of criticism but because he is entitled to an impartial review.

As to the people who wrote these chapters, I believe, when we as a government were good enough to put them to work on projects, it should not be for the two or three men who try to maliciously besmirch the proud record of Massachusetts. As governor of Massachusetts, the responsibility of finding out who these people are rests on my shoulders. As governor, I will demand of Harry Hopkins that these men be removed from the payroll."

Harry Hopkins, the Works Progress Administrator, calmly responded: "It sounds like the publishers must have started it all. It has the earmarks of an old trick." As if all this were not enough to upset Governor Hurley, a

HILL OF CHURCHES, TRURO

WEAVING

PRINTING

recent foe, Governor E. D. Rivers of Georgia, jumped on the bandwagon. The *Standard-Times* went on to report:

"That 675-page Guide Book of Massachusetts criticized by Hurley," Rivers said, would be considered for purchase "so our children may be informed as to the deplorable condition of the courts and penal system in Massachusetts . . . I am going to write for a copy . . . I also hope that after we adopt this Massachusetts history as a textbook we can persuade producers to dramatize the Sacco-Vanzetti episode for the stage and screen. You know they did that for *A Fugitive from a Chain Gang* and *Tobacco Road*."

Antagonism between the two governors arose earlier when Hurley refused to grant extradition of James Cunningham, Negro robber, who was arrested in Massachusetts as a fugitive from a Georgia chain gang.

The State Librarian did eventually submit a list of revisions. After examining the passages in the guidebook which the State Librarian and Governor Hurley had marked for deletion, Billington noted "they not only requested the publishers strike out every mention of the Sacco-Vanzetti case, but they eliminated all references to strikes, unions, organized labor, welfare legislation, child labor laws and virtually every progressive act in the history of the state. They even proposed dropping Labor Day from the list of official holidays!"

Inside the
Writers' Project

by Joseph D. Thomas

In compiling this Federal Writers' Project anthology, Spinner staff made several trips to the National Archives and the Library of Congress. Our main interest was the work produced by the New Bedford district office, which covered all of Bristol, Plymouth, Barnstable and Dukes Counties, and most of which was never published. We researched stacks of administrative correspondence, memorandums and documents, and were rewarded with an insight into the character and energy of those who worked on the Federal Writers' Project. We have also been fortunate to talk to some of the writers about their work on the Project.

When Merle Colby, the Project's Assistant State Supervisor in Massachusetts, began canvassing editors, educators and writers in 1934 for their reaction toward an ERA writing project, the prospects for such an undertaking seemed remote. Two years later, Colby reflected on his accomplishments:

> The composition of the project is unusual in that all racial groups in Massachusetts in any numbers have at least one worker, with the exception of the Chinese . . . The project has had at least two worthwhile results: the recognition by the community of the writer as a social unit and the prevention of mental erosion among academically and professionally trained persons.

Colby viewed the project as a salvation for the white collar worker, "saving" them from physical labor. The liberation "from swinging a pick in the ditch out in Randolph or from

shoveling dirt on frozen Fisher Hill was a service to the community as well as the individual. Before the writing project, many trained persons were forced to classify themselves as mechanics, laborers or clerks."

The New Bedford district office was headed by G. Leroy "Roy" Bradford, a Fairhaven native and former editor

with the New Bedford *Times*. The office was located at the former Mary B. White elementary school on Pleasant and Maxfield Streets.

While the district offices focused their attention on community projects, they experienced problems of parochialism, patronage, political favoritism and general chaos. Carl

Far Left: Cove Street roadwork and breakwater rehabilitation, September 10, 1938. WPA photograph from the National Archives. *Above:* A group of local writers from the Project, with their friends and associates, enjoy an outing somewhere on Cape Cod. Those identified are: front row (seated) far right, Julia Keane; second row (kneeling), 3rd left Evelyn Silveira, 4th left Eunice Turgeon, 9th Left Frank Manning; third row (standing) left to right, unknown, Anderson, Charlotte Bonney, unknown, Bertrand Levesque, Madelyn Flannery, unknown, unknown, Gerald Gauthier, unknown, unknown, Margaret McKenna, Roy Bradford. The photographer of the portrait was probably James F. McKenna. Courtesy of Al Saulnier.

Malmberg, Secretary of the Artists and Writers Union of Provincetown, expressed outrage at the way in which payment of wages was handled. The irregularity of payments, the haphazard delivery of checks and the amount issued made it impossible for the workers to know what they were being paid for and when.

An instance of the slipshod and uncoordinated manner in which the payrolls are handled is reported by two Provincetown writers who went all the way to Hyannis to try to collect their overdue pay. They were informed by the Hyannis paymaster that the checks had been in the office for some time, but they had not been mailed out because there was a lack of stamps! Surely, it is a ridiculous situation when the government cannot get hold of stamps to conduct its own business.

Meanwhile, at the New Bedford Writers' Union, Local 15, concern over the lack of membership, financial problems and public relations were the order of the day. Since the Writers' Project drew heavily from the ranks of the various writers' unions, new memberships were being encouraged from within the Project itself. Local Writers' Union Secretary Evelyn Silveira, at a July 28, 1936 meeting, recorded the suggestion "that we vote by mail and also have a field day on the Cape at some beach and in that way probably more members would attend and become interested." While the union did supply many writers to the Project, most of those hired were unemployed college graduates, free-lance writers and desperate individuals with basic writing skills from all over Southeastern Massachusetts.

In the summer of 1936, a delegation of Massachusetts Writers traveled to Washington to lobby members of Congress and the Democratic National Convention. Their mission was to urge politicians to go on record in favor of continuing and expanding WPA Federal Project #1 (Writers, Artists, Musicians and Actors) and all other professional white collar projects and to request continued federal control over these projects. The delegation was headed by Frank Manning of Boston. Delegates from Salem, Worcester and New Bedford (represented by Eunice Turgeon) were on hand.

At their meeting with FWP Director Henry Alsberg, the group expressed their concerns about maintaining quotas and giving writers more opportunity to do creative work — to which Mr. Alsberg gave assurances on both items. Alsberg went on to advise the writers that new projects in folklore, ethnic and Indian studies and community history would soon be underway.

In Boston, a discussion between writers and supervisors on October 23, 1936, addressed many of the writers' concerns. One writer commented about work methods:

> If a group of writers are sent out to write reports on sewers, construction, etc., is not this the same as the artists on the easel project? Writers cannot do creative writing after working six hours on the sewer project.

Weary from the work on the state Guide, some writers suggested finishing up all Guide work before embarking on creative writing:

The drawback is that the Guide has been a long time project. It is difficult to preserve enthusiasm and spirit when the work goes on without seeing it in print. Short projects . . . would be of benefit to the community and an inspiration to the writers. We should not put ourselves in the position of writing into a vacuum . . . A bureau could be set up to hand out (short-term) assignments to keep the workers going from one assignment to another.

Said another:

Working in the field I am always being asked 'What is to be done with all this work?" I have to explain that it is going to be put into depositories . . . for posterity and where historians can have access to them in the future . . . What is all this work leading to and what will the town be gaining by it?

To which supervisor Edwards replied:

You have brought forth a fault of the administration. We have never given the public sufficient information of our accomplishments . . . In response to criticism, I have tried to explain that if it had not been for this federal money, real estate taxes would have been raised. A few years ago, doctors had to serve

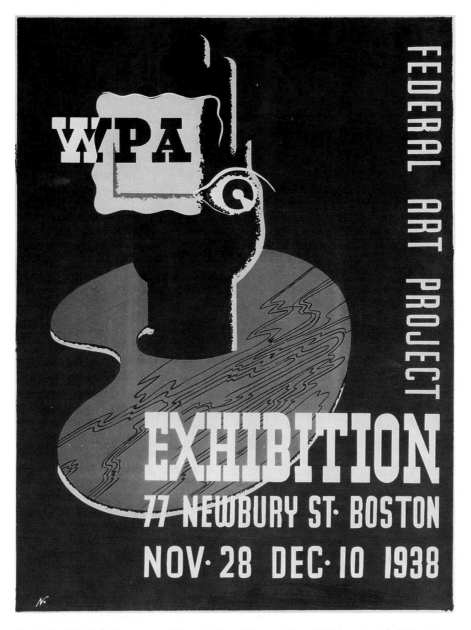

Far left: The WPA Art Project supported the production of 21 panels (over 250 ft. in perimeter) of historical murals for the Durfee High School Auditorium. The scenes depict Indian villages, Portuguese explorer Miguel Corte Real, King Philip's vision of the rise of the city, and others. The series, one of the largest and finest examples of WPA art, was painted by John Mann between 1935 and 1940, in a studio in the Weetamoe Mill which also housed headquarters for the WPA in Fall River. The panel shown here is entitled "Sealing of the Freeman's Purchase with the Presentation of Turf and Twig." *Above:* Federal Art Project poster. From the Library of Congress.

the unemployed without money. But people soon forget these things unless we point them out by means of our bulletins, etc.

Eventually the conversation reverted to the recurring topic of money:

The matter of the prevailing wage — 24 hour week and a minimum wage rate of one dollar an hour. In October the prevailing wage scale was instituted in New York City. It should be the same in Massachusetts . . . The writers here should be getting the same as those in New York.

Several months later, the problem of money would surface again, this time in a larger way. Roosevelt had recently begun his second term and his WPA program was in full force. However, a proposed dismissal of workers on the writing projects brought ire to the ranks and a plea for the President to recall his humanitarian principles and his pledge to keep America working. A telegram to FDR from one boston writer reads:

BOSTON MASS JUNE 10 1937
PRESIDENT FD ROOSEVELT
WASH DC
FEAR GRIPS OUR PEOPLE
HERE LIKE A NIGHTMARE
SET THEM FROM FEAR STOP
YOU CAN DO IT
GRACE KELLOGG
MASSACHUSETTS WRITER

Despite pleas from thousands of workers, business people and politicians, personnel quotas were established and layoffs ensued. In July, 1937, New Bedford Mayor Leo J. Carney wrote the State Director in Boston an angry request to end the quotas and hire one particular writer, Antoinette Coleman, who "is eminently qualified for assignment."

Her need for employment is great, so great in fact . . . she would be willing to accept a position as typist or secretary.

Mayor Carney called attention to the fact that the Writers' Project occupied free quarters in valuable space provided by the city: light, heat, telephone and supplies were accommodated; and many people employed there were not even residents of the city.

By late 1937, local writers were producing much material including histories of the different ethnic groups and studies of the fishing, cranberry and textile industries. Sponsorships were sought from businesses and community organizations to cover publishing fees; new ideas were being advanced by writers, supervisors and sponsors.

A memorandum from Roy Bradford to State Director Muriel Hawks on April 20, 1938 suggested that the Federal Writers interview the few remaining whaling captains, mates and seamen still living in Southeastern Massachusetts. These stories should be preserved, he urged, "as a particular type of Americana far too valuable to be lost."

Every year, every month, yes, even every day that it is

neglected means the chance that one more mine of information has left behind hardly a memory. It is unfortunate, yet I suppose natural, that friends and relatives of this dwindling band of whalemen pay little if any attention to their garrulous recitals.

Ms Hawks okayed the project. She was optimistic that a book of whaling yarns could eventually be published. No such book by the FWP was ever published.

Another major work, planned and never published, was a 500-page book entitled *The Portuguese in New*

England. This book was to be a novel-like recounting of the Portuguese experience in New England — tracing patterns of immigration, work, custom and cultural aspects of Portuguese life. Material originated from many sources — from academic treatises to personal observations. We have included several excerpts from the unedited version of this collection in our anthology.

Several books of local interest that did get published were *Whaling Masters, Cape Cod Pilot, New England Hurricane* and *Fairhaven, Massachusetts.* Today, *Whaling Masters,* published with the Old Dartmouth Historical Society and

printed cost-free by Reynolds Printing, ranks as one of the most useful reference works relating to whaling. *Fairhaven, Massachusetts,* a 60-page town history, published in 1939 and sponsored by the Board of Selectmen, was well received by local critics. The *New England Hurricane,* a best seller published in record-setting speed, received high praise from *Newsweek:* "The text to each picture and the short account of the hurricane are superb, the full tragic drama brought home to us with all its force and meaning, without any cheap tricks of writing."

The *Cape Cod Pilot,* released in June 1939 and hailed by *Time* magazine as "the boldest and best of the American

Guide Series," increased the literary prestige of the Project and brought a measure of acclaim to author, Josef Berger, who used the pseudonym, Jeremiah Digges. Berger, struggling to feed his family on the pittance he earned as a free-lance writer in Provincetown, was often dependent on food given to him by the Portuguese fishermen he befriended. The *Cape Cod Pilot*, written in the first person, is an anecdotal journey through places and time along U.S. Route 6 on Cape Cod.

Former Project writer Jerre Mangione, in his book *The Dream and the Deal*, notes that the *Cape Cod Pilot* "marked an important stage in the maturing of the Federal Writers' Project — humanizing its national image and strengthening so many writers' dreams to be able to function as creative individuals rather than as extensions of the giant writing apparatus controlled from Washington D.C." Many writers were further encouraged when Berger won a Guggenheim Fellowship in recognition of his work in the *Cape Cod Pilot*.

The work represented in this anthology is a small sampling of the diverse subjects covered by the writers in Southeastern Massachusetts. The historical and subjective interpretations expressed by the writers are often biased and typical of attitudes prevalent during those times and they do not reflect editorial opinion of Spinner personnel. We hope the readers will view these interpretations for what they are — responses shaped by the values, prejudices and sentiments of aspiring writers in the 1930s.

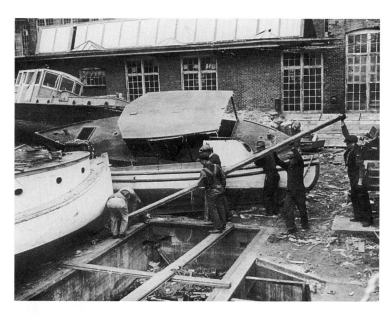

Opp. page: a librarian from the WPA Library Project talks about books to children in Dartmouth, February 1941. *Left:* In the wake of the '38 Hurricane, WPA crew cleans up debris in the mill yard of the City Manufacturing Co., foot of South Street, New Bedford. *Below:* "Pope Beach — WPA clearing away wreckage and looking for bodies," Fairhaven, October 3, 1938. WPA photographs from the National Archives.

Above: CONTINUATION SCHOOL Recreation Project in Fall River, November 1937. WPA photograph from the National Archives. *Right:* Instructor Reynolds gives direction to students taking Art Instruction at Falmouth Center on Cape Cod, 1937. WPA photograph from the National Archives.

In Search of the Federal Writers

by Linda Donaghy and Marsha L. McCabe

In working on the Federal Writers' Project feature, one of *Spinner*'s challenges was to try and locate writers from the Project who worked out of the New Bedford office in the 1930s. This was not an easy task, for most of the writers are deceased and those who remain seem to have left few tracks. We had some success, nevertheless: two in-person interviews, one with Mr. Hooten Squire of Westport and one with Ms Eunice Turgeon of East Orleans. We also interviewed the son of James McKenna and the daughter of Irene Posey. We talked with Mr. Gerald Gauthier from his home in Florida and with the son of Elsie Moeller from West Newton, Massachusetts.

In particular, we wanted to know about the writers' experiences working on the Project and the circumstances that brought them to it.

Hooten Squire

At his Westport farmhouse, Mr. Hooten Squire shared memories of his tenure as a federal writer. Mr. Squire entered the world of the Depression as a recent graduate of the Wharton School at the University of Pennsylvania. "There were no jobs anywhere. No one had any money." The WPA served as a temporary answer for Mr. Squire.

"Originally I worked out of the Fall River office," he said, "assigning people to WPA projects. Then I was assigned to work on the Federal Writers' Project in the town of Westport. I had the education."

Mr. Squire and Ms Irene Posey worked as a team doing historical research. "We were very much in the field." said Mr. Squire, "searching for Indian burial grounds, or old houses where hotels were. We would document these by taking pictures and writing descriptions. We also interviewed lots of older folks, most importantly, to establish where their parents were born so we could find out how they came into Westport. We worked long hours — sometimes 50-60 hours a week."

There was one occasion Mr. Squire remembers clearly: "Mrs. Roosevelt showed up one day at a meeting of writers at the town hall in Westport. She wanted us to join the Writers' Guild of America. I didn't want to get in any labor union. That's when we quit."

Following his job as federal writer, Mr. Squire took a job at Lorraine's Coffee Company of New Bedford and soon became manager of the Lorraine's store in Fall River.

Eunice Turgeon

Eunice Turgeon expressed surprise that anyone could be interested in the federal writers fifty years later. She greeted us in her home in East Orleans, near Nauset Beach, and shared her memories of being a federal writer. "It was a stop gap job for me," she said, "but interesting."

A graduate of Pembroke College, Ms Turgeon explained she had been living off tips from a waitress job at an inn in Wareham, then sold lighting fixtures for the New Bedford Gas and Edison Light Company. Though it was the depression and there were few opportunities out there, she felt she wasn't getting anywhere. When she appealed to friends and family, a friend mentioned the Federal Writers' Project.

Ms Turgeon emphasized that she was a researcher, not a writer. As a biology and French major in college, she had good research skills and could make full use of them on the Project. She was assigned to research old town records in Dennis on Cape Cod. Much of the material was in a musty vault. Here, she had access to old town meeting minutes and other town history. She also got much information by talking to the town clerk. At the cemetery, she researched tombstones.

"We would turn all the material over to Jim McKenna. He was in the office — tall and gangly, witty and helpful. And I remember Frank Manning very well too. He had such fluency, such a vocabulary. When they were going to cut the FWP way down, a group of us went to Washington to ask them not to."

As a federal writer, Ms Turgeon was making $24 a week. From there, she went to another WPA job, working for the welfare department with WPA funds. "Here my job was to determine eligibility for WPA applicants. I was now making $37.50 a week."

"Working as a researcher was fun but temporary," said Ms Turgeon, who left New Bedford in 1939 for Boston and a career in the Navy.

Irene Posey (From an interview with Priscilla Smith, her daughter)

After graduating from Wellesley College, Fall River resident Irene Posey took an unlikely route: She became a social worker in a shoe factory, working with immigrants as the director of their Americanization classes. She was greatly interested in the different ethnic groups. Her work in the shoe factory became a training ground for work she would do during the Depression.

In 1933 she worked as district supervisor for the National Recovery Act, then became a social worker for the Emergency Recovery Act. In 1936 she worked as a writer for the FWP and, in the years following, became a

supervisor of the Federal Health Survey and of research on the Historical Records Survey. She also distributed surplus food and clothing through the General Relief program.

Ms Priscilla Smith describes her mother as a woman on the move. She made 18 different trips to Hawaii to visit friends before she died on November 26, 1985.

James McKenna (From an interview by James E. McKenna, his son)

James McKenna was a newspaperman and he brought the skills of a lucid, careful reporter to his work on the Writers' Project. After earning his degree in English at Holy Cross College, he worked at the *Worcester Telegram and Gazette* and later at the New Bedford *Times* as a financial writer. He had a reputation of being able to make a story out of anything.

McKenna found himself without a job when he left the defunct *Times* for a job at *Time* magazine in New York doing newsreels. At the last minute, he decided not to subject his family to the move. In search of a job locally, he made contact with another former newspaperman, Roy Bradford, who was now the director of the FWP for the district. McKenna was hired.

His son James remembers the FWP office at the Mary B. White school, which looked like a newspaper room. In fact, many of the workers came from newspaper backgrounds, victims of the closing of the *Morning Mercury* and the merging of the *Times* and the *Evening Standard*. As a federal writer,

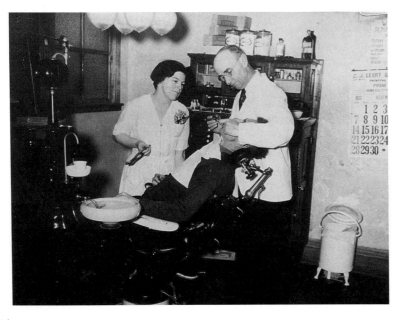

Left: WPA Dentist clinic in Fall River, November 1937. WPA Photograph from the National Archives.
Right: Clock Repair Project, Fall River, April 1936. WPA photograph from the National Archives.

McKenna wrote for the Narrative Reports project which described progress of the WPA programs. He also wrote on New Bedford history for the Guide Series and produced an extensive narrative on the history of the 1928 textile strike. During the strike, he had served as Secretary of the United Textile Workers Union in New Bedford and later he was Secretary of the New Bedford Writers' Union. Finally, he became a WPA coordinator, overseeing many of the achievements of the WPA projects in New Bedford.

Elsie Moeller (From a telephone conversation with Rodman Moeller, her son)

The Federal Writers' Project was fulfilling to Elsie Moeller in terms of interest, but not financially rewarding, especially for a single parent of a teenage son. But Elsie Moeller always wanted to be a writer and her tenure on the FWP gave her the opportunity to practice her craft.

During the war, Ms Moeller worked as a riveter in a California shipyard, uncommon for a woman with a college education but a job she was proud to do. Later, she did research at the Old Dartmouth Historical Society. The publication of her novel, *Pack a Bag,* published in 1955, about her world travels as a high school girl, was the climax of her writing career.

Lucretia Norton

Lucretia Norton, the daughter of a famous whaling captain, Ichabod Norton, was born and raised in Edgartown on Martha's Vineyard. From early childhood, she was interested in the Island, its people and its traditions. In later years she became a source of information for the historical society and the Edgartown Public Library.

Her work as a Federal Writer — gathering folklore and material for the local guide — fit her nature and enthusiasm, though it appears her FWP writings were never published until now. She left behind notebooks, rather than books, at the Dukes County Historical Society where she worked for several years. Her notebooks contain information on the

Portuguese immigrants to Martha's Vineyard, the Old Historic House of Great Harbor, logbooks of Vineyard Haven and other subjects. She died in 1944.

Left: After hurricane repairs on West Rodney French Blvd., New Bedford, September 9, 1938. WPA photograph from the National Archives. *Right:* Atlantic Avenue washout, Fall River, September 28, 1938. WPA photograph from the National Archives.

Narrative Reports from the WPA

by James. F. McKenna

Editor's Note: Since the Federal Writers' Project was a pool of trained writers within the W P A , they were responsible for publicity projects for the other sections of the W P A. On Wednesday, September 23, 1936 New Bedford observed "W P A Day" and all of the projects in the city were open to the public. James McKenna wrote the following account, which we have abridged, of the various projects in New Bedford under the Ashley administration. Later the same year New Bedford's "perpetual mayor," Charles S. Ashley would retire from public office and this article is very approving of his management of the W P A projects in the city.

New Bedford's accomplishments under the various federal Emergency Relief Programs have been a source of wonder to thousands of visitors to the city, including city, state and federal officials, and a source of pride to Mayor Charles S. Ashley and the successive directors of the works programs in Massachusetts whose cooperation made them possible.

Since the latter part of November, 1933, when the Civil Works Administration Program started in the city, a vast amount of money has served to provide employment to many thousands of needy persons with families dependent upon them and to give New Bedford a series of improvements that have already been enjoyed by tens of thousands. That the original and dominating purpose of the program, to provide relief employment, has been rigidly adhered to in the city is evidenced by the fact that of the $4,535,433.90 spent, $3,836,799.56, or more than 83 percent, was paid out by the federal government as wages to project workers in the city. Latest complete employment figures are those of August 1, when 1330 men and 473 women, a total of 1803, were employed on operating projects.

When the Civil Works Administration Program started late in 1933, New Bedford boasted one of the finest municipal plants in the United States. Excellent streets,

municipal buildings, schools, parks and recreational facilities, and a $6,500,000 water supply system were all included. While the market crash in 1929 marked the beginning of the depression in most sections of the country, New Bedford, as the leading center of the world for the manufacture of fine textiles, had been suffering losses from the readjustment of the textile industry for several years prior to then. This made a program of rigid economy in municipal expenditures imperative and as a result plans for further extending and improving the various municipal institutions were all held in abeyance.

An instance of this was the case of the New Bedford High School. The original trim of the structure was terra cotta. It had become cracked, loosened, and a serious menace to the safety of the students attending the school. The cost of replacing it was far more than the school committee could afford to spend from its annual appropriation and hence it wasn't done.

Under the CWA, approval of a project to replace this terra cotta with Indiana limestone, a more attractive and permanent trim, was obtained. A total of 52 unemployed masons, masons' helpers, stonecutters and laborers were given work. The result was a more beautiful building and the elimination of a condition which had been threatening tragic consequences.

While many communities rushed into the Civil Works Program without any definite program of their own, Mayor Ashley delayed New Bedford's entrance into it a few days while he made a study of its possibilities and held several conferences with officials at Boston.

The principal result of these conferences was an agreement by the state CWA officials to approve a project for razing the old Bristol Mill buildings. These and the land on which they were located had been turned over to the city in lieu of taxes by a defunct corporation and, during several years of idleness, had become a menace to the neighborhood.

This was one of the first projects undertaken. It served many purposes. First, it provided employment to 296 workers engaged in tearing down the building, 24 workers employed to remove piping, and 99 workers who cleaned and sorted the brick and

lumber salvaged from the operation. The demolition project left a tract of 17 acres in extent, fronting on the Acushnet River and located in a congested neighborhood where hundreds of children had been without a convenient playground. An attractive feature was the high wire fence which entirely surrounds the land on two sides abutting heavily travelled streets. A section of six acres was immediately made available for community gardens and the balance was graded and developed as a playground, 82 men being employed for this purpose. A second project for developing this tract was construction of a bulkhead to eliminate the cove which cut deeply into the land.

Before the razing of the mill buildings was completed, however, a huge supply of materials such as cleaned brick, lumber, piping, steel beams, etc., began to be available for use elsewhere. This made possible construction projects for which the city itself would not be able to appropriate even the money necessary for materials.

The first construction project for the use of these salvaged materials was the municipal garage. Buildings formerly used by the New Bedford Street Department had been turned over and remodelled for use of the New Bedford Vocational School. The completed work gave the city one of the most modern and spacious municipal garages in the East. Land immediately surrounding was graded and seeded to make it most attractive. Materials which went into this building included more than a half-million bricks salvaged and cleaned at the Bristol Mill, 247,730 linear feet of four and three inch planking and miscellaneous lumber from the same project besides steel "X" beams and other materials.

Left: Portion of the bathhouse, breakwater and seawall at Municipal Beach, built under the federal relief program, are visible in this 1988 photograph. *Above:* The carefully crafted stone wall along Rural Cemetery is a glimpse of the several miles of stone wall construction made by the WPA and CWA along cemeteries, beaches and other areas throughout the city. Photographs by Rachel Barnet, 1988. *Right:* Warming house and skating rink on Brock Avenue in the south end. City infirmary is in the distance. WPA photograph, November 1937, from the National Archives.

Other projects which the demolition of the Bristol Mill building made possible included a new children's bathhouse at the municipal bathing beach, a 14-car garage for the Water Department yard to replace a dilapidated wooden structure, an addition to the Vocational School for welding shop classes and a coal and wood building at the City Infirmary.

At the Municipal Bathing Beach, patronized by thousands during the hot summer days, facilities were not adequate for many years. When originally established the buildings at the beach were hurried to the extent that a section in the center was temporarily constructed of wood. Before this could be made permanent the curtailment of city expenditures was started and hopes for further work there in the near future abandoned.

The federal relief program permitted the undertaking of various projects there which have resulted in one of the finest municipal bathing beaches along the Atlantic coast for any city in New Bedford's class. The bathhouse provides every modern facility for child bathers and has permitted use of the beach by thousands of children who were previously kept away because of the congestion which existed previously.

The center portion of the existing buildings was reconstructed, a plank wall with an unsafe iron rail was reconstructed entirely in concrete, a concrete wall was built along the edge of the covered stone pier, jetties were extended out into the waters of Clark's Cove to create a new beach, a seawall of concrete on the beach portion of the waterfront to further beautify and protect the shoreline and other improvements undertaken.

After the demolition of the Bristol Mills had started, the city came into the possession of the old Acushnet Mill property, from which most of the buildings had been removed, the Whitman Mills property and finally the Potomska Mills property. These paved the way for more building projects and provided hundreds of workers with employment.

Acushnet Mill demolition provided employment for 82 workers. At the Whitman Mill the city decided on demolition of only a large weave shed on which project 297 workers were employed. In addition 21 men received $2,966 in wages on a project for removal of piping from the building. The other Whitman Mill buildings were prepared and put into proper condition for their preservation. Sections are now in use by the Federal Emergency Relief Administration commissary, a planing and sawmill to cut and prepare lumber for various projects, and by the women's sewing and allied projects. The Potomska Mill demolition has been a WPA project. Peak employment on this project was 493 men.

At the City Infirmary the most important project was the two-story dormitory addition which relieved a congested condition. This is a two-story brick structure with modern dormitories on the first and second floors. These have been equipped with 114 beds, now occupied, to provide the needy aged at the institution with a degree of comfort impossible to obtain prior to the construction. The wood and coal storage building was previously mentioned. Then extensive alterations to the barn provided an east section for cows, horses, grain storage and harness room, the west section for cows and the center for

general use as a potato cellar. A poultry house further increased the farm facilities.

City owned cemeteries have been vastly improved under the local program. The largest undertaking in this group of projects was the reclamation of a 15 acre tract at Rural Cemetery that was covered by weeds and brush. This entire area has been reclaimed, roadways built and the tract graded until it will soon be available for burial purposes. Development of this tract provided employment to a peak of 816 men.

New boundary walls at Rural Cemetery extend for 2,119 linear feet and involved nearly 20,000 square feet of grading. At Oak Grove Cemetery 2,000 linear feet of wall, involving 63,000 square feet of grading was built and along the Grape Street boundary of Rural Cemetery 1,201 linear feet of wall was constructed. In addition, buildings have been painted and repaired, 7,877 feet of fencing renewed, graves of veterans of the Civil, Spanish-American and World War marked and the cemeteries, including Pine Grove, generally improved.

One of the most attractive buildings constructed is the new warming or community house at Buttonwood Park. This replaces an old wooden structure which was on the verge of collapse and had outlived its usefulness as a shelter for skaters during the winter. The new building is located on the shore of the park pond, which was increased in area by 56 percent and deepened under another project. A block paved ramp runs from the waterfront entrance down into the water for the use of skaters and a covered 10 by 10 feet porch is available for spectators.

tennis courts and extensive alterations to the keepers' house besides several minor improvements.

Marine Park, on Pope's Island in the middle of the New Bedford-Fairhaven Bridge, has come into existence since the advent of the federal relief program. This is principally made land, the city having erected a wooden bulkhead to make a place for the dumping of stones collected by the Street Department and other solid fill. When the filling was completed, welfare labor was employed to level and grade and then surface the tract with a loam covering. Shrubbery was donated by the Garden Club of Buzzards Bay, which also supervised the landscaping of the new park. The WPA completed the work with the laying of water mains through it to provide a source of water for sprinkling purposes. This park has greatly enhanced the entrance to the city from the east on route 6 and a

parking place in it affords a splendid view of New Bedford's attractive and busy harbor.

Playgrounds in the city have been greatly increased with the addition of the Bristol, Acushnet and Potomska Mill tracts. In addition to the grading of these and their development for the children, with baseball and soccer fields for the older folks, there have been extensive improvements to the previously existing playgrounds and parks. In the West End, in the rear of the City Yard, a 479,340 square foot of land has been filled in and graded to serve as a West End Recreation Field with cricket, baseball, soccer and other fields for sports.

These new playgrounds and athletic fields are all located in sections where it has been customary for large numbers of children to resort to the streets for play purposes either because of the lack of a convenient playground or because the existing

In increasing the area of the pond a swamp on the northwest side was eliminated either by being included in the pond or by being filled and graded to permit landscaping and general improvement of the area around the pond. Buttonwood Brook, which runs through the park, was beautified by rip-rapping, construction of concrete culverts, and spanning of it by several rustic bridges.

Other accomplishments at Buttonwood Park include a Recreation Building, two new tennis courts, the woods cleared of brush, walks laid out and the 1¾ mile bridle path improved. A spacious and attractive bear den is nearing completion. Brooklawn Park projects have resulted in making it most attractive in addition to

providing more extensive recreational facilities. Brooks in the park were cleared and walled, the park pond increased in area and walled around with concrete. A lodge equipped with showers and other facilities, was constructed with an additional bowling green, two new tennis courts and a cricket field laid out as further improvements. In this park also the woods were cleared of brush and their beauty enhanced. At present a new garage and storage building is under construction with materials salvaged from the Potomska Mills being utilized.

Hazelwood Park, the third of New Bedford's large park areas, has acquired a new boundary wall which extends 2,053 linear feet, two new

playgrounds were too small to attract them. To assure a maximum utilization of the increased recreational facilities made available, an extensive and comprehensive recreational program has been conducted under the WPA, opportunities for unemployed boys and girls.

Rodney French Boulevard, which runs along the shore of Clark's Point down along Clark's Cove to Fort Rodman and thence easterly and north along the shore of New Bedford Harbor, has been protected and made doubly attractive by the construction of a seawall and rip-rapping along the shore with a general clearing up of the beaches. The seawall is of concrete and it has made possible the grading and seeding of the park land stretches lying between it and the roadway. Walks have been laid out, trees planted where they were needed and other improvements undertaken to complete the work. Currently a new

stone pier is being constructed on the East Boulevard and beach improvements, rip-rapping and allied work being done.

At the city-owned piers in the commercial section of the waterfront improvements have been underway, the outstanding one being the new city wharfinger's building. Of appropriate architectural design, this was built with about 50,000 salvaged bricks and contains office, workshop, storage and other necessary space.

Sewer and surface drain construction work has also played an important part in the local program. The largest single item in this line was the Rodney French Boulevard sewer and force main which connects 11

sewers running easterly and emptying into the harbor. The situation was one which the State Board of Health had condemned, but because of the cost the city was unable to undertake its correction. The sewers were connected by a sewer which runs to Apponegansett Street where a new pumping station was constructed, also as a WPA project. Sewage is pumped at the station into a force main connected to the main interceptor on West Rodney French Boulevard. A total of 165 men were employed on the sewer project and 48 on the pumping station. The second largest sewer project was the Plainville Road drain which eliminated a flooded condition that had been a source of

complaints from abutting property owners. This work employed 140 men. Other sewer and drain projects provided several hundred others with employment and greatly improved the sewer system of the city.

Police Stations also were renovated, the Central Station being remodelled on the interior to provide more adequate facilities for the various divisions. An addition to the garage at the Central Station was also built.

The principal new acquisition by the Fire Department is a new No. 9 Station. This is a most up-to-date building, constructed of salvaged brick and two stories high. There is space for two pieces of apparatus, with the upstairs devoted to sleeping rooms,

Far left: Entrance to the bear den at Buttonwood Park Zoo. *Left:* Seawall at East beach along East Rodney French Blvd. with Teledyne Rodney Metals in the background. *Right:* Apponegansett pumping station, near East Beach. Photographs by Rachel Barnet, 1988.

distribution to the needy. About 15,000 red pines were set out on a tract of 15 acres and other work accomplished.

Street work undertaken under the relief programs was not extensive, although grading, and in some cases surfacing with bituminous macadam, was done on a total of 39 streets, or a lineal distance of 9.17 miles. At the present time a granolithic sidewalk construction project is underway. A total of $194,000 is to be spent on labor on this project and it is proposed to build 58,000 square yards of walks.

Numerous small projects have been undertaken for the employment of women in the city, but the principal source of employment for them has been the sewing projects. Under the CWA and ERA the peak employment on sewing was 426 but under the

WPA this has reached 571. Mattress making and comforter making brought $18,789.38 more in payrolls for women and girls.

The sewing project has produced 33,086 items of men's apparel, 29,891 items of women's apparel, 2,029 children's, 3,493 girl's, 12,686 boy's and 43,234 miscellaneous under the ERA. The largest production under the WPA has been 11,639 men's and boy's shirts, 18,739 men's and boy's pants, 15,418 women's dresses, 15,210 pieces of women's underwear and 21,426 flat pieces. The products have been of a wide variety and made to meet the needs of everybody, from the tiniest baby to men and women. Every item has been distributed to the needy, originally through the Board of Welfare and more generally through the FERA commissary.

baths, reading rooms, office and other accommodations for the men. Other fire stations in the city were repainted and repaired but the elimination of the old wooden No. 9 Station was the principal item.

In addition to acquiring new garage and storage buildings at its yard in the city, the Water Department had a project for constructing a new garage at the Quitticas Pumping Station in Freetown. This building is 180 x 24 feet and accommodates 15 machines. The department owns approximately 1,600 acres of land surrounding Little and Great Quitticas Ponds and of this total more than 1,200 have been cleaned out by WPA projects. Peak employment on this saw 162 men at work.

In addition to protecting the water supply system by clearing out the underbrush, the project produced more than 3,000 cords of cut wood for

Of the nearly 300 projects undertaken in New Bedford, a majority have been of minor importance and can be considered only as a group. These are mostly isolated items such as the watch tower on the municipal parking lot. This is an attractive octagonal shaped tower, 25 feet high and 13 feet across the center at the base, to permit the police officer on duty at the lot to have a clear view of the entire area and more efficiently watch over parked cars and guide motorists to available spaces. Stone for

Far left: Sewing Project (Sunday) at an Army base in South Boston, November 1938. *Left:* New Bedford Vocational School Gymnasium on Hillman Street, 1937. *Above:* Watchtower built in municipal parking lot (behind City Hall), 12′ x 12′ and 22′ high construction, covered with copper and a base of stone. A spotlight provided on roof is manipulated from within. May 1937. WPA photographs from the National Archives.

the exterior of this was obtained from the Rural Cemetery development project.

Perhaps the largest construction project now uncompleted is the Gymnasium of the Vocational School. This will be two stories high, 140 x 70 feet. It is situated on the southwest corner of the school lot.

One of the special features of the New Bedford program has been the extremely low cost of administering it and preparing the plans for the multitude of projects. Mr. Minor Wilcox, administrator under the CWA and ERA, is the coordinator of WPA projects, acting for Mayor Ashley. Inspector of Buildings George Gardner and his regular staff have been in charge of all building projects and in a great majority of instances have prepared or supervised the preparation of all plans for projects involving construction work.

While Mayor Ashley has been the directing force behind the local program since it started, with Mr. Wilcox tending to the executive duties, department heads have contributed greatly to keeping administration costs at an absolute minimum. Statistics on the first $1,300,000 spent revealed the percentage of cost chargeable to administration at only 3.16% and officials consider that since then that percentage has been reduced rather than increased.

With the WPA program still continuing, Mayor Ashley is confident of bringing about even more valuable additions to New Bedford's facilities. The principal objective is a seaplane ramp for Homer's Wharf, recently acquired by the city, and plans for which have been declared by aeronautic experts as the finest they have ever seen.

A Guide to
Island Places

by Lucretia Norton

Editor's Note: We have selected three of Lucretia Norton's unpublished Guide Series contributions for this anthology — Nomans Land, Gosnold and Gay Head. Ms. Norton followed a format used by all writers for the local Guide Series. Under sub-titles such as Geography, Archaeology and Ethnology, Racial Elements and Customs of Dress, Norton takes us on a cultural tour through Island towns and settlements in and around Buzzards Bay.

Through Ms. Norton's eyes, we become acquainted with these bleak, beautiful, windswept islands at a quieter time in their history. We arrive with the British explorer, Gosnold, and taste the "excellent sweet water," greet the Indians and feel the light and stony soil.

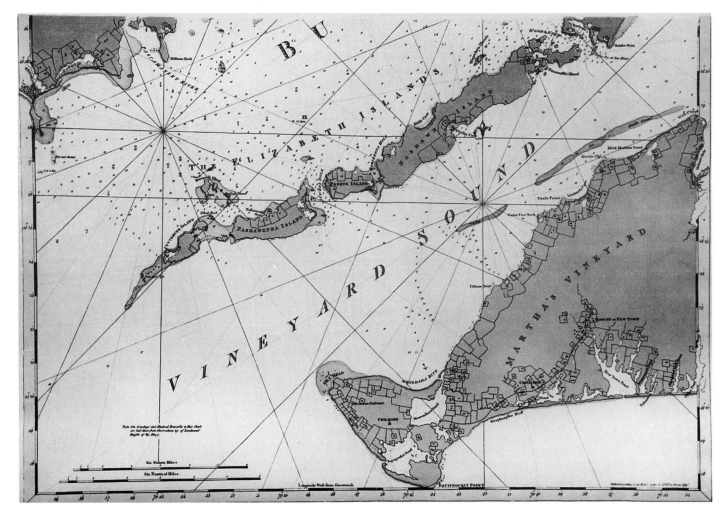

During World War II, Nomans Land was bought by the Navy to be used as a bombing base by the U.S. Naval Air Station at Quonset Point, Rhode Island. Today, though the island is still used by the military for dummy-bomb exercises, tranquility has returned and with it, there is sanctuary for fowl and

vegetation. A dispute still exists: prevent private development by leaving it with the military, or drive out the military presence and gain public access, while risking private development.

Above: 1776 map of Buzzards Bay, from *The Atlantic Neptune* by Joseph F.W. Des Barres. Considered the first great marine atlas of North America, *The Atlantic Neptune* was produced for the Royal Navy and used by the British during the Revolutionary War. This chart of Buzzards Bay continued to be the most accurate and widely used map of the bay until 1846 when a new chart was issued by the Federal Government. Courtesy of the New Bedford Whaling Museum. *Far Right:* "Nomans Land," a watercolor by Amelia M. Watson painted around 1888, views the island from Squibnocket on Gay Head. Courtesy of the Dukes County Historical Society.

Nomans Land

Geography and Related Subjects

The island of Nomans Land lies in the Atlantic Ocean about six miles south of Gay Head and three miles from Squibnocket, the nearest point of Martha's Vineyard. It is one and one-half miles long and one mile wide. The island is a mass of glacial drift and at the present time consists of swampy bogs alternating with grassy ridges and pastures strewn with stones and boulders. Hollows, a few feet across, occur at intervals along the crest of some of the ridges. Most of the beach stones are of quartz, in many forms, and granite or gneiss. On Stony Point are five acres of clean stone.

The island is, for the most part, made up of small hills with intervening swamps. In several places dams have been made at the outlet of the outer swamps making beautiful artificial lakes. The largest, Rainbow Lake, is situated near the southeastern shore and is approximately three miles in circumference. Ben's Pond is one mile in circumference. Near the southeastern part are two other lakes: Sisson's Pond and Lake Katherine. Near the shore at the northeast is one natural lake measuring two-thirds of a mile in circumference.

On March 26, 1602, Bartholomew Gosnold, in command of two ships, the *Concord* and the *Dartmouth,* left Falmouth, England on a voyage of discovery to the new world. Following an uneventful voyage, they first sighted land near Cape Ann and sailing southward around Cape Cod, they passed between the islands of Nantucket and Martha's Vineyard. They cruised along the southern shore of Martha's Vineyard and on May 22, they came to an uninhabited island, which is now known as Nomans Land. Casting anchor south of the island in eight fathoms of water, part of the company landed to explore the territory.

When Gosnold and his companions landed at Nomans Land, it was a "disinhabited island," but the two journalists of the voyage give detailed accounts of its natural features and called the place "most pleasant." Also many springs of "excellent sweet water" were here found. Gabriel Archer, in his accounts of Gosnold's voyage states: "Here we had cranes, stemmes, shoulders, geese and diverse other birds which there did breed and had young. In this place we saw deer; here we rode in eight fathoms near the shore where we took great store of cod — as before at Cape Cod, but much better."

Today geese and wild duck are to be seen in autumn in great quantities, also various kinds of hawks and Arctic owls. During the winter of 1926-27, 43 white Arctic owls were killed or captured as well as 40 hawks. In spring, many varieties of birds, migrating northward, stop to rest on the island, including scarlet tanagers and grosbeaks. There are a few pheasants and a colony of muskrats has been imported which appear to be doing well. The importation of Chinchilla rabbits has been too successful and they have become so numerous that sportsmen are allowed to kill large numbers of them.

The early account of Gosnold's voyage describes this little island as "full of wood-vines, gooseberry bushes, whortle-berries, raspberries, eglantine." At the present time, low bushes, producing various kinds of berries are found everywhere. The shady stretches near the shore produce quantities of coarse sea grass with seed heads not unlike ears of wheat — a very welcome source of food for small birds. There are now no large trees on the island, only a few stunted and gnarled silver poplars and cherry trees about six inches in diameter. Beach palm bushes and the wax myrtle, sweet pepper berries, reeds, grasses, and all flora indigenous to this locality abound. Marine plants cast upon the shore are many and varied.

There are abundant traces of former Indian habitation. On the north point of the island excavations have revealed the existence of a workshop for the manufacture of arrowheads and other stone weapons. Deer antlers, oyster shells, clam shells have been found three and four feet below the present shady surface, on a layer of peat. A well, sunk near the shore revealed a pine cone, and peat bogs disclose skeleton leaves and even seeds.

Gosnold, in his account, mentions the bones of whales he saw laying on the beach at Nomans Land. Bones of many kinds of ducks and sea fowl, especially those of the Great Auk, have been uncovered. Many tools and weapons, fragments of pottery crudely ornamented with circles and spheres of different colors painted upon before being baked, stone hammers and tomahawks, arrow and spear heads have been found on Nomans Land. The shell heap is a never ending source of interest.

Early History

A representative of the Duke of York proclaimed the authority over this island, and on August 3, 1666 granted it to William Reeves, Tristram Dodge, John Williams, and William Nightingale, conditional upon the establishment of a fishing trade, construction of a harbor within three years, and the annual payment of one barrel of codfish as a quit-rent.

These conditions were not fulfilled within three years and the grant was forfeited. According to the statement of John Williams this was due to "the default of his partners," and upon his petition the grant was renewed to him on June 28, 1670, "to settle a fishing trade there." There is no record of this trade being established.

Matthew Mayhew under patent owned the island, followed by Governor Dongan, who sold it to Jacob Norton, in whose possession and his heirs it remained for over half a century. After the death of Jacob Norton in 1743, the island came into frequent litigation among various claimants.

The first record of any settlement here is in the early part of the 18th century. With the purchase by Jacob Norton in 1715, the first English people came here to live. Jacob and family resided here. In 1860 George Butler came to the island and built a house and a grocery store near the landing. This building yet remains, with a platform extending into the water. At one time a mill stood near a farm house and one of the mill stones can still be seen. The power which turned the stones to grind corn and grain was furnished by a windmill.

Another industry was dressing and salting codfish.

Naming Nomans Land

The island of Nomans Land has the distinction of being the first land touched by Gosnold in 1602 and from him receiving the name of "Martha's Vineyard." This title became attached to the present island bearing the name, but the reason for the change of names is not understood. Since the first name given by Gosnold, a second name it bore was "Hendrick Christiansen's Eylant" in 1616 and "Ile de Hendrick" in 1646, both having reference to the Dutch explorer of that name who probably visited it. The curious name of "Dock Island" appears on a map of 1675, but it is not repeated in later charts.

In 1666 it was first called "Nomans Land," also the Isle of Man. The Indian name was Cappoaquit. The origin of the name "Nomans" is not known. It is usual to attribute it to a combination of two words, No Man's Land, as descriptive of its ownerless condition, but while this is the easiest conclusion it does not seem to be the correct one. The word is scarcely ever divided and its almost universal spelling is Nomans Land from the earliest times.

There was a great Powwaw on Martha's Vineyard called Tequenoman when the English came and he is thought to have had jurisdiction over, and ownership of, this small island, which came to bear the last half of his name (Teque)Nomans Land. This name became attached to the island at that time and has been the only title ever since.

Archaeology

A discovery of great importance to historians and scholars has recently been made on the shore of the little island of Nomans Land. A large rock with an inscription chiselled upon it was found several years ago on the western shore at the foot of a huge boulder from which it evidently fell many years before. The stone is a hard, dark-blue quartz, and because of its unusual appearance, an examination was made which revealed the resemblance to Runic characters such as were used in Greenland and Iceland a thousand years ago.

The inscription translated into English reads: "Leif Erikson 1001."

There are two lines below which are so obliterated that their exact meaning cannot be determined. A tracing of the inscription has been made, and scientists and experts in European languages of the past centuries have examined it to ascertain its authenticity. They have not yet agreed, however, that the inscription is genuine, but, with the knowledge which we have from history of Leif Erikson and the voyages of the Norsemen, the discovery of the rock on Nomans Land with its Runic inscription furnishes interesting proof that it was upon these shores that the Norsemen landed when they reached the New World.

It has long been known that Leif Erikson made a voyage of exploration to the New World about the year 1000 A.D. and accounts of his voyages are given in the sagas of Greenland and Iceland. At first these accounts were in the form of ancient epics or lyrics, but about the year 1200 A.D. they were put into writing in both countries. These agree with the essential facts of the visits of the Norsemen to the American coast.

Government

Nomans Land became part of the township of Chilmark in an act of October 30, 1714. Since this date, it has remained in the township but occupied a small share in the affairs of the town. For years at a time the island was scarcely mentioned in the proceedings of the annual town meetings.

Early Indian Folklore

The time came when Moshup, the giant with a single eye in the center of his forehead, who lived in a cave near the present Gay Head lighthouse, felt he was being crowded out, and that there would soon be no room for such great fellows as himself. He was too good to attempt the destruction of others and too proud to complain, and after many sad communings with himself made up his mind to a course of action which, while it might remove the last remnant of his gigantic tribe from the earth, yet seemed for the best.

By this time he had an infinite number of sons and daughters; these he sent to play on a beach which in those days joined Nomans Land to Gay Head. He then made a mark across the beach at each end with his toe, and so deep that the water flowed through and rapidly cut away the sands — so rapidly, indeed, that the children were in danger of being drowned. The boys held their sisters above the water. Then Moshup called and told them to act as though they were bent on killing whales, whereupon they were all turned into killers (a fish so called). For you must know our giant was a magician as well as the fountain of all wisdom.

American Folklore

During the Revolutionary War, a British warship came to Nomans Land. The troops landed and seized all the cattle. Without oxen to plow and prepare the ground, no crops could be raised. One old woman begged so pathetically to keep her pair that an officer relented and her oxen were returned.

Left: Homestead of the caretakers of Nomans Land, Cameron and Annie Wood, the last inhabitants of the island when they retired in 1939. Annie Wood, in *Romance of Nomans Land,* wrote of the climate: ". . . The winters are mild with no snow and very little ice. Flowers are in bloom until December and garden produce can be planted in the middle of March. It is a spot where God's pure air abounds and where every breath partakes of cool bracing sea breezes; . . . where sound refreshing sleep is assured." *Right:* As caretakers, the Woods' duties were caring for livestock, sheep raising and game preservation. Sheep-shearing was a major industry and help was often imported. Here, one of the 12 children of seasonal laborer, Elmer Lawrence, fetches water, one of the many chores performed by children. Photographs circa 1925, from the Stan Lair collection, courtesy of Mr. and Mrs. Eugene Baer.

Gosnold

The township of Gosnold in the County of Dukes County is composed of a chain of twelve islands, large and small, situated between Vineyard Sound and Buzzards Bay. The islands are Nonamesset, Onkatanka, Ram, Uncatena, Monahanset, Naushon, Weepecket, Pasque, Nashawena, Penekese, Gull and Cuttyhunk. They were incorporated as a town on March 17, 1864.

Naushon, the largest island, is 7½ miles long, 1¼ miles wide and 5,560 acres. The length of Cuttyhunk is 2½ miles and the width is three-fourths of a mile. Gull, the smallest, is less than ¼ mile in length.

The Indian name Naushon means "between," Nonamesset, "the little island," Monahanset, "the little fishing place at the straight," and Nashawena, "the third shell place."

History

The history of Gosnold may be said to have begun in 1602 when Bartholomew Gosnold, with his companions, landed on the rocky islet of Cuttyhunk, the most westerly of this group of islands, which he named Elizabeth's Island in honor of his queen. As recorded by John Brereton, "one of the voyage," and Gabriel Archer, "a gentleman in said Voyage":

"On the eight and twentieth of May we entered counsel about our abode and plantation which we concluded to be in the west part of the island. This, on the western side admitteth some in creeks, or sandy coves, so girded, as the water on some places of each side

meeteth, to which the Indians from the main do oftentimes resort for fishing of crabs.

"We determined to fortifie ourselves in the little plot of ground where we built a house and covered it with sedge which grew about the lake in great abundance; in building whereof, we spent three weeks and more.

"In this island is a stage or pond of fresh water, in circuit two miles, in the center whereof is a rocky islet containing near an acre of ground full of wood, on which we began to build our fort and place of abode, disposing itself so fit for the same.

"The nine and twentieth, we

labored in getting us sassafras, rubbishing our little fort or inlet, new keeling our shallop and making a punt or flatbottom boat to pass to and fro our fort over the fresh water. The powder of the sassafras in twelve hours cured one of our company that had taken a great surfeit, by eating the bellies of dogfish, a very delicious meat.

"The thirtieth, Captain Gosnold, with divers of his company, went upon pleasure in the shallop towards Hap Hill to view it and the sandy cove, and returning, brought with him a canoe that four Indians had there left, being fled away for fear of our English, which we brought into England.

"Began, some of our company that before vowed to stay, to make revolt; whereupon our planters diminishing, all was given over.

"We set sail and bore for England, the three and twentieth of July we came to anchor before Exmouth, in England."

This landing and twenty-five day stay in New England is the beginning of the island's history. The following year, 1603, mention is made of an expedition of Sir Humphrey Gilbert under Captain Martin Pring, who visited this group of islands - 'the bark goes homeward with sassafras, (Indian name, pauame) and arrives safe" is in the record of that expedition.

Exploration became more frequent. These shores were touched by Henry Hudson in 1609, and in 1611 by Captains Harlow and Hobson and Captain John Smith. In 1615 this chain of islands was described by De Laet in his voyage, and in 1619 the Englishman Dermer explored this part of the shore line. All of these sailed along this coast before the arrival of the Pilgrims in the *Mayflower,* and the era of exploration merged into that of trade and settlement.

The many deeds and legal papers dating from the year 1637 reveal much of local history. The island of Naushon was owned by Thomas Mayhew, Sr.

and his heirs from 1641 to 1682 - a period of 41 years. In 1682, he sold this property to Wait Winthrop of Boston, Mass. The correspondence between members of the Winthrop family suggests the reason for this purchase.

A letter dated July 7, 1682, written by Wait Winthrop to his brother, contains the following: "I am going tomorrow towards the island it being profered to me as an extraordinary thing at the price, which I have agreed for if I like it when I shall see it. 'T is said to be seven or eight miles long, and were two miles long generally, and most of it good land, tho somewhat unsubdued."

On September 16, 1682, this letter of that date to his brother contains this statement: "I have purchased the island, but know not whether it will be for the best, it being a very rugged place. It may be worth something in time; when I see you shall give my thoughts about it."

The deed of sale of Naushon from Matthew Mayhew to Wait Winthrop for the sum of 400 pounds is one of the turning points in its history. At this time the destiny of the island to be held as a single estate was settled. The next change of ownership took place in 1730 when John Winthrop sold it to James Bowdoin of Boston, Mass.

During the ownership of Thomas Mayhew depredations were committed upon the shores of Gosnold, probably on Pasque Island. "One Mondaye night the 18, 9, 1667 about 2 or 3 a clock in the morning, by reason of the violence of the wind, my vessel drove ashoare in the harbor at the west end of that island next to Quicks-hole. My self, and company went to warme ourselves at an Indian house. The Indians saied the vessell and the goods were theirs, wee answered noe, they had no right to it.

"About an hower & halfe after wee being returned to the howse the Indians came also and toll'd us they had determined all together we should neither have vessell or goods, they would take them. They tooke away my chest, a suite of cloathes, 2 pre of shooes, all my tooles, my saw, my axe.

"They took away my new Hatt and a paire of new shooes from my sonne; my vessell of 15 tunns with all due furniture belonging to it, and a foresail; to spare my cables and anchors I desired of them but they woulld not gyve them unto mee. My freight aboard, my leads and lyne with divers other things out of my chest and vessell."

This declaration was attested upon oath and reported by Thomas Mayhew to the governor of New York, whose agent, Colonel Nichols, replied as follows:

"It is not possible for me to give full advice at this distance, therefore I must leave very much to ye prudence and the dictates of a good conscience; which two ingredients are proper in all matters of great importance."

Tarpaulin Cove of Naushon Island was used as a haven for pilots. It was a most strategic spot. Often a privateer captain became ruthless in his

"Fishing shacks on Pasque Island," painting by Lemuel D. Eldred, 1873. Private collection.

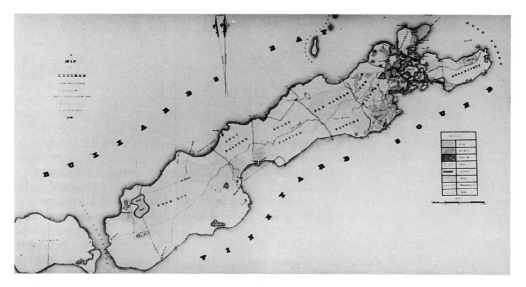

methods and easily slipped from privateering to piracy. An example of this is shown in 1689, in the account of a privateer, Captain Pound, of the King's frigate *Rose,* and his armed men, and his encounter with the sloop *Mary,* a police craft ordered by the Governor and Council to cruise in search of the pirate. In the conflict the captains of both vessels were wounded, which resulted in the death of Captain Pease of the *Mary* on October 12, 1689.

In 1696, H.M.S. *Falkland* arrived in this cove, battered and forlorn, after a long mid-winter voyage from England. The *Falkland,* a 54 gun ship built in 1690, by order of the British government, was the first ship of war built on this side of the Atlantic.

Of this voyage, Captain Hancock writes: "We were much in want of Water and Wood, our mast and rigging very out of repair, a greatly many men very sick, and so we have now, & buried eight. Our Fore Mast is faulty being sprung by a Clapp of Thunder what I believe must come out, and our mainmast we have cut shorter."

In the introduction of the log of H.M.S. *Falkland* is the following petition for spiritual compass orders:
Lord let thy Grace dwell richly in my hart
And make me skillful in thy havenly Art
And let me understand and be soe wise
To know uppon what point my havenly Country Lyes.
And having set my Course directly thither
Great god preserve me in the Fowlest weather.

No name is more closely connected with hidden treasure and piracy than that of Captain Kidd, and it is known that his last port of call, before being captured in July 1699, was Tarpaulin Cove on Naushon of Gosnold Township.

Vineyard Sound was one of the favorite haunts for French privateersmen, affording an easy escape to seaward in case an expedition was sent out against them. The French Watering Place on Naushon was probably so named

because of its use by these French privateers.

These stories of pirates and privateers using Gosnold as a convenient port continued until the outbreak of the Revolution, and Tarpaulin Cove became a favorite haunt of British vessels. The keepers on these islands must have had difficulty in preserving the good will of the British officers and at the same time protecting the stock entrusted to their care.

The outbreak of the Revolution brought great anxiety and fear to the people of this coast and the record of the year 1775 is replete with mention of loss of sheep and cattle from Pasque and Naushon Islands. The owners asked to have troops stationed on these islands, and on September 13, 1775, "billeting barracks & firewood for thirty men from June 29 to July 13 and fifty men from July 13 to September 30" were ordered by Congress.

The logbooks of H.M.S. ships contain frequent mention of this locality, and life must have been exciting with British vessels hovering along the coast.

One Dr. Gilson, a Tory, described as "a short well set man, and had on when he went a way a reddish sheep skin coat, dressed with the wool side inside and a scarlet waist coat," was placed in the custody of Barachiah Basset, Esq., of the Elizabeth Islands, for being "an enemy to the Liberties of this Colony" and the record states that Dr. Gilson was held prisoner at Naushon in June 1776. During this month the island was visited by the illustrious John Paul Jones.

Several distinct raids took place on Naushon, and in May 1778, came a devastating descent upon the island. The British troops carried away all the live stock.

The coastwise shipping which had its beginning hundreds of years ago grew to amazing proportions. The warning signals on this rugged coast consisted of flares or beacons set at certain points. In the 18th century there was a lighthouse, an inn, several small houses, the Revolutionary barracks and farm houses on the island. The Cove was place for the gathering of all the inhabitants of the island, and the farmers had a good trade in meat and vegetables with the visiting vessels. Shipping was of such interest that the daily newspapers gave space to maritime news as: "A Providence brig, a Newport schooner, and a Rhode

Island sloop, all whalers, went ashore at Tarpaulin Cove" (*Boston News-Letter,* 1786).

The newspapers during the War of 1812 relate many depredations made by British warships, and again Naushon was used as a base by British men-of-war.

The *Telegraph* "announces that the ship *Perseverance,* Cook, 135 days from Batavia, ashore at Tarpaulin Cove, and bilged. We are happy to hear that all the coffee is got out of the *Perseverance* dry and in good order; that the sugar is not much wet, and that the property is in a far better state than could be expected."

January 18, 1814: "The Swedish schooner *Dragon* was boarded on Saturday by a barge from H.M.S. *Nimrod* and permitted to proceed, and went into Tarpaulin Cove" (*Boston Daily Advertiser*).

May 18: "H.M.S. *Nimrod* anchored in Tarpaulin Cove on Wednesday, captured two smacks and a sloop, attempted to cut off the Nantucket mail packet, and chased a sloop on shore" (*Columbian Centinel*).

The whaling industry was the next interesting maritime pursuit. The whale ships often spent a night or two at the Cove after leaving their home port and, returning, these whalers stopped for a final "brushing up" before reaching their destination.

No doubt the flavor of venison lingered long in the memory of these sailors and great was their appreciation of fresh, island mutton and turnips grown on Naushon on their return from the Pacific Ocean, Japan Sea or Arctic shores.

A record has been kept of the number of vessels which passed the Cove, through Vineyard Sound, in the year ending June 1829, total 11,653, and in the year ending 1830, 12,603.

The busy, bustling days of long ago are a great contrast to the present serene solitude of the cove in Naushon. In 1842, John M. Forbes arranged to buy Naushon, which includes Nonamesset and Uncatena, and this estate has been in possession of the Forbes family since that date. This family, as the last "masters of Naushon," has emulated its predecessors in high ideals, and thus far the island has the unique reputation of being untainted by commercialism.

Geography and Related Subjects

The geological formation of Gosnold is of the Miocene Tertiary period. Professor Koons, who made a study of glacial "kettle holes," says there is no more remarkable region on the whole line of terminal moraine than on the islands of Uncatena, Nonamesset and Naushon. On the tops of the hills, stratified material consisting of sand and gravel is found and considerable area is covered with boulders.

A slate which the Indians scraped into water and drank when they received any bruises, and traces of a light red earth used by them when going to war, have been found within the territory of Gosnold. On the island of Naushon and Cuttyhunk the soil is fertile. On Pasque, the soil is light and more stony than any of this group of islands.

An original catalogue made by John Winthrop, F.R.S. in 1800 notes that on Naushon he found "fragments of shells dug up to 30 feet deep in making a well three miles from the sea; great quantities of other shells were found in the same place. No water was found — and a piece of red cedar petrified in a short time."

The island of Naushon is well-wooded, and early records show that sassafras trees, the roots of which the Indians boiled and drank for fevers, and a root called Dram-root, so called because it warmed them like a dram, grew abundantly. The red oak, the bark of which the Indians called "touch-wood," was used to kindle fire which was done by striking two flints together. The beach plum which never grows higher than the knee, is found on the barren sand-beaches; this is a very pleasant fruit. The wild indigo wood is found here. The juice of this "rubbed on horses keeps the flies from stinging them." A sort of Sena, which dyed an excellent black, and myrtle berries, which made candles and soap, were found on these islands.

The fauna is composed of fish and shellfish indigenous to the coast. Wild fowl, land birds of many varieties, turtles, harmless snakes, rabbits, butterflies, deer and moths are found on this chain of islands.

The natural resources consist of springs of fresh water and good pasture land on the larger islands. Agriculture has been a feature of the larger islands, with sheep raising the industry. Naushon, the largest of the group, has a fresh water pond of 55 acres and the highest hill, being over 200 feet above sea level. On the

Far left: Map of Naushon from *The Atlantic Neptune* marine atlas. The Island features a fresh water pond of 55 acres in the southwestern part and Mary's Lake, over 15 feet deep. Courtesy of the New Bedford Whaling Museum. *Right:* Today, on tiny Penekese Island, can be found the ruins of the Leper colony (background) abandoned in 1921, fresh water ponds, wild vegetation, a horde of sea gulls and the Penekese School (for delinquent minors). Photograph by Joseph D. Thomas, 1984.

southeastern shore is Tarpaulin Cove and Kettle Cove is on the northeastern shore.

The climate is mild and salubrious. The description given by Brereton of Gosnold's voyage in 1602, and his settlement on the island of Cuttyhunk, voices the opinion of the present generation. "For the agreeing of this climate with us (I do speak for myself and so I say justly do for the rest of our Company), that we found our health and strength all the while we remained there so to renew and increase, notwithstanding our diet and lodging was none of the best, yet not one of our company felt the least grudging of inclination to any disease of sickness, but were much fatter and in better health than when we went out of England. Leaving this island with as many true sorrowful eyes as were before desirous to see it."

Gosnold in literature
"The isle is full of noises,
Sounds and sweet airs, that give delight and hurt not.
Sometimes a thousand twangling instruments
Will hum about mine ears, and sometimes voices
That, if I then had wak'd after long sleep,
Will make me sleep again; and then in dreaming,
The clouds methought would open and show riches
Ready to drop upon me, that, when I wak'd,
I cried to dream again."
The Tempest

Edward Everett Hale in 1902 made the statement that the island of Cuttyhunk may be the one described

by Shakespeare in "The Tempest." This may seem an unwarranted statement, but Marshall Shepard, in a most interesting paper read before the Dukes County Historical Society in 1917, sets forth some convincing evidence.

"The Tempest," it is thought, was published between 1605 and 1610, just after Gosnold had returned and Archer and Brereton had related vivid accounts of the new land recently explored by them.

Gosnold's patron was the Earl of Southampton, who likewise was Shakespeare's patron, and the poet listening, may have received inspiration for this play, as the descriptions are similar to words and phrases used by Brereton.

As Edward Everett Hale suggested, Miranda may, after all, have been a Massachusetts girl.

Above: Cuttyhunk, seen through the camera lens of Fairhaven historian Charles Harris, around 1900, looking northeast toward Nashawena Island. *Courtesy of Fairhaven Academy. Far right:* The Gay Head cliffs and light house, photographed by Joseph Tirrell around 1890. *Courtesy of the New Bedford Free Public Library.*

Gay Head

Gay Head is a small town on the western peninsula of Martha's Vineyard. Explorer Bartholomew Gosnold, in 1602, named this peninsula Dover Cliff, after the clay cliffs of his native land. The Indian names for this territory were Aquinniuh, meaning "the meadow under the hill," and Kuhtuhquetuet, "the place of the rising ground." The name Gay Head was given by the English settlers before 1662, for its gaily colored cliffs, visible when approaching from the western sea.

Geography and Related Subjects

The Gay Head peninsula terminates in one of the most striking headlines of the Atlantic coast, a unique exhibition of nature in one of her most colorful moods. The varied clays of this cliff rise to an elevation of 145 feet. Their geological formation has never been accounted for. The theory is that during the glacial age, erosion carried these materials from their source and deposited them here where they built up as delta formations at the mouth of a great river. Each color represents the deposit of material from a certain region.

Subangular masses of sandstone are found embedded in the strata, apparently ice-rafter, possibly from the Connecticut Valley. Here, also, are beds of dark brown lignite, iron pyrites and crystals of selenite and resin hardly distinguished from amber. Visitors to Gay Head as early as 1786 found many signs of volcanic action. Springs of water contained certain iron and alum, others weakly tinctured with sulphurate hydrogen. This is the only part of our northern seacoast where mineral springs are found.

From a boat offshore, with the rays of the afternoon sun playing on the cliffs, the beauty of the coloring is seen to best advantage. Every shade of red, yellow, blue and gray may be picked out in various gradations. The appearance of the cliffs is like that of a great paint pot with drippings of many colors left streaked diagonally on the surface.

The rate of erosion of the cliffs is alarming and it would seem that the ocean waves to the north and south would soon join hands over their finished work. It is a matter of great concern that no action is being taken by any agency to prevent the destruction of these cliffs. They are a national asset, as worthy of protection as the Niagara and the Grand Canyon of Arizona.

Fossil remains have been found in sands which abound in sharks' teeth and bones of whales. In these clays were found a molar tooth of a young rhinoceros, the bones of a camel, the bones of a horse of the pleistocene period which ended with the final retreat of glacial ice within 25,000 years of the present time.

The natural resources consist of an abundance of clay, springs of fresh water, good meadow land and facilities for fishing. Agriculture is not extensive. The soil is well adapted for crops and is fertile in some localities. When the native cranberry is suitable for harvesting, the entire community is engaged for one day in this occupation.

The flora of Gay Head consists of many varieties such as Mayweed, Ground-nut, Canker-weed, Shore Goldenrod, Woo Grass, sensistive Fern Root, Copper Leaf and Bulrush. The Cat-tail Flag, and Cooper's Flag of whaling days, so-called on Gay Head from its use of caulking casks, also grow. The fruitage of wild nature surrounds many deserted cellar holes of ancient structures. There is an abundance of herbs used for medicinal purposes by the Indians.

Early History

Gay Head has always been known as an Indian community and the Indians have made every effort to maintain the rights bequeathed to them. The earliest sachem of this territory was Nohtoaksaet. At his death, about 1670, his younger son, Mettack, became sachem, and in 1681 drew up the following deed:

"I Mettack Sachem att Kuhtuhquehtuet and Nashauakquetget as far as Wanummuset:

Know yee all People that I Mettack

and my principal men my children & people are owners of this: this is our land forever. They are ours, and our offspring forever shall enjoy them:

I Mettack and we principal men together with our children and all our people are agreed that no person shall sell any Land; but if any person will stealingly sell any Land: take ye your Land because it is yours forever: but if any one will not perform this Covenant he shall fail to have any of this Land at Kuhtuhquehtuut and Nashanaquetget forever:

I Mettack sachem and my chief men speak this in the presence of God it shall be thus forever" (*Mass. Archives*, XXXI, 10).

The authenticity of this deed has been questioned. After the death of Mettack the sachemship fell to his son, Joseph. On April 25, 1685, Matthew Mayhew received the grant of the "Manor and Lordship of Martin's Vineyard" from Governor Thomas Dongan of New York. At once, Mayhew purchased the whole peninsula of Gay Head from Joseph Mettack, and immediately granted unlimited leases to the white settlers of Chilmark. This caused trouble and the Indians complained of their treatment to the "Society for Propagating the Gospel," who purchased, on May 10, 1711, for 550 pounds, the lands at Gay Head.

In 1714 this society was obliged to dig a ditch across the neck, four feet wide, and two feet deep, and erect a heavy gate to keep the white settlers on their own land. These intrusions were unnecessary because the Indians were ever kind and considerate.

After the revolution, their lands were made a state reservation, and in 1862 this reservation became the "District of Gay Head," by an act of the General Court in Boston.

True to tradition, some of the Gay Head Indians found the lure of the sea irresistable, and they soon established a profitable fishing industry. Worthy of note are the small stone sinkers which these men used in hook fishing for flounder and tautog. The weaving of hand nets with a tongued netting needle, using the becket hitch, is a common practice.

The use of beach grass, called in Gay Head dialect "pukapweb" was only recently abandoned. The local expression to "waphan-a" means to braid beach grass into roping for the basket making. A unique type of pack basket or "back basket" was woven of beach grass and the carrying strap was woven in fancy openwork patterns. The only beach grass basket now in existence is in the possession of a woman, formerly of Gay Head, now living in New Bedford, Mass. Another occupation was the use of corn husks made into strips for mats. Another use for these husks was filling for the "under" bed, the "upper" bed being filled with the feathers of geese.

Certain old women were adept in the preparing and administering of medicines and many of these teachings have been handed down to posterity. The absence of magic and ritual is noticeable. All the remedies were formulated from the indigenous flora, gathered under proper weather conditions and always dried by that great healer and strengthener, the sun.

To catch, clean and roast a white-footed mouse and feed it to a patient was a sure remedy for some ailments, and an eel-skin placed around the waist would cure cramps and rheumatism, while oil from skunks was most effective in relieving congestion of head and chest. Certain of their 70 herb remedies would dispel the presence of a "Toppai," the ghost or spirit sometimes occupying the mind.

The tilling of the soil was done with oxen, and an ox team was the motor power used during the lobster season at Gay Head.

Among Gay Head family possessions may be seen several small wooden mortars, as well as a large one, nine inches high, five and one half inches in diameter and three quarters of an inch deep. The material for these mortars is sassafras wood and the pestle is a purely aboriginal utensil made of stone.

The Indians at Gay Head were the last to accept the religious teachings of the white settlers. In 1663, the sachem Mettack accepted the new theology and became a missionary to his people.

In 1696, it is recorded: "At least 260 souls, who have here at their charge a meeting house already framed." This meeting house was also used as a schoolroom, for in 1702 it is recorded that two school-masters, Josias Hassawit and Peter Chavin, taught during the winter season. At this time and until 1870, the school system was under the control of the State of Massachusetts. The "cause of education" did not flourish until 1889, when the town of Gay Head gave sufficient financial support to lengthen the school terms and provide several teachers.

Left: Up-island sheep grazing is depicted in an 1888 watercolor by Amelia M. Watson. Courtesy of the Dukes County Historical Society. *Right:* Gay Head Indians employed the services of oxen for plowing their fields and to assist them in the servitude of a growing tourist population. Tourists and sightseers were carted around in ox carts (as shown here) from the ferry landing at Gay Head to the pavillion and to see the various sights. Stan Lair collection, courtesy of Mr. and Mrs. Eugene Baer.

Gay Head Light by Laura Jernegan Spears
Page from artist's sketchbook, May 1888

The patriotism of Gay Head began at the time of King Philip's War. One Japhet Hannit was captain of an Indian company. In 1675 it was written of him that "good Japhet was very serviceable to both those of his nation and our's on the Island; for being firmly set, if possible, to maintain and reserve Peace, betwixt the English and the Indians here, and being an Indian captain, he was employed by the English to observe and report how things went among the Indians" ("Indian Converts," by Experience Mayhew).

In the War of the Revolution one Anthony Jeremiah, a Gay Head Indian, was in the first American naval battle, when John Paul Jones captured the English ship *Serapis,* the greatest and most unique victory of modern times. In the admiral's account of the battle he often spoke of Anthony Jeremiah, who was Gay Head's first naval hero and for many years the only full-blooded Indian in the United States Navy.

The first church was organized about 1693 and the preachers usually acted as school teachers, with the Indian Bible, primers and catechisms for text books and the meeting house for a school room.

In 1698 there were 260 souls reported as attending church services at Gay Head; in 1747, the number of men, women and children was 112; and in 1786 there were reported to be 276 Indians living in Gay Head.

In 1727 only one English house had been built and a visitor in 1736 stated that they suffered much from cold during the winter weather although peat was procurable and plenty.

The Indian men spent most of their life on the water and became most expert whalemen. Gay Head has been the scene of many marine disasters since its settlement by the English. On the night of January 14, 1782, a vessel was driven ashore on the reefs, two miles from the cliffs and 12 men were drowned.

The following description given by a traveller is on record of the early history of Gay Head:

"Here, on a dreary point, nearly cut off from the main body of the island by a couple of fresh water ponds, dwells a scanty remnant of the aboriginal inhabitants of Martha's Vineyard.

"A number of ordinary cattle may be seen browsing upon luxurious grass, but no signs of cultivation or improvement are visible except a few lonely, unpainted wooden houses and several sorry patches of corn or kitchen vegetables, weed-grown, neglected and forlorn. But the welcome we received from the light-keeper was worthy of his personal fame and the glorious Flag under which he serves" ("A Summer in New England," by Porte Crayon, *Harper's,* Sept. 1860, pages 4-8).

Far left: Young Gay Head man holding his ox-team, circa 1920. Stan Lair collection, courtesy of Mr. and Mrs. Eugene Baer. *Left*: "Gay Head Light," by Laura Jernegan Spears, May 1888, from a sketchbook she kept, while on a whaling voyage with her father, a captain. *Right*: Gay Head Light and tourists, 1887. The lighthouse keeper's house (background), torn down in 1902, was considered unsafe for human habitation after four of the keeper's children died within a 15 month period, presumably from the drinking water taken from a nearby spring. The keeper, a Gay Head Indian, wore two uniforms, one for duty and one to greet the tourists who arrived by the hundreds off the Gay Head Steamer from Cottage City. Courtesy of the Dukes County Historical Society.

On the dangerous rocky ledge of Gay Head, called the Devil's Bridge, the U.S. Government, on February 22, 1799, under President Adams, established a lighthouse to be erected on this island and the height above sea level is 172 feet. In 1858-9, through the influence of the Supervisor of Lights, Constant Norton, the Government built a first-class lighthouse at Gay Head. The lamp was purchased from the French government for ten thousand dollars and was the most powerful light on the Atlantic Coast. It contains 1,003 prisms of cut and polished crystal glass, scientifically arranged by Fresnel into sections so that if flashes every ten seconds, three white and one red flash. The works are so finely balanced that one can move the great lantern, which weighs over a ton, with very little effort.

The original proclamation of President Adams concerning the acts of the General Court of Massachusetts is preserved at the lighthouse. Not until 1870 was a road from Chilmark to the lighthouse laid out. It is the only public highway in the town.

From 1862 to 1870 endeavors were being made to create this reservation into the District of Gay Head and at last April 15, 1870 "the town began its independent career with nothing in the treasury and the sandy peninsula to work out its destiny" (*History of Martha's Vineyard* by C. E. Banks, 1911).

In 1873 the town was severed from Chilmark office and on February 14th the Gay Head Post Office was established.

A life saving station was placed in commission December 20, 1895, with a crew composed of native surfmen. The crews have generally been of Indian extraction. The record of this station is one of great efficiency and notably brave work.

The wreck of the *City of Columbus,* occurring on the night of January 18, 1884, was the most appalling in the history of this coast. The toll of the sea from this unnecessary wreck was 121 persons and is the greatest disaster in the annals of Gay Head.

In 1891 the U.S. Battleship *Galena* was lost on the south side of Gay Head. All hands on board were saved by an Indian crew who showed their usual heroism.

Eight Indians from Gay Head took part in the Civil War - six in the navy and two in the army. In 1918 Gay Head had the honor of sending more men to the World War, in proportion to its population, than any town in New England.

Archaeology and Ethnology

Early folklore consists of 28 hero episodes and eight tales pertaining to a female deity. Animal, reptile and weather lore and tales of witchcraft, pirates and buried treasure correspond to that of other tribes and towns.

Indian contributions to the language: The Indian name for tautog was "taut-auog" meaning sheep's heads and the name of the bivalve called quahog may be derived from their name for it — poquahock. Places such as "mash-atan-auke" which has corrupted into "shot-an-arrow" and "shot higher hill" meaning "the great hill land," are from the Algonguin language. The name Kugh-tuh-quick-e-wutt, meaning "at the going up" was

called Catackutcho in a deed 1687.

Early records show that nokekick or nocake was indispensable when traveling or hunting. Nocake soup or corn, ground and boiled, was almost a necessity. Other savory dishes are hulled corn, succotash and corn meal bread.

Outstanding Indian Characters

The religion of the Indians on Martha's Vineyard was a form of Polytheism and the worship of many gods existed until 1643, when, under the influence of the early missionaries, a Chief Hiacoomes joined the first founded church.

Meetings were held in his wigwam and the known converts were Hichqsad, a chief converted in 1646; Tawanquatuck, an Indian sachem; Ammapos, the daughter of the sachem Cheshchaamog and wife of Wammamauhkamun; also Manchquannum, the mother of Sissetome, who became an Indian minister. (*Mayhew and the Indians* by E. A. Hallock.)

Other outstanding Indians were Cheesehahchamuk, a sachem of the Algonquin tribe, and Josias, a sachem of Takemmy (Tisbury) who sold land to the first white settlers of that region. The sachem of Sowchacomkacket in 1660 was named Wampamaq. He was the son of Adommas "queen sachem" as she was called. The earliest sachem of Gay Head was Nahtoaksaet who died in 1670. His youngest son Mettack became sachem of this territory and his name appears in several recorded deeds.

Teachers and preachers in the Indian dialect were Japhet Hannit, Wauwompohque, Josias Panneu, Peter Abquanhut, Silas Paul, Thomas Jeffers, and Anthony Jeremiah, the only full blooded Indian in the United States Navy during the Revolutionary War.

Government

The town of Gay Head, since its incorporation, has yearly elected a Board of Selectmen. Town and government positions are held by Indians. The late Edwin Devriss Vanderhoop represented Dukes County at the General Court in 1888.

Folklore, Customs and Legends

Martha's Vineyard Folklore

by Lucretia Norton

Editor's Note: In 1936, Henry Alsberg and John Lomax, the Project's first folklore editor, sent a letter to the state directors reminding them that gathering material for the Guides offered an incredible opportunity for the gathering of American folklore. They asked for information on "wishing seats, wishing wells, swamps or quicksand with sinister properties, localities with beneficent qualities; stories of the relationship between people and animals; early settler narratives." The instructions were greeted with derision in some states and with enthusiasm in others.

In 1938, John Lomax was succeeded by Benjamin A. Botkin, whose vision and qualifications gave the program respectability. Until Botkin and the Federal Writers became involved, folklore was the preserve of scholars. Now it became a viable aspect of the nation's identity. Two valuable contributions to the Project were the Slave Narrative

Collection *and* These are Our Lives, *a collection of oral histories. As Botkin pointed out, "living lore was responsive to the mood of the moment but behind it was the accumulated wisdom of generations." In 1944, Botkin edited an anthology called* A Treasury of American Folklore, *the first of a series of best selling books on the subject.*

The Legend of Devil's Bridge

The Indians believed in a giant named Cheepie-unk. He agreed to build a bridge of stone from Cuttyhunk to Gay Head and this contract read: "I, Cheepie-unk, between the hours of sunset and before the cockcrow in the morning, do agree to build a bridge from Aquinnah to Cuttyhunk. If I fail to finish said bridge of stone before cockcrow, this compact is null and void."

One dark night he began his work and the bridge would be in place. But some said: "We do not want a bridge." Then an old squaw, one of the cunning ones, lighted her torch and waved it where the cock would catch the flare. Immediately, with flapping wings and out-stretched neck, the cock crowed long and lustily. Cheepie-unk had to stop building, the bridge was unfinished, and the opposing party triumphed. This is the legend of Devil's Bridge.

Amelia M. Watson's watercolors appear on the next five pages and on pages 35 and 44. Amelia M. Watson (1856-1934), from East Windsor Hill, CT, taught at Martha's Vineyard Summer Institute, 1878-1902, a successful, non-accredited college with an enrollment of over 700 students. During summers, accompanied by her mother and two sisters, she resided at various places up-island, and had ample opportunity to paint the countryside. An acclaimed illustrator, her most well-known work appears in Henry David Thoreau's two-volume set, *Cape Cod*, published in 1896. The books illustrated in color, are filled with miniature paintings of plants, animals, still-lifes and landscapes. *Left:* "On the Road to Gay Head." *Right:* "On the Road to Gay Head." Courtesy of the Dukes County Historical Society.

The Legend of the Trustram Weeks House

In Week's Lane in the township of Gay Head stood an old, abandoned house. This empty, weather-beaten building was the first church erected in the town and in it were held religious services by itinerant preachers and the early Island ministers and teachers, especially for the Indians of Gay Head.

These Indians possessed strong, musical voices and it was told that the rafters of the old church frequently shook from the vibration of chants and hymns of praise. Later, the building was occupied as a home by one Trustram Weeks. He also was a singer, a man whose strong bass voice was often heard as he led his family in song.

There were those who said that, although the old house stood unoccupied for many years, in passing at night one could distinctly hear music sounding through the ancient rafters and in the attic shadowy forms were seen moving about and kneeling in prayer. (Told to writer by an Indian named Ann Job, a woman employed as family laundress. She died many years ago.)

The Legend of Abel's Spring

Abel's Spring near Abel's Neck, in Gay Head, derives that name from a noted Indian dignitary, former owner of that neck of land, whose signature on a deed reads, "I, Able Abel, Indian man." Near the spring is an Indian burial ground where Hiacoomes, the first Indian convert, was buried with his hatchet, and bow and arrows.

It is said that stones were arranged around the grave and a fire kept burning until the stones were red hot, thus driving away any evil spirit from his last resting place. Since he was buried here, the spring of water has never ceased to flow.

The Legend of Great Swamp

On entering the town of Gay Head the highway passes over Black Brook which flows from Great Swamp, the haunt of goblins and witches and uncanny noises. The swampy ground, overgrown with sweet-pepper, bushes, black alder, wild roses, swamp honey-suckle and briars is full of hiding places for ghosts and they are said to live there even at the present time.

Hundreds of years ago all the Gay Head Indians had straight hair but a certain squaw got into bad company such as witches and adepts of the so-called black art of the Great Swamp. Having more than the usual amount of a woman's curiosity, one day she was discovered peering into a kettle containing some magic brew, whereupon the witches shook her, clawed her eyes out and snarled her hair.

So, ever after that time, all her descendents are called "Snarly-haired."

Popular Names of Animals and Plants

Wood-pussy for skunk.

Locust for the periodical cicada of Martha's Vineyard. Only the male is musical and the chorus suggests the croaking of frogs.

Reindeer moss the common moss growing in open fields on sandy soil and classed as Caladonia rangifernia.

Copper-leaf or false wintergreen

Shore Goldenrod, growing near salt water creeks. The botanical name is Scirpus Lacustris.

Cooper's Flag or *bulrush,* used in caulking casks. The botanical name is Scirpus Lacustris.

Dangle berries, the Gaylussacia Frondasa

Bonaparte's Crown, The Spurge

Smelling Leaf or *Bible Leaf,* habitually used on the island of Martha's Vineyard to place in the bible and diffuse its fragrance. The botanical name is Costmary.

Other popular names are: *Mayweed, Ground-nut, Canker-weed, Wood-grass, Hog-tush, Iceland Moss* and *Running Ivy.*

Weather Lore

Vineyard cats are always more playful before a storm.

The croaking of a tree-toad is the sign of approaching rain.

The whistling of a robin is an indication that showers are coming.

If water boils away rapidly the rain will continue.

A circle around the moon indicates that rain will fall during the following day.

"Rain before seven, clear before eleven."

"Rainbow at night, sailor's delight, but rainbow in the morning, sailors take warning.

"Thunder in the morning, showery all day."

"Winds that change against are always sure to be backward run."

"Wind from the east, bad for man and beast. Wind from the west is softest and best."

"The farther the sight the nearer the rain."

(These are familiar sayings on the island.)

Wart Cures

To cure a wart "take a white bean, split it and rub the wart with each half. Then throw the two halves of the bean into a well of water." Or, "wet the wart with castor oil as many times a day as convenient, being careful to let it dry thoroughly each time and the warts will disappear very rapidly." To touch or handle a toad will cause warts to grow on the hands. (From an old account book of Charles B. Snow (1840-1863) in the Dukes County Historical House.)

Aug. 28, 1888. By Amelia M. Watson

came from New Bedford to gather it."

"The honeset that grows near streams, swamps and marshes is good for the system. A tea is made by pouring boiling water on an ounce of the herb. Taken hot it will sweat, taken lukewarm it will vomit, and taken cold, it will purge."

"A tea made from the bark of the bayberry will cure dysentery. Also grind the bark, bake it and it's good as snuff."

(Remedies given by Aunt Biah Diamond in *The Old South Road to Gay Head,* 1926, by E. S. Burgess.)

Omens and Superstitions
(From the older people of the island.)

Tradition seems to have preserved one superstition about Abel's Spring in Gay Head — that cattle can see or feel presence which is not observed by humans. "When cattle in a certain field come near the Mittack rock and the thickets about the burial stones, they become strangely excited, leaping and bellowing as they do nowhere else." Also, "a light is sometimes seen there, but the light is in no man's hand." (*From The Old South Road of Gay Head,* 1926, by E. S. Burgess.)

An extra plate unintentionally set on the dining-room table will bring an unexpected guest.

When the housewife drops the dish cloth on the floor it is a sign that guests are coming to the house.

If you hit your elbow, that is a sign that you'll receive a letter.

The bride, in order to have a happy marriage, must on her wedding day wear "something old and something new, something borrowed and something blue."

If a sore throat is to be cured, bind the neck with a piece of red flannel. Burn the flannel when the throat is cured, and toss the ashes over two crossed sticks of wood.

A branch cut from a willow held in the right hand will indicate where a spring of water may be found. The branch will bend toward the hidden spring.

If a black cat chooses to make his home with a family, he will surely bring good luck.

Folk Medicine

"Steep mayweed and drink it for there's nothing like it for a broken bone — why, it'll almost set a bone itself."

"The ground-nut or Indian potato was much used. It may be eaten raw or baked or boiled."

"We gathered canker-weed and used it for some months, and many people

Customs Pertaining to Life and Death

Proposals of marriage were sometimes written by the suitor and sent to the maid of his affections. In many instances, the young man asked the father of the young woman if he might "pay attention" to the daughter, and if the father consented, the lover called on Wednesday and Sunday evenings of each week.

The front or "best" room was the place of reception and the length of the visit was determined by the burning of the candles. If the candles used were short ones the caller left early, but if the maiden were in love

with the youth, she previously arranged to have lighted the tallest and largest candles. This mute but eloquent sign was also a help to the shy young man who became quite sure of acceptance before making his proposal.

The maiden so honored would be busily engaged in preparing linen sheets, woolen blankets, quilts and garments for the "hope chest."

The custom of "publishing banns" was followed on the island of Martha's Vineyard in the early days of its settlement. These marriage intentions were sometimes announced by the minister from the pulpit and printed forms were fastened near the church entrance so that all who passed were able to read the "intentions" of the persons named in the documents.

The church was the favorite place for the wedding ceremony and after the newly wedded couple reached their future home they were serenaded by their friends. The bridegroom was expected to dispense cigars and confectionery to the group assembled outside.

The simple custom known as "Coming out Bride" was observed. On the first sabbath after the wedding the couple attended the church services dressed with as distinctly bridal finery as they possessed, and to arrive a trifle late in order to receive the attention of the congregation was the correct procedure.

That a death had occurred in the family was at once announced by the placing of a wreath or spray of flowers at the front entrance of the home. If an old person died, a purple ribbon was used to tie the flowers; but pure white was selected for announcing the death of a child, and pale pink for that of a young person.

Carefully kept in an unused drawer of the old "high-boy" or bureau, scented with lavender or geranium leaves, were the garments made ready for that last occasion. Shiftless indeed was the housewife who had not prepared her own "burial outfit" and kept it clean and bleached by sun and dew. (Told to the writer by her mother, who died about twenty years ago.)

Social Customs

In the early days of the history of Martha's Vineyard Island there was much "visiting," especially among the women of the community, and their hands were never idle. They were equipped with balls or skeins of wool or cotton, knitting needles, shearths. These shearths were firmly fastened to the waist and fashioned to hold one needle while the other needle was so rapidly manipulated as to produce a clicking sound.

So much in vogue were these "knitting parties" that it was said that those rounding Cape Poge could hear the clicking of the knitting needles before seeing the lights of Edgartown village.

The annual output of stockings from this town was about 15,000 pair, mittens 3,000, and wigs for seamen 600. The old custom of rolling the knitted portion of the stocking as tightly as possible so as to stretch its length is still followed.

Another very old custom was the gathering known as a "donation party." When an individual or a family seemed to be in need of the necessities of life, members of the community would assemble at that home at a certain fixed day and hour, bringing with them articles of clothing, food, fuel, etc. A meal was prepared of which all partook, taking great care that an abundance of food was left.

A "donation party" was also one way of supplementing the somewhat meager salary of the preacher by filling the cellar with vegetables and increasing the size of the woodpile with loads of seasoned oak and pine. (Consultant: Mrs. Johnson Whiting, West Tisbury, Sept. 7, 1936.)

A quilting party was another popular occasion for getting together. Not only were bed coverings quilted, but so were petticoats of silk or satin, capes, infants' slips and hoods. As many as 400,000 tiny stitches were taken in one small garment.

Tea was always served on these occasions and the "menfolk" were expected to assemble to partake of the "cup that cheers" — a custom continued to the present time. (From Rev. William Homes' diary, 1737.)

A time-honored custom was partaking of a vineyard clam-bake. "The smell of hot rock-weed, the hiss of scalding rocks, the approaching succulence of clam, corn fish, lobster, potatoes and a multitude of edible things cooked in that salty smother, and to end the rite with ripe, luscious watermelon was, and is, a repast to be remembered." (From *Martha's Vineyard Summer Report,* by Henry Beetle Hough, 1935.)

On the salt water one of the memorable institutions was the whaleboat race. The first one was held in August 1875 when the whaleboats from New Bedford, Fairhaven, and Edgartown contended. The Edgartown boat became so famous that the sport died out years later because this boat won every race. The boat in question is now the property of the Dukes County Historical Society and is "anchored" on the grounds of the society's house in Edgartown.

Bartering was another early custom, not only among neighbors, but with ships entering the harbors of Martha's Vineyard. The pilots would exchange knitted mittens, stockings, caps, pies, and other cooked food for molasses, sugar, tea, coffee, spices, even Holland gin and Jamaica rum. The housewives were rich in such supplies.

"Opening the pond" in West Tisbury is a custom in which the work of some members of the community benefits all. In early spring, about late March or early April, depending upon the weather conditions. Tisbury Great Pond is opened to the ocean so the herring may enter the pond and spawn.

This opening calls for the efforts of oxen or horses with plows, or strong men with stout shovels. Volunteer help is always available and the occasion is honored by groups of spectators.

After the spawning season is over, the opening is laboriously closed by men, unless Nature assists by a severe storm, in which case the work is done in less time and much more effectively. Later, the pond is again opened to the ocean so the herring may be caught or escape. These are interesting occasions where the efforts of a few are for the benefit of many. (Consultant: Mrs. Johnson Whiting, West Tisbury, Sept. 7, 1936.)

Cranberry Day

A gathering in which all the community shares is that of the annual "Cranberry Day" in Gay Head. The native bogs produce an abundance of berries and on an appointed day, usually in September, all business is set aside, the schools are closed, and old and young assemble in the bogs. During the noon hour, all partake of a "basket lunch" together and the labor of the day is mingled with jests, games and songs. (*Vineyard Gazette*, September, 1935)

House Moving

A rather common custom on the island of Martha's Vineyard is that of moving houses. Being sea-farming as well as farming communities, men frequently decided to "change the moorings" of their houses as well as of their boats. Many a house built in Lambert's Cove has been moved to Vineyard Haven, from West Tisbury to Chilmark, from Sengecomtucket to Edgartown. This latter town claims title of having the most travelled houses. By actual count, forty-eight houses have been moved from one part of the town to another part, not only once but three or more times.

In early days oxen were used as the motor power but later this tedious and careful business was accomplished by a horsepower capstan and four sets of rollers. Accomplished during a period of several weeks, the buildings suffered little damage and an abandoned house is something foreign to Vineyard traditions.

Buried Treasure at Cottissimoo

Cottissimoo, meaning "a great spring of water," was the Indian name given that beautiful body of water now called Lake Tashmoo. A woman of great age lived on the banks of Tashmoo and died many years ago. She told the story that from a vessel lying in Tarpaulin Cove, across Vineyard Sound, came a small boat with two men aboard.

They rowed the boat up the Herring Creek into Cottissimoo and, landing at a great rock on the eastern shore, buried a large bundle. Some folk thought that a member of the crew had died of small-pox and been buried near the rock by his mates; but others were of the opinion that the bundle contained treasure from some pirate vessel.

As few people cared to trifle with a case of small-pox, the spot was undisturbed for many years. However, one dark night several adventurers armed with shovels and spades and lanterns proceeded to dig around the rock searching for gold. They dug and dug and at last came upon the bones of a man. One picked up the skull, extracted a tooth as a memento and drove his spade deeper into the ground.

With a yell, he sank to his armpits while all manner of strange, uncanny noises were heard. The other members of the party pulled up the half buried man and then fled without looking back, for fear evil spirits were following them.

The story closes with the statement that the man who found the skull and the buried treasure was later afflicted with small-pox and there has been no treasure hunting around that rock since that midnight hour of long ago.

The Skipper Borrows His Leg:
a Provincetown sea yarn

by Josef Berger

clement e daley 1988

I see where they've been digging down for Injuns in the burying ground over to Eastham. Here's a two-ply piece in the paper, fitted out with pictures and all, about the Boston Society of Archy - Archy - well, anyway, about 'em bringing up seven skeletons of Injuns, with their arrowheads, fish-hooks, pots and one thing and another.

The feller in the paper goes on to say the Injuns buried all that gear with their dead so's the spirits wouldn't go short of nothing. Well, him and all them historical professor fellers is guessing wrong on that! You know why the Injuns stowed down all that dunnage with a dead man? Not so's he wouldn't go short, but so's he wouldn't come back for nothing when he seen he was short!

Yes sir, them savages was a lot sharper than us — some of us, anyway. I see young Tony over there in the corner, baiting me with a grin. All right, Tony. but I presume you never knowed Cap'n John Santos. Died before you et out of a spoon, I presume.

Well, Cap'n John was a cripple, but he wasn't shorebound by it. Skippered the trawler *Hetty K* and contrived to get around real handsome on a hand-tailored leg which come all the way from Switzerland. And was Cap'n John proud of the furrin piece of jury rig! Swiss yodelwood, he said 'twas, the genuwine as a low-line doryman's

alibi. It was one of the show-sights in town, back in those days, to let folks from up-Cape watch Cap'n John dance a "chamarita" down to the Atlantic House without once nicking the ballroom floor. He hadn't wore it six months before he copper-bottomed it just to make sure the worms wouldn't get to him before his time.

When the Portland Gale struck in '98, the *Hetty K* was thirty miles off the back-side of the Cape and making a run for it. That was November 11. Presume you've heard of the Portland Gale. If Father Noah'd been out in that he'd have added a couple fathom to the keep of his craft and shipped a couple of extra elephants for ballast.

Well, as I say, Cap'n John's vessel was caught in it, and on November 12 here she come, rounding the Point into Provincetown Harbor, standing in under bare poles with her lee rail under water. And Cap'n John wasn't aboard. In the fight she'd had riding out that storm, him and two of the crew was washed overboard, and he was never seen here again — never, that is, but the once I'm going to tell you of.

Two days after the gale'd abated, Joe Barcia, working with the wreckers on the beach, picked up Cap'n John's wooden leg. He fetched it home to Maria, the widow. But the Cap'n's body was never found, not then, not later, and 'twas a mite queer that his prize mast should come in clean

unstepped from the whole of him, because he was overboard, and when the Cap'n had on that wooden leg he had it on fast. It set the whole town talking. The widow signed up men to comb the back-side beach for the body, and the wind turned nor'west, which always brings drowned men ashore there, and the other two that was gone overboard did drift in. But no Cap'n John. There was some talk that the sharks might have got him, but the wooden leg come in clean as a beach pebble, with not a mark on it. Oh, there was all kinds of yarns afloat in town!

Maria was hard took by the Skipper's going. Married thirty years, they was, and never shipped a twister once in all that time. When Joe Barcia brought the leg back, Maria petted it and talked to it, just like it was the Cap'n himself, and gradually she got kind of moony over it. When she wasn't coddling it in her arms she kept

it stowed away in a spice cupbcard with the door locked.

Joe Barcia was a mite betaken with the widow, and when he seen how she was carrying on with that leg, he was sorry he ever fetched it to her — and a mite worried about her too. One day he come to the house and warned her.

"If I was you, Maria," he said, "I'd take that leg and give it to me. And I'd take it out thirty miles to sea and weight it with half a dozen net-leads and drop it under water. You can't never tell."

But Maria wouldn't listen. She wanted to keep that leg just like other women hang on to their babies' first shoes.

Nothing more come of it till the night of November 10, a year later. One year wanting a day, of the night when the Portland Gale struck here. And that night Maria Santos had a dream — or anyway she decided next morning it must have been a dream.

She'd set up in bed, about midnight, she said, and there before her, standing straight as two yards of pumpwater on his one leg, was Cap'n John. He looked at her and smiled. Then he hopped over to the bedside. Holding himself with one hand to the starboard bed post, he canted over and whispered:

"Barometer's falling, my dear. And win's from the no'theast. I'm in for a spell of heavy weather, and I'll be wanting my store leg to steady me when it's all hands on deck."

Then he pinched her cheek, the way he used to do, and at the cold touch of his hand — dear as the widow'd held her man — she let out a screech. The Cap'n give her a sad look then and cleared into thin air.

Next morning, as I say, the Widow Santos decided she must have dreamed it. But all the same, before she went to bed she took the Skipper's leg out of the spice-cupboard and left it near the hearth, where he could pick it up in case he made another call for it.

She didn't sleep sound that night. Outside a breeze of wind come up, and in a couple of hours it turned into a living no'theast gale. The rain drove a drumbeat on the windows, the house rocked like a forty-foot flounder-dragger, and the big willow tree outside howled like as if the yoho bird of every dead sailor in hell had come to roost to it and see which could sound off the most severe.

This time the Widow Santos was

awake, and knew gospel-sure she was awake, when she heard an easy thump-thump-thump across the floor downstairs. Then the door shut to. She was afraid to go below. She stayed in her bed, shivering, until finally she dropped off to sleep.

Next morning she went to look if Cap'n John's leg was still in the corner by the hearth. It was. Yes, the leg was there, but when she picked it up it was wet, wetter'n a drownded shark! And down one side of it was a row of long clean grooves, like scrimshandering on a piece of whalebone.

Widow Santos set down, shaking and feeling kind of bilgey to the stomach. But she noticed there was water on the floor where the leg had been and wet spots on a couple of other floorplanks. Sometimes it come down rain hard enough to go in by the chimney, and she decided that was what must have happened. And the marks on the wooden leg — well, she

told herself, they must have been there before, and she just hadn't seen 'em.

All the same, the poor woman was so upset that she took sick thinking and fretting over it, and she called in Doc Atwood that same morning. The Doc, when he got through sounding for a misery and not finding nothing sprung, told her she must have something on her mind. She said yes, she had. And then she told him the whole of it.

"I'd like to have a look at that leg of Cap'n John's," Doc Atwood said. So she give it to him to take an observation, and when he'd gone over it — still wet and showing them long, clean grooves — he looked hard at the widow.

"You've seen these marks before, Widow Santos?"

She was so gallied by that time, she said yes, she was certain sure she'd seen 'em.

"Well," the Doc went on, "that

explains why they never found the Skipper. Seems to me they should have knowed it in the first place!"

"Why, what do you mean, Doctor?"

"These marks, Widow Santos, is the marks of sharks' teeth," he answered. "Plain as plain! And they say you left this leg over there in the corner all night?"

"Yes, Doctor," the widow gasped.

"But it's wet, Widow Santos. The leg is wet."

"Yes, Doctor. But it's the rain done it. The rain - do you hear? the rain done it, Doctor!" She was screaming now, gone clean whacky in her fear.

"Widow Santos," the Doctor said, after he'd calmed her down a mite, "I'm going to ask you to have one of the men take this thing out and weight it down and drop it in the sea. Yes, it's wet, all right. But this water, Widow Santos — I've put my tongue to it, and this is salt water!"

clement e daley 1988

Washington Swapped Shoe Buckles with Yankee Hatch (*Attleboro*)

by Roy Crandall

Colonel Israel Hatch, who was my host at the Steamboat Inn in Attleborough as well as the White Horse Tavern in Boston, was entertaining a distinguished guest. He had noted the arrival of a superb private coach and four and had hastened to receive the dignified stranger — a man about six feet, four inches in height, clad in a rich costume. His face was calm, his mien was one of lofty dignity. The upper lip protruded slightly because the dentists of 1785 were not as skillful as those of 1936 and the upper dental plate that the newly arrived traveler wore was a clumsy affair. It might have come from the forge of a smith. Colonel Hatch had seen service in the Revolutionary War and he suddenly grasped the fact that his guest was named George and that his other name was Washington.

He was a bit flustered, but not for long. Great men were not novelties. John Quincy Adams had dined at his historic Attleborough tavern more than once, the orotund voice of the mighty Daniel Webster had rolled through the broad spaces of the dining room in friendly argument and Washington's famed friend and ally Marie Jean Paul Roch Yves Gilbert Motier, known affectionately to all liberty loving Americans as Marquis de Lafayette had also stretched his legs under the heavy oaken dining table in Hatch's historic hostelry.

And now the roof covered the idol of the nation, the great and beloved Washington.

The date? No quien sabe, but it was between 1780 and 1799 for Colonel Hatch did not acquire the even then ancient garrison and inn until the first year above set down and Washington passed on near the close of the last one.

It was in the days of small clothes, knee breeches of silk or satin for the great, fustian or leather for the lowly. Washington was richly clad. For years his clothes had been sent from England, but at the period now under conjecture they were from Philadelphia. The buckles on his low shoes shimmered for they were of tastefully cut steel enriched with crystal. Colonel Hatch liked those buckles; he thought them as fine as the best pair he was possessed of; those he reserved for unusual historic or social functions. He began to ponder and to plan though he did not fail to show appreciation of the distinguished figure confronting him. Personally he took the guest's cloak and hat, as well as those of two unidentified associates, and leading the gentlemen to comfortable chairs he ordered refreshing toddies and then hastened to the kitchen to order dinner. Such was the custom when our country was in its early teething troubles.

There were no printed menus in those days; the guests at Colonel Hatch's numerous hostelries never saw one, but there was food in plenty. Venison was to be had for the shooting, wild ducks were as plentiful as mosquitoes in New Jersey,

George Washington and Colonel Hatch make their exchange. Illustration by Stephen Cook, 1988.

partridges, pheasants and quail were cheap, and nearby waters were literally crowded with oysters, clams, scallops and lobsters. The fish swam fin to fin.

When Washington and his friends were summoned to dinner the board fairly groaned beneath the load of delicacies for banquet boards had even greater reasons to groan than now.

Colonel Hatch was asked to join the party. The bottle marched across the board four abreast and Hatch told the Great Commander that he had served under him in repelling the British, had been a captain in fact. All ice was

melted; all reserve departed. Hatch, who might with justice be described as the first of the Massachusetts "hustlers," might also be described as one of the best of the Yankee traders. A real one would rather swap than buy. Israel proved it ere the party left the table by sending a servant to bring his best shoe buckles and offering his now happy and jovial guest an even "swap," buckles for buckles.

And, so runs the tradition, Washington accepted, removed his buckles and substituted those handed to him by the hotel keeper.

The Pioneer Jewelry Maker of Attleboro

by Roy Crandall

Rochambeau, whose generous parents had endowed him with the name Jean Baptiste Donatien de Viemura, and who added to it by earning and adding the titles of Comte and Field Marshall, was encamped with his French army within eighteen miles of Attleboro, "the Jewelry City," in 1780 and thereon hangs the tales of "The Furrener."

In every army one will hear of deserters, or "meet up" with stragglers. Such a one is said to have been "The Furrener," or Foreigner, and yet American jewelry manufacturers must, if justice rules, look back on him as the pioneer patron of the great art and industry on which the fame and progress of Attleboro rests. "The Furrener," so called by early historians, was the first man to make jewelry in the country we now live in. The place of his arduous one man task was in South Attleboro, and legend, tradition and generation-by-generation lore has it that he straggled from the army of Rochambeau, to the sparsely settled frontier clearing, which is now Attleboro, and went to work at a tiny, tumble-down and abandoned forge, located less than two miles from Attleboro's now busy heart. There the jeweler's art had its American birth.

Early writers followed the path of early pioneer settlers and gave the Frenchman no name, he was simply "The Furrener," or the Frenchman, but later workers and writers treat this mysterious man better. They blame the ignorant early dwellers of the sparsely settled area for a descriptive title rather than a name and declare the soldier-artisan had declared himself as "Le Fournier." Those to whom he named himself knew nothing of the French language, he of little English and "Le Fournier" became by daily usage "The Furrener."

So runs the tale. Le Fournier it is agreed came in 1780. The French army was less than twenty miles away. Le Fournier felt no personal love for America and no especial hatred for Britain. He was just a soldier in Rochambeau's army. He came because he had to. His mind was not on warfare, but on craftsmanship, for he had worked as a jewelry maker in France.

Possibly he had brought some of the tools of his trade with him, but of that there is no proof. The ancient forge, which was merely a tumble-down brick pile, attracted him. He set it in order and went to work. His first effort was making buttons, largely intended for military uniforms. They were in great demand. The button production was slow, for the worker had no moulds, crude tools and his material had to be widely sought for. The first buttons were of brass, but, as months passed, buttons of brass appeared covered with gold-fire gilt, so-called. Where Le Fournier got his gold is a mystery. His champions believe he had some gold trinkets on his person and that they went into a melting crucible. Where he got mercury (for fire-gilt requires the blending of gold and mercury and the subsequent evaporating of the mercury by heat) is an even greater mystery, but fire-gilt buttons did come forth from the crude forge of the mysterious foreigner and he sold them readily. Soon he had a helper, one David Brown. Settlers found the work and the proprietor interesting puzzles and boys and girls went constantly to the forge. Adults followed and thus the seed of an industry, new to our land, was sown.

Besides buttons, small trinkets appeared. The Frenchman was undoubtedly skillful and versatile, friendly but uncommunicative. That is excused; he talked to nobody who could understand him for there were no French people in the settlement.

More than 156 years have passed since this French artisan toiled against seemingly insuperable obstacles to plant the seeds of a new industry in partial wilderness, but the fruits of his efforts become manifest to the outlander who first visits the city that leads all other American settlements in making ornaments of precious metals. It is today the "Jewelry City" and it has sent its name to India, China, Siam, Burma; to all lands in fact where man's natural love of ornamentation created a demand.

From Le Fournier's patient assistant, David Brown, the art was developed after the Frenchman "passed out of the picture." How he passed is not known. Historians do not even venture to conjecture. No story of his death or disappearance is even offered. There is a divergence of opinion to the time he spent here; some say three or four years, but the North Attleboro Historical Society advances the claim that he worked here for nearly a quarter of a century and that David Brown was his assistant for nearly that long. That Brown learned the art of jewelry making from the Frenchman is assuredly true and that his knowledge was considered of great value is shown by his partnership with Obed and Otis Robinson, who opened the first well-equipped jewelry factory in 1807 and took Brown in as equal partner and general manager. That first shop was on Commonwealth Avenue in what is now North Attleborough. The neighborhood is still known as Robinsonville. In 1812 the firm was enlarged by the additions of Mark Baldwin and Milton Barrows. Soon thereafter there was built what was called the "brick shop." It is today a prosperous jewelry making plant. The major output for years was metal buttons for the uniforms of Army and Navy officers, Police and Firemen.

Brown knew button-making well, for he spent years watching Le Fournier mould and polish gold plated brass buttons for uniforms. Attleboro supplied them to the "boys of blue and brass" for generations.

The Legend of Daddy Pope
(New Bedford)

by Mary I. Fogarty

"Daddy Pope." Illustration by Stephen Cook, 1988.

Bang! Bang! A scamper of bare feet, a confusion of shouts and squeals, and a hurried rush of small bodies tumbling headlong over the stone wall surrounding old Daddy Pope's huge apple orchard. It was an oft repeated performance and the sight of the owner, standing with legs spread far apart, long white hair tossing wildly, small eyes glaring savagely beneath grizzled brows, and gnarled hands tightly clutching an old rifle, remained long in the memory of the young rogues who raided his orchard.

Old Daddy's family had scattered, unable to stand the irritable old fellow, and he lived alone except for the hired man who was almost Daddy's equal in temper and disposition. They made no friends and welcomed no callers. Gradually, as Daddy advanced in years, the orchard, neglected, failed to tempt even the youngsters so that he was left more and more to himself. He never relinquished his watchfulness, however, and every night he was seen going his rounds, peering here and there, his rifle cocked in readiness for any marauder.

Finally, Daddy was missed from his haunts and his withered servant reported that the old man was gone.

His spirit did not long remain at rest, however, for shortly after his death a late home-comer, to his everlasting fright and horror, saw the bent form of the old man prowling among the trees of the orchard, now almost as gnarled and grizzled as himself. The story spread like wild-fire and, thereafter, those who were unable to avoid passing the estate after dark did so with bated breath and quaking knees.

Today the huge estate comprises many thickly settled blocks in the heart of the North End of New Bedford and although the ghost of old Daddy Pope hasn't been seen for many years, old residents sometimes wonder if he doesn't occasionally wander forth, seeking vainly for the trees which were his only interest in life.

Note: The old Pope Estate extended from what is now Sawyer St. to Coggeshall St.; from Acushnet Ave. to Ashley Boulevard.
Consultant: Mr. John Reilly, cor. Pleasant and Linden St.

Mill Hill
(New Bedford)

Mill Hill, now known simply as Mill Street, as the beginning of the main road to Cape Cod, with all its quaint beauty and appeal in earlier days, held a rather unique place in the history of New Bedford.

Here was formerly a rather steep hill, rising gradually from the meadows with their neat farm houses. Well up toward the top of the hill, between what are now County and Hill Streets, stood an old grist mill, close by a force well, which was the only source of well water for these settlers. Consequently the mill became a rendezvous for the farmers, who gathered here daily for their drinking water. Many a tale of romance and adventure was told under the arms of the old mill, which may still be seen in Westport, where it was later moved. From the mill the street got its name — Mill Hill, later changed to Mill Street.

Just above the mill was the old Hathaway homestead, one of the show places of the town, and a source of endless delight to natives as well as visitors. The rose window, valued at $1,500, was particularly beautiful, even though it slightly bulged when the house was moved from where it originally stood. In the living room was a huge crystal chandelier of unusual beauty. It was an exact replica of that in the House of Lords in England. Both the rose window and the chandelier still remain and the present occupant of the house is very

The Devil's Blowhole
(New Bedford)

by Mary I. Fogarty

willing and proud to show them to those interested in seeing them. The house was further graced by a large, rounded conservatory in which there was a fountain of running water. The fountain was moved to the Hathaway home at the corner of Hill and Mill Streets.

Both the street and the homestead have lost the glamor of their early history, but remain to inspire the reminiscences of "old timers" to keep alive the charm of old New Bedford. (Consultant: Mrs. Mae Walters, Maxfield Street)

The Acushnet River, though small, has many attractive spots along its shores to invite the picnicker or the lover of nature, but there was one spot that was strictly shunned by the amateur sailor of the past and watched with a wary eye by even the most experienced navigator. About half-way across the river heading towards Devil's Rock on the Fairhaven side,

sudden unaccountable gusts of wind of great velocity and force would arise and either force a craft off its course or capsize it. This happened so often that mariners sought the cause. But no explanation could be found for the fact that, on otherwise calm water, they should be struck by this wind, which was sometimes of gale proportions. So the tradition grew that the spot was in the possession of the Devil, who thus lay in wait to destroy the unwary, and it was named the Devil's Blowhole.

On one occasion, a bright, summer day, made especially for the delight of picnickers, a whole family, accompanied by several neighbors, pushed off from the foot of Wamsutta Street. The small craft was filled to capacity, but no one felt even the slightest fear, for the guidance of the boat was in the hands of a wise and experienced sailor. Suddenly all this was silenced, for such a blast of wind struck the group that they became not only speechless but breathless.

"The Devil's Blowhole! The Devil's Blowhole!" someone whispered fearfully, as they looked from one to another in alarm. A scream rang out, one of the girls leaped to her feet, lost her balance, and toppled over the side. For one breathless moment no one moved. Then as if moved by one impulse they all rushed to the side of the boat. In vain did the sailor cry out a warning, and over went the boat, throwing bodies headlong into the water. All were lost, victims of the Devil's grim playfulness, according to old timers.

The only survivor of the family spoken of was a small child, too young to join in the pleasures of the older members. He had been left in the care of friends. All through his life, and he lived to a ripe old age, he was seen to loiter around the vicinity of Wamsutta Street, looking over the water as if in tribute to those whose loss affected his life so much.

(Consultant: Mrs. G. D. Maxim, 191 Kempton Street, September 22, 1936; The story was given to Mrs. Maxim by Alonzo D. Rogers, the sole survivor of the family in the story)

The Stone Wall Legend

by Herman P. Wilson

The observer who has ridden or rambled over the New England countryside must have been struck by the prevalence of the stone wall, that typically Yankee device designed to divide fields, meadows, pastures, and even woodlots. The walls, built at the cost of painful toil, serve not only the purpose of dividing the land as does "bob wire" in other sections, but they serve as a repository for the innumerable rocks which ever and again rudely jar the farmer from his daydreams as he follows the plow.

While most of the walls date from a period whence "the memory of man runneth not the the contrary," each year sees additions and repairs to them on many farms, and even today on a few farms one may see the tremendous pair of wooden wheels, joined by a heavy axle bearing a stout chain, which serves as a lever to remove the stones from the earth and also as a means to transport them to their destination. This contrivance removes many of "the back aches in an old stone wall."

But frequently, if the rambler leaves the beaten track, stone walls are found in locations which puzzle the discoverer to divine the reason for their erection. Long stretches of wall extend through weary leagues of swamp and woodland, where neither man nor cattle are apt to trespass. A firmly established local tradition explains these useless walls as a product of the first Public Works program in America but no records on

the point exist. An older legendary account traces them back to the Indians. According to this account, after King Philip's War, the settlers were faced with the problem of disposing of numerous Indian prisoners. History records that many were sold into slavery and lesser numbers were slain. Tradition and history agree that large numbers of captive Indians were apportioned among the settlers to be used as servants or slaves. But here authentic history leaves them, while tradition continues their "short and simple annals" a little further.

Attempts to make them earn their keep at routine farm work were futile, the legend says, as they invariably took advantage of the first opportunity to decamp, often taking with them such plunder as appealed to their primitive fancies and was not too firmly attached to the free-hold. Naturally this unpleasant habit was most discouraging to their loving masters, upsetting the orderly routine of the farm and necessitating the waste of considerable valuable time and effort to regain the missing property, human and otherwise.

As it became painfully evident that these Indian slaves were a liability rather than an asset to those who tilled their former hunting grounds, it became necessary to find work for them wherein they could not annoy their conquerors by escaping to the woods where they had formerly roamed, free as the wind. Happily,

Stone wall in the woods of Dartmouth. Photograph by Rachel Barnet, 1988.

some early Harry Hopkins conceived the ingenious idea of putting the Indians to work in groups so that two or three armed White guards might curb the roaming proclivities of the toilers. And what better project could be found for such groups than the building of stone walls, thereby killing two birds with each stone, clearing the land and dividing it into fields.

This idea met with instantaneous success and acclaim, the word "boondoggle" being applied then only to useless work with a jackknife. In fact, so well did the idea and the Indians work, for many a weary moon (weary to the Indians, at least), no attempt was made to find other work for the slaves. As time and the Indians went on, however, so did the walls until at last each farm was neatly walled off with mathematical

exactness and still the settlers had to find work for the idle hands of their slaves, lest the devil take over that task as is reputedly his want. So the indomitable spirit of optimism which had led their fathers across the wide Atlantic and with a boundless faith in future real-estate values, the settlers went ahead, by proxy, building stone walls where they believe future toilers would "tickle the soil with a hoe and make it laugh a harvest."

And even when they had walled off all the prospective farm sites in the district, their zeal for labor was so great that they kept right on building walls, even in the most unlikely locations. Just how the affair ended, tradition does not make clear. Since it is certain that the supply of rocks did not fail, it is fair to assume they must have run out of Indians.

Destruction Brook, near Russells Mills, So. Dartmouth. Illustration by Edward Seager, 1856, courtesy of the New Bedford Whaling Museum.

The Legend of Destruction Brook (Dartmouth)

by Herman P. Wilson

Sources:

F. H. Macy, deceased, late of 95 Court St., New Bedford.

This legend and that of Destruction Brook were told to the writer by Mr. Macy many years ago. He credits them to William Wing who owns land on Destruction Brook. Mr. Wing makes a practice of lecturing on the region's tradition and history and refuses to let the writer "steal his thunder."

On the Destruction Brook legend, he admitted that the story as told is substantially correct but said the stone wall legend should be confined to a single wall on his land. Mr. Macy did not make this limitation.

At the little agricultural village of Russells Mills in the township of Darmouth a small stream called Destruction Brook flows into the larger Paskamansett River. Just before joining the larger stream the brook flows through a mill pond and turns the wheels of an ancient grist mill.

In this vicinity the brook forms a feature of an idyllic pastoral scene, but only a few miles nearer to its source in Deerfield Swamp the surroundings are so completely altered that the ominous name of the rivulet seems entirely appropriate.

On either bank of the stream, at frequent invervals, are quaking bogs of the type locally reputed to be "bottomless," while occasional small stretches of even more forbidding quicksands await the unwary. The countryside hereabout is gloomy and depressing, the scattered woods, chiefly of cedar and other conifers, being interspersed with tangled swamp growths.

The stream was once, before trespass signs prevented, a favorite with trout fishermen, but they confined their sport largely to the lower end of the stream. Occasional bolder spirits braved the dangers of the upper reaches of the brook, and numerous cases of sportsmen being rescued by rope from the slimy clutches of the bogs are known to the writer.

But even a person familiar with the brook and its surroundings must be at a loss to account for the name, unless equally familiar with the history and traditions of the district. An old folk tale, passed down through a number of generations, still survives to account for the portentious title.

According to the legend it was a common, if reprehensible, practice of the Indians to harass early settlers of the district by forays and night raids, running off the livestock of the scattered farms. Then, having no use for the stolen cattle and horses, the raiders would head the stock into the swamp and drive them into the bogs to their destruction.

From this vengeful practice arose the name — Destruction Brook.

The Underground Railroad in New Bedford

Editor's Note: The documentation of Black history is one of the major achievements of the Federal Writers' Project. Throughout the South and elsewhere former slaves were interviewed and their stories were arranged by state in a multi-volume work that was named The American Slave: a Composite Autobiography. *Of course the runaway slave narrative had been a major genre during the days of anti-slavery agitation and thousands were printed by abolitionist groups in their propaganda war. But never had former slaves been interviewed so extensively and systematically. The interviewing took place over seventy years after the end of the Civil War and, had the project been delayed until after the Second World War, a great opportunity would have been lost. Here we have the story of slavery told from the slave's point of view and in the words of the ex-slave.*

The language of the interviews is an interesting problem. In the facsimile reprints of the typescripts the work of the editors is very evident and a tension can be seen between the effort to record speech patterns exactly and the concern on the part of the interviewers that the language sounded too much like racist caricatures of Black English. The stereotype was complicating communication between the Black speaker and the audience. Even in a massive oral history project the racism of history and literature was working to rob the Black man and woman of a true voice.

While Massachusetts had fewer former slaves to interview than the southern states, we do find some good material, including Elizabeth Carter Brooks' memories of Harriet Tubman; Isabella White recalling being sent to freedom in a barrel of sweet potatoes; newspaper articles on Henry "Box" Brown, who had himself shipped to New Bedford in a box; and William Henry Johnson who was given the opportunity to study law while living in New Bedford.

The Slave Trade
and the Underground Railroad

March 13, 1923: In clearing away the debris from the lower Union Street fire, a tunnel was revealed under the old Mansion House, built by William Rotch in 1795. The tunnel could be followed but a short distance. The entrance was of steel and stone and a little beyond it was clogged with dirt and stone and it is not known just where it will lead.

There were many theories, most of which are too fanciful for serious consideration, such as one that it was used to shanghai sailors for whaleships. This theory is that the sailors were made drunk in the Mansion House, that became a hotel after the death of Mr. Rotch, and that the sailors were carried through the tunnel or secret passage to the docks where they were landed on the ships.

The answer to this is that in the days of shanghaiing the waterfront was a lawless place and the victims were made drunk or doped in the sailors' boarding houses and it would not have been necessary to use a tunnel. Half the sailors were taken aboard the ship drunk anyway and it would not have attracted attention if a stupefied sailor was carried through the streets of the town and landed aboard ship. There was no need for subterranean passageways. Furthermore, the Mansion House in whaling days was a highly respectable inn and was frequented by men and women of high degree, such as the Adamses, celebrities in politics and business.

The more likely explanation of the underground passages and rooms is that they were used to hide fugitive slaves. The Quakers, who were the most important people in this city, were abolitionists and New Bedford was the most important station of the Underground Railroad. Fugitive slaves were sheltered here while awaiting transportation to Canada.

It would be a very reasonable assumption that the subterranean rooms were used for this purpose. They were a part of many houses in these parts, in some of the old houses in old Dartmouth and Potomska. It is a pity that the history of the activism of the Quakers with reference to the Underground Railroad does not exist, except in tradition.

Far left: "At the Whipping Post on a Southern Farm." *Right:* "Passage to the North." Illustrations by Robert A. Henry, 1988.

Back in the fifties, when the fugitive slave law was being enforced, word was brought by an express carrier, S. P. Hanscom, who rode on horseback all night from Boston, that the brig *Acorn,* with a force of U.S. Marines and deputy marshalls aboard, was to make a raid on the slaves in hiding here. This was a matter of such consequence that Mayor Rodney French ordered the bell of old Liberty Hall to be rung to give alarm to those who were harboring slaves here.

Incidentally, there is another side of slave history, in which New Bedford figured, that is not so creditable. Many New Bedford men were engaged in the slave trade. Whaling was an excellent cloak for the business and a ship would be fitted for a trip to the African coast for a cargo of slaves, under the guise of fitting for a whaling voyage and without attracting any attention.

The foundation of a few New Bedford fortunes were made in the slave trade. The old files of *The Mercury* contain reports of trails of some men of prominence. But that early story is forgotten and later generations do not suspect things that the old files would reveal. (*Boston Sunday Globe Scrapbook,* pages 74-75, at Free Public Library)

Below: Elizabeth Carter Brooks, was elected president of the National Association of Colored Women in 1896 and founded New Bedford's Home For The Aged in 1908. Courtesy of Carl Cruz. *Right:* "Shelter." *Far right:* "Delivery." Illustrations by Diedra Harris-Kelley, 1988.

The Story of Harriet Tubman

by Warren E. Thomson

This is the story of a heroic Negro woman, as told to me by Mrs. Elizabeth Brooks, colored founder and president of the New Bedford Home for the Aged.

"I remember Harriet Tubman well, although I was a young girl at the time she was in New Bedford. Nobody called her Harriet — she was always 'Mother Tubman.' She was short, very strong and very black. I think she was the strongest-willed person I ever knew. I've known her to pound at the base of an aching tooth with a stone until the tooth was loosened, then pull it out with her fingers. So you can see she was fit for the work of guiding runaway slaves north on the 'Railroad.'

"Mother Tubman's home was in Auburn, New York, but she frequently came to New Bedford. Usually it was with a 'parcel,' as they called runaways. Altogether she helped between three and four hundred people to escape from slavery. Most of them she led to New Bedford.

"One of Mother Tubman's favorite methods of bringing slaves north was to go among them in disguise. She pretended to be an old woman. She'd find the slaves that wanted to escape and make them promise to say nothing to anyone else. Then, when

"Mother Tubman almost always managed to get the runaways through, even when they became discouraged and wanted to give themselves up. Once a man, Henry Carrol, who came up here to New Bedford later, wanted to rest while he was making his escape. The party was almost in sight of Philadelphia, but Henry was dog-tired. Pursuers were close behind them, but even so Henry wanted to rest for a little while. 'Henry,' said Mother Tubman, 'get up. We'se got to move along. Remember, Henry, dead niggers tell no tales.' Henry got up.

"Mother Tubman had many a narrow escape from capture. I remember one she used to tell of. She was in a train riding south. She was going to meet John Brown — she was supposed to help him in a few days, when he was to make the attack on the arsenal at Harper's Ferry. So Mother Tubman was riding to join him, dressed the way she usually was when she traveled by railroad, as a Negro servant.

"In those days trains had posters up inside the cars, carrying notices. Mother Tubman didn't look at them, because she couldn't read. But all of a sudden she heard the man in the seat behind her speak her name. Then she realized he was reading it from one of the posters up in the car, because he went on to say that a reward of $10,000 was offered for her capture, dead or alive. That's how much the Southerners thought of her activities.

"Well, Mother Tubman never took any part in John Brown's Raid. She got off the train at the very next station and came right back to New Bedford. She was hidden in an underground station on the southeast corner of North and Cedar Streets here when the raid took place."

she was ready to make a trip, she'd come to the place where they were working, shooing along a flock of hens. 'Shoo, shoo,' she'd call to the hens in a singsong voice. 'Shoo.' Then she'd be right next to a slave who had wanted to escape. 'Shoo, north tonight, shoo, shoo, meet me in the old graveyard, shoo, shoo.' Then she'd move off, and nobody would know she'd said a word to the slave.

"She did that until she had every slave warned. Then, that night, she met them in the graveyard and they started the trip north. They traveled by night and hid during the day, at least until they reached free soil. Usually Mother Tubman took them to Philadelphia, where there were many underground stations, then took all those farther north who wanted to go.

William Henry Johnson

by Warren E. Thomson

Before the Civil War, New Bedford was one of the most celebrated of the northern terminals of the "Underground Railroad." A tablet recently erected on French Avenue records that Rodney French, later mayor, ordered the ringing of the bell at Liberty Hall on the passage of the Fugitive Slave Law, to give warning of the rumored visit of revenue officers.

The discussion over the incident has led some of the Negro population to propose some sort of memorial tablet to one of these fugitives, William Henry Johnson, who died 30 or more years ago.

The interesting thing about Johnson is that he was the second colored man admitted to the bar in the United States. The first was Robert Morris of Boston.

Johnson was a picturesque character at the bar a half century ago, and had a story behind him that was entertaining. He was born in Richmond, Virginia, in 1811, and his master was Andrew Johnson, a famous owner of running horses. William Henry was his star jockey, but after a time he grew too heavy for riding.

The greatest race in which his master was interested was about to come off and it was necessary for William Henry to reduce. This was before the invention of the "daily dozen" and diets, and his master resorted to a device which had the warrant of custom in old plantation days.

William Henry was buried in a stable heap for 22 of 24 hours each day, and even his head was covered to the depth of a foot. He was given a pipe to breathe through and in the two hours he was released, he was given a single meal of bread and vinegar. William Henry's weight came down and he rode and won the race. It brought $50,000 to his owner, and the latter gave William Henry $250.

William Henry was tired of being fertilized to check his growth, and he made a bargain with the crew of the schooner *Tanting,* loading with flour, to take himself, his mother, and his brother to New York. His masters' daughter, aged 17, gave him $25. At the last minute the brother decided not to leave.

The schooner went ashore on Sandy Hook. Johnson swam with his mother to a rock and a boat from a British ship took them off. After working for a while on a farm at Jamaica, Long Island, William Henry went to New York and found a job washing dishes at the Astor House.

One night the well-remembered voice of his owner was heard at the door asking if Johnson lived there. William Henry assumed the voice of a woman and sent the man three houses up the street. Then William Henry ran out, and calling upon John Jacob Astor, told him of his predicament. Mr. Astor shipped him on the sloop *Rodman,* Captain Charles Wood, to New Bedford. For a while William Henry worked for Seth Russell at $6 a month. Then he secured a job as waiter in the Mansion House, kept at that time by Mrs. Doubleday.

He learned to read and became janitor in a lawyer's office. Timothy G.

Coffin, a leading lawyer of the section, assisted him, and Francis L. Porter, another lawyer, gave him law books. Johnson studied hard for a long time. Mr. Porter would explain nothing, but advised him where to find the knowledge he was seeking.

George Marston, later Attorney-General of the state, questioned Johnson one day and told him he felt he was qualified for the bar, and in 1866 Johnson was admitted. As one of the two colored lawyers in the country Johnson was summoned to represent colored clients in other states. At one time Johnson defended many liquor dealers in prohibition times. Then Johnson became satisfied of the evil results of liquor and he joined a temperance society. Thereafter his services were no longer at the command of violators of the liquor law.

Mr. Johnson was a captain of the Independant Blues, the first colored military company organized in New Bedford, and he was the first colored member of the City Council. It is these circumstances that have led to the thought of a memorial for him. Incidentally, Mr. Johnson was twice married and had 22 children.

(From *Boston Sunday Globe Scrapbook,* pages 60-61 (July 19, 1925), at Free Public Library)

Kidnappings in the North

by Warren E. Thomson

Although many Northern cities swore that no escaped slave should be returned from inside its precincts, attempts at kidnapping occurred. The New Bedford *Evening Standard* for September 2, 1850 prints an excerpt from the *Providence Post,* which says that "an attack was made on Henry Box Brown, the fugitive slave, in our streets on Friday, by some men, whose purposes were not fully disclosed. We are told that Mr. Brown was twice attacked, while walking peacably through the streets and that at one time the attempt was made to force him into a carriage. He proved too strong for them. His friends think the object was to get him on board a vessel bound to Charleston or dispose of him southward in some other way."

At approximately the same time a similar attempt was rumored to have been made in New Bedford. There was great public excitement in the town, but the *Standard* refused to believe it was a real kidnap attempt. However, on September 6, 1850 it printed a letter from a committee of citizens who had investigated the rumor. Excerpts from the letter:

"Mary, the colored girl, says three months ago she lived in Baltimore, where under the laws of Maryland, George Whim claimed her as his property. She wanted to be free (Who would not be free?) and so took advantage of a favorable opportunity and left for the North, with her two children . . . Six weeks ago Mary arrived in New Bedford. She wished to obtain work, as directed to the Franklin House . . . Last Saturday, while employed at this house, two men entered the room in which she was engaged.

"Mary declares that one of these men was George Whim. The other man, she asserts was Sheriff or Constable Hayes of Baltimore. She is sure that she is not mistaken, either as to Mr. Whim or Mr. Hayes, as she has unfortunate reasons for remembering them both.

"She further declares Mr. Whim said, 'this is my girl. I am looking for you. Do you remember me?' and that she was greatly confounded at his sudden appearance; that he declared his determination to carry her back, then seized and attempted to put irons upon her; here she cried out, when several of the girls of the house came in and interposed and there was a struggle . . . The interruption gave Mary an opportunity and she ran out of the house and gave the alarm. This is the substance of Mary's statement."

The letter goes on to give corroboration of Mary's tale and protest strongly against such kidnapping attempts. It is signed by H. Johnson, J. W. Smith, Edward W. Parker, John Kelley, J. B. Sanderson, D. W. Ruggles and Samuel Thomas.

This seems to be one authentic case of an attempted kidnapping of a fugitive in New Bedford and there have been records of other efforts of slave owners to recover their property. So far as is known, none such succeeded, which is one reason for the fact that New Bedford became a haven for escaped slaves.

Far left: "Kidnappings in the North." *Right:* "Sweet Potatoes." Illustrations by Deidre Harris-Kelley, 1988.

Isabella White

by G. Leroy Bradford

That she was shipped as freight over the "Underground Railroad" that came to New Bedford, was the story told to friends and acquaintances by the late Isabella White of that city. Mrs. White died on February 6, 1924. According to the New Bedford vital statistics in the office of the City Clerk, her age at death was "about" 79. Her story that she came north as a child in a barrel marked "sweet potatoes" has never been verified but was quite generally accepted. The death record indicates "parents unknown" and in the dim uncertainty of the past Mrs. White was never certain to whom she was indebted for her escape to a free state.

All she knew was that when about four or five years old she was headed up in a barrel among others containing sweet potatoes from a place where there were a few white folks, lots of "cullud" people and a big farm. She came "no'th" somewhere, presumably New Bedford. Her definite recollections were confined to the time after she was taken into the home of the late Miss Amelia Jones, where she spent the greater part of her life in various pursuits as a domestic.

Older residents of New Bedford recall that it was Mrs. White's idea that parents she did not remember, simply put her in the barrel confident that "quality folks in the no'th, regardless of who they were, would care for her." After that, like Topsy, Mrs. White declared she "jest growed."

Her barrel shipment has frequently been questioned by scoffers who pointed out that freight service in the 1850's was uncertain and at best, a tedious trip, far too severe and long for a child of tender years to have survived.

It had however some support from white persons in a position to know. Miss Agatha Snow, 10 Hawthorne Terrace, recalls her grandfather Loum Snow telling how Isabella White came north in a barrel and how he had her cared for until she was old enough to enter the employ of the Jones family.

This recollection does not include an admission from Mr. Snow that the small negro child was shipped to him, but in view of the fact he was an ardent abolitionist and known to have purchased the freedom of other slaves, it is not difficult to imagine he may have been expecting something more animated than sweet potatoes from the south when a barrel was received by him sometime in the 1850's.

From These Strains

The Lebanese of Fall River

Editor's Note: Following the publication of the Massachusetts Guide in the spring of 1937, the Federal Writers began researching the ethnic and racial groups in the state. This work project, at one point entitled "From These Strains," was also referred to as the "Survey of Racial Elements." The project received much support from ethnic and racial organizations, including financial sponsorship.

The newspaper Swedish Consul *and others guaranteed financial sponsorship for work on the Swedes; the Associated Jewish Philanthropies and the* Jewish Advocate *agreed to sponsor Jewish Study. Groups representing the Irish, Negro, Armenian, Albanian, Chinese, Latvians, Finns, Russians, Scotch and Italians were also considering such sponsorships.*

The International Institute had given assurance that the histories of the smaller racial groups would be published in a single volume.

Assistant State Director, Bert James Loewenberg, wrote to Henry Alsberg expresssing concern that the racial survey be submitted to a learned society or university press to assure its success.

The success of this survey depends not so much upon the procurement of active sponsors but upon its point of view and scholarly attainments . . . Adequate studies of American racial elements constitute a gap in our historiography and those which have already appeared are, for the most part, marred by a lack of perspective.

As of 1940, a list of publications submitted by State Director Muriel Hawks to the Boston office included "The Albanian Struggle in the Old World and New" and "The Armenians in Massachusetts." Most of the work performed by the hundreds of Massachusetts writers on ethnic or "racial" elements was never published.

The five selections we have included are a small sampling of FWP writings on the many ethnic groups in Southeastern Massachusetts. Some of the work is not original, nor is it comprehensive or scholarly. Though the writings often reflect the stereotypical attitudes and politics of the times, they are valuable as a major attempt to gather these histories and may be appreciated for what they reveal.

Early Beginnings and Demographics

Though most of the people in this city who come from that country generally designated as Syria are called Syrians, they are not in the strict sense of the word Syrians at all, but Lebanese. Practically all the people in this city come from that section surrounding Beyrouth on the Eastern Mediterranean Sea which is designated as Mount Lebanon.

The reason for the misnomer "Syrians" for these Lebanese furnishes an interesting story. The present country of Lebanon is situated in Asia Minor on the Mediterranean Sea. To the south lies Palestine; to the north, Turkey; and to the east, Syria. In appearance, language (Arabic), and customs, the people are very similar to their neighbors. However in religion, grave differences manifest themselves. The Lebanese are mainly Maronite Catholics, one of the oldest of the Catholic religions; whereas the neighboring Syrians are Mohammedans.

As early as 1860, Lebanon had attained a degree of semi-independence in having a Christian governor and in having their religious freedom guaranteed by France,

by Irene Posey

and Nathan Kaplan

A Lebanese family, photographed shortly before their emigration to America around 1910. Courtesy of Stacie Hallal.

England, Italy, Belgium and Spain. However, up to the close of the World War, Lebanon, Syria and Palestine all belonged to Turkey which had united all three countries under the name of Syria. In 1926, France was granted a mandate over Lebanon. During the latter part of 1936, Lebanon was granted total independence. Since Lebanon was a part of Syria when the first wave of immigrants arrived in 1890, these people were officially listed as Syrians. One hopes that this listing, erroneous as it is in view of Lebanon's independence, will be changed in the future.

Lebanon in 1890 was an agricultural country with hardly any industrial development; most of its people owned their own little farms in which by dint of hard toil they secured an existence. A spirit of restlessness existed among some of these small farmers; they were eager to attain some of the riches of the newly-heard-of America. Upon arriving in America, they turned to trading in dry goods for a living. The peoples of neighboring or the same village lived in close proximity of each other in the larger cities. When migration to the smaller

cities occurred, we find a repetition of the above phenomenon. Furthermore, since the people possessed different customs, language and religion from others of the community, colonies were formed in the various cities.

Soon after settlement in the smaller cities, most of the Lebanese turned to the industries of their particular neighborhood for a living. They have prospered and many are skilled workers at present. Though an agricultural people in Lebanon, these people are predominantly city dwellers in the new world. As a result, one finds practically none of these people in Barnstable, Dukes and Nantucket counties. Likewise, in Plymouth and Bristol counties, nearly all of the Lebanese are located in the urban centers. Of the nearly 3,000 Lebanese and Syrians living in the five counties mentioned, close to 2,000 reside in Fall River.

The original intentions of many of these people were to secure wealth and then return to Lebanon. With the passage of years, these ideas have been completely altered. Most of the people have settled in a particular district of this state, bought their own homes,

CORIATY'S VARIETY STORE

and adopted America as their country.

The city's polyglot population experienced its first impressions of the Lebanese around 1890 when a few immigrants sought employment in cotton mills, which it was easy to obtain even with ineptitude, or followed the example of the preceding Greeks by embarking in the fruit business, or venturing into the peddling line despite the handicap of unfamiliarity with English. Their increase in representation proceeded fitfully, notwithstanding that the Lebanese pioneers had managed to make their lot fairly satisfactory among a strange people.

While storekeeping is the "colonists" most engrossing pursuit, the textile industry absorbs not a few. Their adaptability was determined in the homeland, and locally it has been

tested successfully in silk weaving as well as in the production of the finer fabrics of cotton.

While members of the race may be located in different sections, unlike most other settlers, they have but one colony. That exists in Flint village, or the east end, being restricted to Harrison, Quequechan and Jenks Streets in the main, south of Pleasant Street. This settlement is in the French section of the city. They settled here because most of them speak French quite fluently and, by their contacts with the French-Canadians who settled here earlier, are able to accustom themselves to America that much more quickly.

Lebanese people are to be found expressing themselves freely in social contacts with other people. Clannishness, group segregation, or

passive utilization of the elements of citizenship do not have a restraining effect on activities. Politically, the doctrines of the democratic party make the strongest appeal to the majority. The ambition to be treated as a factor in politics unaffected by racial distinctions led one of the outstanding representatives to enter the scramble for seats in the city council two years ago and to get himself elected a member of the city committee. Defeat did not daunt him, and again this year he entered the office-seeking fray by offering himself for the office of county treasurer. To eke out the scant profits of a variety store in the Globe district, the aspirant has become a weaver in the Charleton factory.

Religion

There are approximately 200,000 Syrians and Lebanese, foreign-born and American-born, living in the United States. With regard to their religious adherence they are divided as follows: Maronites, 90,000; Greek Orthodox, 85,000; Greek Catholic, 10,000; and Protestants, 5,000. The remaining 5,000 are scattered among the Mohammedans and Druzes.

Fall River is represented by two of these four sects — the Maronites and the Protestants. The Maronites, who claim allegiance to the Roman Catholic Church, are said to have the largest number of adherents both in America and Lebanon. While they have conformed to many of the practices of the Occidental Roman Catholic Church, they still retain many

of the eastern services for baptism, marriage and burial as well as their feast days. They celebrate Mass in Syriac instead of Latin and the gospel is read in Arabic for the benefit of the people. Their parish priests may marry while they are in minor orders or before they are ordained. The Maronite Catholics represent the overwhelming majority of Lebanese in Fall River.

The other religious group among the Lebanese in Fall River is the Syrian Protestant Congregation which is located on Harrison Street in the city. There, Joseph Zaidan expounds the gospel as taught to United Presbyterians.

Lebanese Catholics settled Fall River in 1900 and until 1911 attended services celebrated each week at Notre Dame and St. Anne's churches by a Lebanese priest from Boston. In 1911 Rev. Gabriel Corkemaz of Boston spent three months in this city, during which time he purchased a tenement at 286 Jencks Street and converted it into a church.

Upon the return of Father Corkemaz to Boston the pastorate was given to Rev. Ignatius Savegh who had been called from Lebanon. He administered the parish's affairs until 1920. From 1920-1929 Rev. Caesar Phares took charge of the parish. During his pastorate the property on Jencks Street was sold and the land upon which the present church stands was purchased.

On July 14, 1930 Rev. Joseph Eid took over the duties of pastor of the church. He proved to be a

Opp. page: Coriaty's Variety Store (1940), at 243 Eastern Avenue, was owned and managed by Kally Coriaty. *Left:* Father Caesar Phares (insert) and the Jenks Street tenement where the first Maronite Catholic services were held. *Bottom:* Father Savegh in 1912. Photographs courtesy of St. Anthony of the Desert Church.

conscientious worker, a fine organizer and a benevolent pastor towards his people. It was during his early pastorate, while he was still a young man that the idea of a church for the Lebanese was conceived and consummated.

The founding of the first Syrian Roman Catholic Church in Fall River represented something of an event throughout Massachusetts, as can easily be gathered from the account of the ceremony taken from the records of a local newspaper:

"Parishioners of St. Anthony of the Desert Church, their members greatly increased by prominent Syrian personalities, delegations of Syrian colonies, relatives and friends from many near and distant New England communities and state and municipal officials thronged the vicinity of

Quequechan and Alden Streets yesterday for the solemn and impressive ceremony of the blessing and dedication of their beautiful and attractive new church edifice, the realization of their hopes and prayers for a quarter century."

Causes for Lebanese Immigration to the United States

One of the primary expellant factors in Lebanese immigration was their desire to find freedom from political oppression. Lebanese had long been dominated by the Turks and desired to seek freedom in the countries across the seas. That they found it upon coming here cannot be doubted nor can their appreciation for American democracy be fully understood by those who have become accustomed to

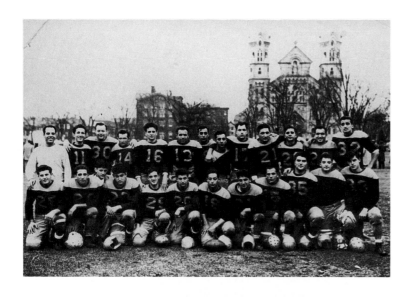

it. It is a significant fact that the picture of the first Syrian family in America, that of Arbeely, was taken with a placard on which was written: "THE CHILDREN AND I HAVE HAPPILY FOUND LIBERTY!"

Another expellant factor in Lebanese immigration was their desire to escape military duty. Every steamer bound for North or South America was crowded with Lebanese Christians who were anxious to avoid military draft. This desire to avoid military draft finds expression in the present day attitude of Lebanese in this city who say they are not Syrians at all. To say they were Syrians at the time of

their emigration from the country would have meant that they were admitting they were liable to military service under the Turks. Thus, the aversion of Lebanese in this city to being called Syrians.

A further cause of Lebanese immigration to this country was more attractive than expellant. It concerned those Lebanese who had been in the United States and had returned to Syria. Their apparent prosperity acted as a conspicuous and never-failing advertisement for the United States. The sight of a European-dressed Syrian in the interior of the country was often enough to label him as having been to America.

Another factor in Lebanese immigration was religious. Christian Lebanese are a decided minority in Syria. Christians in Syria have never been entirely free of restrictions placed upon them because of their belief.

Top left: "Roughriders" parish football team, 1942. *Left:* 1920 First Communion class with Father Savegh. Present are James (Najib) Abdullah; Elias Rashed; Lena Praffa; Elias Elias; Nazira Kalif; Nicholas Kalif; Alice Rashed; Jamel George; Josephine Praffa; Solomon George; Assad Ameen; John A. Monsour. *Right:* the former St. Anthony of the Desert Church with Father Eid (insert). The church was taken down in the 1970s. Photograph courtesy of St. Anthony of the Desert Church.

74

Church of St. Anthony of the Desert,
for the Syrian Catholic parish, situated at the corner of Alden + Quequechan Sts.
Fall River, Massachusetts, U.S.A.
Construction begun April fifteenth — cornerstone layed by Rev Joseph Eid. D.D.,
pastor, May 4th — Dedicated by Rt. Rev Bishop James E. Cassidy, D.D., Oct. 12th, 1930.
— Temple of God — Gem of Art —

Housing

In Fall River, as has been remarked previously, Lebanese settled mostly in the Flint section of the city. Although Syrians in other sections of the country are not, as a rule, industrial workers, in Fall River many of them are engaged in the city's factories. As a consequence, it might be expected that housing would be more of a problem among them than among their compatriots elsewhere. Such, however, is not the case. It is true that the section in which the Lebanese have settled is one of the poorer sections of the city, but it is by no means a squalid or unsanitary district. A Mrs. Houghton writing of the Syrian immigrants' housing conditions had this to say concerning the question: they are "superior to most immigrants' colonies, of whatever people, in any part of the United States."

A survey made by the Immigration Commission showed that living conditions among the Syrians on an average were slightly better than among all other groups including native born. It was further discovered that "taking boarders" is an institution almost unknown and the average occupant per room is less than among most other nationalities.

Prominent Personalities during Development

Rev. Joseph Eid, Ph.D., D.D., pastor of St. Anthony of the Desert Maronite Catholic Church:

Father Eid's life is extremely interesting. He was born in Mt. Lebanon, Syria in 1896. He attended the schools of the small village where he was born and later attended the Jesuit University at Beyrouth. While there he studied philosophy and theology. Later he moved to Rome where he obtained his doctor of Philosophy degree and the degree of Doctor of Divinity. He was ordained in 1924. He then took up missionary work in the Orient where he labored for some years following his ordination. He was later assigned to France doing the same type of work. While in France he received an invitation from the then bishop Daniel Feehan urging him to take over the duties of administering to the colony of Lebanese in Fall River. He took over the duties of pastor of the parish on July 14, 1930 and since that time the affairs of the parish have prospered exceedingly. He secured the funds for a new church for the Lebanese people in the city and also was instrumental in securing the present rectory which is part of the church property.

Father Eid is a brilliant linguist, being able to converse fluently in six languages — French, Arabic, English, Latin, Italian and Syriac. He is also a poet of some repute and is the author of several poems which have been rather well-received in French literary circles.

Customs and Practices among the Lebanese of Fall River

An apparently strange fact regarding the Lebanese in this city is their ability to speak Arabic and the fact that so many of them have such a strong admixture of Arabic blood, although they are in no sense Arabian.

This Oriental infiltration in their blood has a profound effect on their lives and their buildings. Speaking of one of the churches (St. Anthony of the Desert) it was written: "As the eyes rest upon the church one receives the impression of comfort and strength. Its architecture is a combination of Occidental and Oriental art. Its Oriental features were originally introduced into Cordova and Granada at the time of the Arab migrations into Spain. The horseshoe at the church portals is often used in Oriental architecture. The effect was introduced into the church interior as well. Similar effects are used in church architecture in Lebanon at the present time."

Another Oriental practice which is prevalent among the Lebanese is the widespread use of the "water-pipe" (nargilah). It consists of a long tube attached to a flask containing water on the top of which there is tobacco burning. It is said by those who indulge in tobacco in this fashion that the smoke is much cooler and smoother than in any other form of smoking.

Annual Banquet — Lebanese American Federation of New England, 1953. *Courtesy of St. Anthony of the Desert Church.*

ANNUAL BANQUET, LABANESE-AMERICAN FEDERATION OF N.E. NOV. 1-1953

The Polish of Fall River

author unknown

Standard Pharmacy on East Main Street was started by William Kuczyuski in 1918. This 1931 photograph shows Stanley Nowak (left) and his brother-in-law, Mr. Kuczyuski. Today, Standard Pharmacy is still family-operated. Mr. Nowak shares the responsibility with his son-in-law. Joseph Rebello. Courtesy of Stanley Nowak.

To avoid giving mortal offense to the most vigorous exalters of Polish nationality and inviting stern rebuke therefore, one must not address them or write of them as "Polanders." It is held to be a term of belittlement, being like "harp" to the Irish and "dago" to the Italians, though applied promiscuously without intended offensiveness. Authoritative information about the harmful signification of the term has lacked publicity hereabouts. To escape rebuke one needs to be told that only "Polacks," "Poles" and "Polish people" are appellations that provoke no rancor and guarantee courteous treatment of a request for Polish favor.

The writer, after long years of innocent employment of the misnomer, leaned in dismay that, in his blissful state of ignorance, he had incurred the penalty for unwisdom when he presented his credentials to a Pole and asked for information about "Polanders." A whirlwind of wrath was stirred and an awesome demand made for an explanation. The plea of common usage of "Polander" was not received as a palliative, for it resulted in the dogmatic and angry comment that American education in European affairs was of a low standard and sadly needed elevating.

Stanley Kania, holding a license for a package store at 276 Fourth Street, in a neighborhood which houses few Poles, was the irate mentor and valorous champion of pure and undefiled characterization of the Polish race without muddling. Under the cooling influence of liberal ordering of canned and bottled goods by customers, the fierceness disappeared from the Kania demeanor and a short bit of autobiography was unfolded for the caller's benefit, without, however, healing the temperamental wound unwittingly inflicted and since reprehended by others who have been interviewed in the quest for Polish data.

In calling attention to a long scar on the forehead, just above the eyes, the spokesman said that just before he had reached his fourth birthday, a vicious Cossack of the Czar's army, which was

persecuting mercilessly the people of Poland, then under Russian dominance, slashed him with a saber, while he was playing on a street. It was only through providence that the weapon did not halve his skull. For six months the victim of the murderous assault lay in the hospital.

Excepting the two years he lived in Detroit, where a younger brother occupied an educational post, which pays $6,000 a year, Mr. Kania has lived in Fall River about forty years. He has just been chosen financial secretary of the Thaddeus Kosciusko Polish American Citizens Club, is an official of a wholesale grocery

company and was represented to the offending inquirer as the one Pole who was the best informed national to be interviewed about Polish activities. Evidently he believes that the unreported praise is his deserving without the right of anyone to demur or to accord to others equal amplitude of historical knowledge.

Before Mr. Kania exuded his indignation, he went to a desk and brought out a large bundle of manuscript. It contained, he remarked, a history of the Polish colony in this city, comprising 7,000 persons, most of whom were American-born. So much time had been given by him to

Opposite: Kuras' Variety Store at Rodman and Tecumseh Streets, was a longtime establishment in the Polish neighborhood. Two 1920 photographs show Albert Kuras with his son, John, and daughter, Louise, posing in front of (far left) and inside (left) his tenement storefront. *Above:* In a 1960 photograph, Mr. Kuras poses inside his same store. Courtesy of Al Cartier, Louise's son.

its preparation that through the data he had been able to collect, Mr. Kania, as the historian, boasted of his ability to name the first Poles to settle here, the first to be born and to die and to detail unerringly the salient facts in the lives of most of the early settlers and their relations.

After having gone to the trouble of getting personal histories and transcribing them, it was not his purpose to yield the opportunity to publish a historical work on the people of his nation just to serve the ends of promoters of the Writers' Project under the auspices of the W.P.A. No words served to disabuse

his mind of the competitive idea, which he appeared to entertain as though it had assumed the form of an obsession, of the possible loss of the glamour attaching to his role as a writer.

Edward Everett considered to be "a singular coincidence of events that our country was constituted the great asylum of suffering virtue and oppressed humanity." The people of Ireland so regarded it in their struggles against Bristish rule and so sought relief by hundreds of thousands. Poland's story is more heartrending, not that there was greater solidarity, but that the soldiery

of the oppressors were more ruthless in executing the governmental policy toward the unfortunate partiots, who remained adamant in devotion to their national ideal and refused to dissemble in order to escape brutality. "The whirlwind of the ukases and manifestoes of the Czars, the hurricanes of the wrongs heaped upon Poland by the Prussians, the maelstrom of Austria's insidious politics," another orator declared, "have endeavored to sap the national life in Poland, and nobody has endeavored to interpose, insamuch as she has been guarded on the one side by the Russian policeman and on the other by the Prussian gendarme."

In spite of that anomalous situation and the open roadway to freedom that ended on American soil, the Poles were singularly slow in seeking the asylum, judging by the local figures on population. Their country was not restored to its original status as an independent nation until the end of the Great War. In the meantime they endured torture. In the hope of freedom they fought valiantly on the side of the allied forces. In the last twenty years the stream of immigration has been dammed up so that Fall River has received few of the 2,000 who have been allowed to enter annually.

Louis Smolinksy, who died on December 18th, was said to have been the oldest pole in point of age and also in length of resident, having come in 1880, but in registering for an old age pension, Anthony Gosciominski gave 1872 as the year of his arrival. The first to land did not go far from the dock of the Fall River Line, finding tenements on Brady, Summer, Spring and Washington Streets, like others who preceded them from abroad.

Poland was not the chief source of the local supply. New Jersey contributed from its hat-making and textile communities and Chicopee attracted a number before Fall River was decided on over Hampden County. Some of the people found work at hat-making in the Marshall factory on Globe Street.

Whatever might have been the number of Poles whhich the tide brought here, after it had turned in this direction, the movement was in progress for years before the pastor of St. Mary's Church, in which a priest of the race ministered to them, recommended the erection of a church for Polish Catholics. In 1898 the dedication of the Saint Stanislaus building on Rockland Street took place. Rev. Hugh Dyla is pastor.

With the creation of a Polish settlement in the territory bounded by Plymouth Avenue and Rodman Streets, another house of worship was deemed necessary. It was called the Church of the Holy Cross. In competition for Polish spirituality, the head of the National Polish Church, who has his headquarters in Scranton, Pennsylvania, made provision for the dissident element of the nationality. Two churches were created. In one, which is near the Roman Catholic edifice, Latis is used in the services; in the other that idiom is discarded for Polish. The tie of nationality is too strong to be weakened by the difference about rubric, one is told upon inquiry.

The Scotch of Fall River

by Irene Posey

With the starting of textile printing around 1832 came the first immigrants from Scotland. They drifted in small numbers and located "below the hill," as the section south of Pocasset Street to William Street came to be named. When the colony grew large enough to warrant more than the makeshift for worship used in 1846, with the help of the Irish Presbyterians a commodious church was erected in 1851 at Pearl and Anawan Streets to which was given the name "United Presbyterian Church." Rev. William MacLaren was among the first of the denomination's ministers to serve the congregation under its own roof-tree. That he was forceful, progressive, and public-spirited, the incident of his election to the school committee the year after coming to Fall River is illustrative. He was with it seven years.

Rev. John J. Turnbull is another Scot whose popularity was not confined to the people to whom he preached. He suffered the loss of an arm before accepting the local call. His ministration embraced the decade, 1875-1886.

Rev. William J. Martin succeeded Rev. Turnbull in 1886. It was on his urging that the novelty of serving breakfasts to poor children Sunday mornings in the church basement was introduced. Those who supported the plan most actively included the musical family of McLeods, whose pride in nationality was whole-souled. Mr. McLeod was leader of the choir and a splendid singer; a daughter was a soprano who developed into one of the city's most accomplished vocalists, while a son, Andrew, was for years connected with minstrel companies. For two years he had been a member of the instrumental band of the E.R.A. and W.P.A. workers.

Mr. Martin's religiousity was virile and fervid, and because of his zeal and learning, at one sitting of the presbytery he was dignified a doctor of divinity. Modestly he accepted the offer, and in the same humble spirit he did not demur when his people assumed the responsibility of commending his merits so as to obtain for him in 1895 a school committee nomination and election for two years.

With the increase in affluence of the original parishioners, they contributed generously to a fund for the erection of a granite structure on a commanding site on Rock Street. That location signified that most of the Presbyterians had found it desirable to select a residential neighborhood of a character more in harmony with their beliefs and habits than developed gradually through foreign intrusion downtown.

Comparatively small as is the record of Scotland's contribution to Fall River's general history, in its relative importance it looms commendably large in comparison. To one William Gilmore it was indebted in our manufacturing infancy for the impulse to the applicaton of power to cloth production when he evaded England's close watchfulness for expropriation of British ideas in this state, by introducing what is known as the Scotch loom, a name changed afterward to Cartwright and a machine superior to the make in use.

No sentimental obligation to a foreigner for becoming identified with the city's industrial expansion rates along with that incurred when the Kerrs of Paisley, Scotland, chose Fall River as the place in Massachusetts in which to establish a branch of their business as makers of cotton yarn and thread. Fourteen acres of the Flint Mills holding, near the outlet of the South Watuppa Pond into the Quequechan River were bought, and with a capital of $292,400 the investors erected in 1890 and equipped a brick factory of five stories, 100 feet wide and 131 feet long. Six hundred persons found work. A son of Scotland, Richard B. Cook, was their superintendent.

In 1893 the success of the enterprise justified an addition of 150 feet to the mill and $500,000 to the capitalization. James B. and Robert C. Kerr represented the family in the management. That was uninterrupted until about 1906, when the Kerr's products were produced under the label of the American Thread Company as a result of company amalgamation.

R. C. Kerr became an official of the buyer and removed to New Jersey for service in the Newark plant. In September 1928 James B. Kerr died; industry felt his loss. His widow retains her Fall River residence. She showed a lively interest in the recent news that the prosperity during her husband's administration, which the depression interrupted, has been revived sufficiently to cause the starting up of long idle machinery.

Scottish connection with local merchandising, a noteworthy incident in gauging racial standing, dates from about 1872. Steward and Hamerton was the firm name over a store on the east side of South Main Street, near Borden, in which drygoods were sold. The partners were Scotch. Mr. Steward was one of the pillars of the Presbyterian church, and he exemplified in his relations with his fellow man the depth and earnestness of religious convictions, tolerance towards dissenting beliefs.

David Morrison was another of the clan to become a successful merchant. With his brothers he established the nucleus of a department store in Flint Village. After a few years here, three of the newcomers went to Chicago. In that city they made good and acquired wealth. The local brother did not suffer through his preference for Fall River in carrying on business, for his scruples caused the villagers to do most of their buying at his establishment instead of going "to the city" to shop. Moreover, he had so bound them to him that in the election that made him a senator party lines were broken.

Mr. Morrison was so rigid a sabbatarian, though without intolerance, that he considered it to be in derogation of the commandment on the observance of the Lord's day if he should use a conveyance to take him over the three miles between his home and the Pearl Street church.

There exists but one department store in the city. It is conducted for R. A. McWhirr Company by two men who as boys began working for Robert A. McWhirr. He had just started as a merchant when Elizabeth Oregan, a teacher, became his wife. The hustling qualities McWhirr displayed made possible the solidity of the foundation of the enterprise on which he had embarked with limited capital within a short cycle after he had left his home in Scotland for America. He did not live to see the wonderful growth that

John C. Milne, Engraving by E.G. William & Bro., N.Y.

attended his venture, which for a time had the appearance of an unpromising investment, but it was large enough in his lifetime to satisfy him that he had left ample provision for his successor in the person of a son who had inherited the talent of the parent. The wife and mother was doubly and grievously bereft when death deprived her of her boy's companionship. She shares with two partners the large earnings of the imposing emporium in which there is a small army of workers.

Robert Nicholson, recognized better as "Bob," is another who, emigrating from Scotland and foreswearing allegiance to the British throne, after

coming here in 1878, entered the ranks of city fathers in 1887 by grace of the votes of fellow citizens. That choice was made three times without prejudice. The councillor and son had their office as contracting masons on Morgan Street and never were accused of skimping on a job.

William and Peter Connell did not remain idle when they exchanged Scotland in 1857 for America in which to promote their ambitions. Peter devoted himself early to the manufacture of brooms, the first introducer of that industry, and became father of a boy who made himself an efficient member of the Police Department for several years.

William Connell was more assertive than his brother by reason of broader aptitude and richer intellectuality, as he had interested himself as a councilman from a southern ward in 1866 and 1867. His interest in education brought about Mr. Connell's assignment to the superintendency of schools 17 years afterward. There were frequent changes in the membership of the committee, but the superintendent was retained for 23 years. He is credited with the passage of the free textbook law for the city. Illness that forced his resignation soon caused his death.

The two sons of Mr. Connell, who was the father of five children, adopted the medical profession; Charles the elder, since deceased, in 1887, and his brother, Arthur, in 1901 and still in practice.

The father of daily journalism, as Fall River has known it, was John Cruickshank Milne, whose life work terminated in 1918. The country of his birth in 1824 was Scotland. Upon the death of his father and mother, his grandparents took him to Nova Scotia in 1832, and in 1835 to this city. His job was secured in the Rodman Print Works. It was in a room set aside by the manager for the benefit of the youthful employees that the youngster obtained his first schooling.

While he was learning to set type in an uncle's shop, a minister, who was to be created a Colorado bishop later on, encouraged young Milne to try for a collegiate education. That prospect was blasted by lack of means. However, he made of himself so good a compositor that his relative took him into partnership and in 1845 the *Weekly News* was launched. In 1859 the firm, which had been alienated politically on the slavery question, took over a struggling newspaper called the *Beacon* and made it the *Daily News* to further Republicanism. In the course of time it became as the family Bible for its readers until, owing to the mortal illness of Joseph D. Milne and the disinclination of the Almy heirs to continue the publication, the *News* was taken over by the publishers of the *Daily Herald* and merged.

The junior Milne was unlike the senior in a variety of ways. He was without any ambition to enter public life, whereas the father was five years

in the City Council and four years in the General Court. In the latter body he commanded broad influence by reason of his ability and fearlessness as an advocate and critic, and his political lampooning of his associates. He was easily the most versatile and individualistic scion of a Scotch household that has ever lived here.

It is not altogether inappropriate to bring this chronicle to a close by reporting the most recent incident involving a representative of the race, who had made good as an officeholder, and who is affiliated with the Caledonian Society and the Burns Club, the latter a social association limited to men either born among the highlands of old Scotia or who are Americans in line of descent. In a heated contest for the mayoralty, Alexander G. Murray sought re-election. He was first city engineer, then city manager and next chosen city executive. the last promotion was received at the polls in 1934, to cover two years. His opponent at that time he had to face again on December 15, 1936. His republicanism was urged as a reason for a democratic city to deny re-endorsement of his candidacy. That his first administration as mayor and his managerial reputation satisfied many democrats of his deserving was revealed when the balloting showed Mr. Murray to have received another vote of confidence. Its size did not weaken the sentiment expressed.

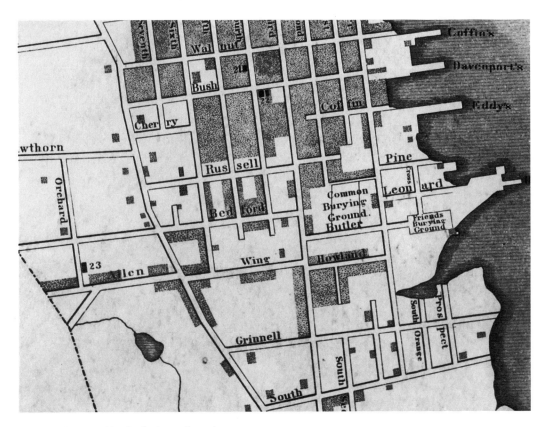

A section of an 1820 New Bedford map shows the early Irish neighborhood district. Block number 23, on Orchard and near Allen Street, marks the "Catholic Meeting House" or St. Mary's Church. Courtesy of New Bedford Free Public Library.

The Irish in New Bedford: *history of Irish Catholic churches*

A half century often makes great changes. If some New Bedford Rip Van Winkle had been sleeping for fifty years, and returning to consciousness, should walk our streets, his surprise and wonder may readily be imagined. When he went to sleep, for instance, there were mere handfuls of Irish in New Bedford and they worshipped in a little wooden church on Allen Street, erected at a cost of a few hundred dollars. Today (Aug. 30, 1887) as he walked through our streets, he would see a fine stone church and chapel, three substantial wooden churches, three parsonages, three parochial school buildings and a hospital.

New Bedford was one of the

pioneer places in New England in the Catholic faith, as early as 1820 having established St. Mary's Church on Allen Street. In 1820 and previous to that time, there were only a handful of Catholics here and their opportunities to enjoy the ministrations of their religion were extremely limited. Once in several months a priest would come from Newport or some other place and stop at some Catholic home for a few days, visiting from house to house, hearing confessions and administering the sacraments. At that time children of Catholic parents were sometimes taken to Boston by stagecoach to be christened.

Among the priests who thus came to New Bedford was Rev. Father

Larasey, an earnest worker, who started a movement for a church edifice. To the little band of Irish this seemed an arduous task, but they seconded the priest's efforts with zeal. Collections were taken from time to time, and little by little several hundred dollars were accumulated. Seamen who were in port from time to time were liberal givers and the gold pieces contributed by them helped materially to swell the fund.

In 1820 New Bedford's first Irish Catholic church was built at a cost of 800 dollars. It was on Allen Street near the head of Dartmouth, and a very unpretentious edifice it was — of wood, one story, not even clapboarded. It was very much like one of the small

country school-houses we see now, the wooden cross above it alone distinguishing it as a place of worship. The site was a very pleasant one, on rising ground, the greensward extending some 150 feet in front, while to the east and rear was the parish graveyard. The grounds were enclosed by a board fence. "A beautiful place it was on a pleasant Sunday," says one of the early residents, reverting to the days of his boyhood. "That part of the town was not built up and one could look from the rising ground where the church stood, off over an expanse of green fields and see in the distance the blue waters of the bay. I can remember the little church as though it were yesterday, and can again seem to see the male parishioners gathered at the front of the building before service and the women kneeling upon the graves, praying." The lot of land upon which the church stood was the gift of Patrick Cluney.

It was a red letter day for New Bedford's Irish when the little church was opened for worship. The building was not consecrated, as the Catholics do not consecrate a house until all the building expenses are liquidated, but Bishop Cheverus came down from Boston and gave the introductory sermon. Father Larasey was the first pastor of St. Mary's church, as the church was named, but for years regular services were not held. It was only once in several weeks that the priest could come, so limited was the number of priests in the diocese. The Reverend Father would come a few days before Sunday, in order to hear confessions and prepare members of the church for communion, and after celebrating on the sabbath he would go on to some other place.

In a small sacristy at the north of the building the first Sunday School was held. The furniture consisted of a desk and a row of wooden benches along the wall. The children sat on these benches and the priest was the Sunday School teacher. Bishop Fenwick of Boston, it is remembered, administered confirmation in the old church. The church was always decorated for Christmas and on that night a midnight mass was held. There was no organ, but on special occasions a music master named Coakley played a clarinet and another musician the flute. Mr. Frank O'Connor of 299 County Street was an altar boy.

Father McNulty was really the first regular pastor of St. Mary's, which for years was more like a mission than an established church. The first mass ever held in New Bedford was a great attraction to the curious outsiders who would stand in the churchyard and listen or look in at the windows.

Among the earlier members of St. Mary's Parish were: John Burke, Patrick Gallagher, Patrick Cluney, Patrick Commerford, Peter O'Connor, John Ryan, Cormack McEllany, Thomas Murphy, Daniel O'Connor, James Gilman, John Hay, Bernard Clark, Dennis Cavanagh, Wm. McGarvey, Morris Buckley, Andrew Kerrigan, Philip Johnson, Peter Murphy, Edw. O'Connell, Philip Nolan, Thomas O'Hara, and James Rotch.

For a long time St. Mary's burying ground was the only Catholic Cemetery in New Bedford, and those Catholics who lived in the surrounding villages brought their dead to be interred in consecrated ground. Mr. Edw. Kavenagh tells of one man bringing his dead child from Wareham in his farm wagon to bury him here.

In those days the present corner of Allen and County Streets, "Dog Corner" as it was called then, was a most unsavory locality, and when the Catholic women went to church they used to go in groups, fearing insult should they go alone.

The church increased very slowly in membership till the railroad was built between this city and Taunton in 1840, establishing connection with Boston. Up to that time there had been nothing to call the Irish here, but with the railroad and various business enterprises many Irish families were among those who came to New Bedford. The old church was enlarged, and then in April 1849 sold and the Universalist Church at the corner of Fifth and School Streets was bought. The old church was moved away, but the lot continued to be used as a burying ground.

The visit of Father Matthew in 1849, renowned apostle of temperance, was an event of great interest to Catholic and Protestant alike. He secured thousands of pledges in New York and Boston and then

Far left: Sketch of New Bedford's first Catholic church by unknown artist, from a 1931 manuscript. Courtesy of St. Lawrence Parish. *Left:* Old farm house on Allen and Cottage Streets, circa 1870, depicts a semblance of the old Irish neighborhood surrounding Dog Corner. Courtesy of the New Bedford Free Public Library. *Above:* Interior of the former St. Mary's Church on Pleasant Street, from Souvenir of St. Lawrence Church, 1895. Courtesy of St. Lawrence Parish. *Below:* The former St. Mary's Church and Grammar school on Pleasant Street around 1970. Courtesy of the *Standard-Times.*

visited many smaller places. He came to New Bedford on Wednesday, September 20, and was a guest at the Mansion House. For weeks the people had been looking forward to his coming and a right royal welcome they gave him. A procession was organized at City Hall, of which Timothy Ingraham was chief marshall, and the line included the New Bedford Band, the Temperance Societies of New Bedford and Fairhaven (7 organizations), the teachers and pupils of the public schools, and members of the City Council and School Committee. The procession moved to the Mansion House and Father Matthew entered a carriage with Mayor A. H. Howland, Alderman Grant of Boston, and James B. Congdon, Esq. The procession moved through the principal streets, which were thronged, to Liberty Hall, and on the way Father Matthew was greeted with showers of bouquets. At Liberty Hall an address of welcome was made by Mr. Congdon, to which Father Matthew responded. The next day Father Matthew went to St. Mary's, which was thronged with people, eager to take the pledge from the hands of the great temperance worker.

In 1853 Reverend Henry S. Henniss was appointed to St. Mary's Parish, and was New Bedford's first American-born priest. Under his labors St. Mary's took firm standing as a parish and it is to Father Henniss that older Catholics refer with tenderest love and reverence.

When he first arrived here he went to the Parker House and was there thrown more with Protestants than the earlier priests who had boarded with Catholic families. Many leading citizens called upon him, and he quickly won their esteem and respect.

He found the parish neither united nor self-supporting, but he was not dismayed. He had a rare faculty for organizing, was a man of great energy and foresight, and entered into the work before him with utmost zeal. In 1854 the increase of Irish made an enlargement of the church necessary, and under the leadership of the pastor an addition was built, nearly doubling the seating capacity. It is remembered that Father Henniss was a remarkably skillful skater and enjoyed the sport. On one occasion he skated from Nantucket to Hyannis. He was also a fine tenor singer and musician and took pains with his choir. Almost the first purchase Father Henniss made after getting the parish in order was the organ later used in St. Lawrence's Church. The first time the organ was played in public was a great day for parishioners and many eyes were filled with tears as the people listened. In 1854 Father Henniss bought seven acres of land in Dartmouth for a new cemetery — the present one. He had the ground graded, laid out, and enclosed in a neat stone wall, and in 1856 all bodies were removed to the new cemetery from Allen Street. He personally supervised the sad and gruesome work of transferring the remains from the old to the new cemetery. His friends believed that his labor and responsibility, in his feeble health, caused his death.

Still the parish increased, and it becoming evident a new church edifice would be needed in the future, Father Henniss with his usual foresight bought land on County and Hillman Streets from Dr. Lyman Bartlett. So much enthusiasm did he arouse among his parishioners that they raised the money ($5,500) in a single year. This was part of the lot where St.

Lawrence's now stands. Father Henniss was pastor of the church for 5 to 6 years and laboring unceasingly for three of these years and laying the foundations for the present prosperity of the parish. For years he had been suffering from consumption and the disease now had such a hold on him that it was evident that his life could not be prolonged. He went to Cuba and to Aiken, S.C., but it was of no avail, and he died in Sept. 1859, at the age of 37 years. No pastor was more deeply mourned. He was so kind, so genial, so quick-witted, that he at once made friends wherever he went, among Catholics or Protestants.

Father Henniss left the parish free from debt and in a very prosperous state. During his pastorate he made rules, some of which are in force at the present time. He established the Scapular, Rosary and Sanctuary Societies, which were later reestablished by Father Smyth.

The next pastor was Rev. Father Joseph P. Tallon, who had been Father Henniss' assistant and who was intimately acquainted with his plans. He took these plans up where Father Henniss had left them. He prepared drawings and specifications for a new brick church to be built on the County Street lot, the plans being similar to the Gate of Heaven Church in South Boston. Measures were taken for the erection of the church when the Civil War broke out and New Bedford received a severe blow to all its interests. The idea of building had to be postponed, but he continued the work of raising funds, looking forward to the time when peace should once more reign. But six months before the capture of Richmond, Father Tallon died, in 1864, at the early age of 31. His unselfishness is shown in the fact

Left: Father Hennis. Courtesy of the *Standard-Times. Above:* Interior of St. Lawrence Church, soon after construction, from a stereopticon, circa 1870. Courtesy of the New Bedford Free Public Library. *Far right:* The constructon of St. Lawrence Church tower in 1880. The superstructure was erected in 1867. Courtesy of St. Lawrence Parish.

that he labored with unabated zeal to provide money for the new church after his failing health made it evident that it would never be given him to build. He was content to sow, even though another might reap.

Jan. 1, 1865, Rev. Lawrence Stephen McMahon assumed the pastorate of St. Mary's. When he came here he found the original lot on County Street, containing 20,000 square feet, paid for

and $13,300 in the treasury. In 1865 he purchased of the heirs of Washington T. Walker a house and lot next to the original lot and still another lot in the rear, for $6,700. This gave 20,000 feet more. The house was moved a little to the west and is the present parsonage. Ground was broken for the new church in May 1866, and the corner stone was laid Nov. 1 of that year. At 10 A.M. on

that day the usual ceremonies of All Saints' Day were solemnized at the church on Fifth Street, Father McMahon conducting them. The house was densely crowded and hundreds were unable to gain admittance. After this service the Catholic Temperance Society, the Sunday School, and the congregation generally, headed by the New Bedford Brass Band, marched to the lot on

County Street, where some 5,000 people had assembled. At 11:30 Bishop Williams and other clergymen, in their robes, proceeded to the southeast corner of the lot where the service was held. The stone was laid by Bishop Williams, and the box placed under it contained a history of St. Mary's Church, a list of members of the Church Fund Society, a programme of the service in Latin, engrossed on parchment, coins and copies of the Boston *Pilot* and the New Bedford *Standard* and *Mercury*. The building operations went on under the closest supervision of Father McMahon, who remained on the ground day after day, and the edifice was first opened to the public on Sunday morning, Dec. 25, 1870 — Christmas morning — when over 600 people attended mass at 5 A.M.

St. Lawrence's Church is a fine specimen of architecture and an ornament to the city. It is of stone, the original plans for a brick church having been discarded and new plans procured by Father McMahon.

In addition to raising about $30,000 for the church building and furnishing and attending to the varied interests of the parish, Father McMahon bought the St. Joseph's Hospital property on Pleasant Street, the building and fitting costing $30,000. It was opened in 1873. The Hospital was also the home of the Sisters of Mercy, who were teachers in the parochial schools.

In 1872 Father McMahon was appointed vicar general of the Providence Diocese, and in 1879 was made Bishop of Hartford. His departure was greatly regretted by Catholics and Protestants, many of the latter being his warm friends.

The next pastor of St. Lawrence's was Rev. Hugh J. Smyth, who assumed charge of the parish Sept. 25, 1879, and proved a worthy successor to Fathers Henniss, Tallon and McMahon.

The membership of St. Lawrence's constantly increased, while the parish financially and spiritually continued in a very prosperous condition. Thomas McDonald was superintendant of the Sunday School, which held its sessions at St. Mary's Church. Other superintendants of St. Mary's School were Frank O'Connor, John McCullough, Michael Kennedy, James Nittleton, Jeremiah Sullivan, John Corish, Maurice Walsh, James Bawson, James Kirwin, Mr. Murphy, Andrew Porter and John Shay.

The devotional societies connected with St. Lawrence's are: the Holy Name, the Scapular Society, the Rosary Society, the Guard of Honor, and the Children of Mary Union of the Sacred Heart.

Father Smyth upon taking up the work of the parish at once turned his attention to the erection of parochial schools. In 1881 he bought the lot on Linden Street, near County, where St. Joseph's School now stands, and in 1883 that building was finished. Father Smyth then purchased land on Acushnet Avenue for the south parochial school, and the building — St. Mary's — was finished in 1885. They are substantial (and are still in use today — 1937). Both schools are carried on successfully under the care of the Sisters of Mercy, who are well fitted for their work of teaching, and both are under the directions of Father Smyth.

The St. Lawrence Temperance Society, connected with the church, was organized Jan. 5, 1865. Among its founders were Michael Kennedy, John Carroll, John Welsh, and others and Mr. McCullough has done a great deal for it. It is still doing good work.

Excerpted from the *Evening Standard* Aug. 30, 1887, prepared by Etta F. Martin.

The Portuguese in New England

Editor's Note: Though "The Portuguese in New England" was originally planned as a book, it was never published. As with all the ethnic studies, it would deal with migration and settlement, customs of living, working, and adjusting to American life. Mrs. Helen Mims, editor for social ethnic studies, pointed out that the contents would include:

The Portuguese worker in strikes, in the IWW, walking home grey-faced from textile or rope mills; the Portuguese fisherman in the parlor of his Cape Cod house, or fighting the fishing monopolies; the urban Portuguese trying to escape from the monotony of factory life by reviving the ancient ceremonial rituals of his homeland; the Portuguese farmer making a go of it in the country around New Bedford, living like a peon on the cranberry farms of Cape Cod . . .

The book will pivot around New Bedford, Fall River, Provincetown, Nantucket, Gloucester, Greater Boston, Plymouth, Lawrence and Lowell . . . The Portuguese story is to be set against changing local conditions, and their reaction to these conditions will be described in terms of the traditions and mentality they brought with them.

In 1939, Mrs. Mims was still editing the Portuguese study. The book was approved for publication and a contract was signed by William R. Freitas, of the Amportus Historical Society of New Bedford, to sponsor the publication. No book has yet appeared.

The excerpts published here, by Elsie Moeller, Stella Vera, Alice Kelley, Michael Regan and the Vineyard Gazette, provide a sketch of the writers' interpretation of Portuguese life in New England. The stories, which are in no way scientific, illustrate attitudes of the time toward the presence of the many ethnic groups.

The Portuguese on Martha's Vineyard

Manuel Silvia of Seven Gates Farm

The name Manuel Silvia being a common one, the subject of this sketch is specifically designated to avoid confusion. Mr. Silvia is worthy of more than a passing mention as having lived in the Up-Islands section longer than any other Portuguese citizen and, while he was not the first to locate west of the Chilmark-West Tisbury line, only one had come before him, the death of his predecessor long before him made Mr. Silvia a pioneer, in a manner of speaking.

Moreover, Mr. Silvia is, so far as is known, the last living resident of the Vineyard who has owned and operated a kaolin pit, an industry that once flourished along Cape Higgon Valley, which industry has long since been abandoned.

Born on the island of Saint George in the Azores, Mr. Silvia went to work when a youth in one of that island's shoemaking shops, which at that time supplied the heavy work shoes worn by the inhabitants.

Then, more perhaps than in later years, the people of the Azores turned longing eyes to the United States, where a few of their race had already located and found conditions very much to their liking. Many of these men shipped out from the islands on the whaleships of New Bedford and Edgartown and it was in this manner that Silvia left his home.

Completing the voyage, he was landed on the shores of this country, a stranger indeed, but he was not long without employment, for friends directed him to Oak Bluffs, where already numerous Portuguese had settled and here he resumed his shoemaking and harness-repairing.

At that time the late Prof. Nathaniel Shales was living and conducting the present Seven Gates Farm. Vastly different in size and aspect from the present select summer colony, the farm was chiefly pasture over which roamed great bands of sheep that grazed among the deserted old farm houses.

There was considerable cultivating done, however, and a number of Portuguese farmhands were constantly employed. Business becoming poor in Oak Bluffs, Mr. Silvia obtained employment on the Shales estate and it was there he spent the early days of his married life. There he learned the language of his adopted country and to practice the customs of its people.

The Azorean Portuguese, such as are commonly known in this section of the country, are villagers or country men. Their community lives in the islands do not differ greatly in principle from those of our other Vineyard people. Thus they know each other well and take an interest in the affairs of one another. When it came about, therefore, that Silvia purchased a home of his own, he moved across the line into Chilmark, locating in Tea Lane, the first of his race to locate in

Chilmark in two or three generations.

His home was a farm, upon which was one of the few low, old fashioned houses in the community. This was at the time when a china clay experimental plant was built and operated at the old brick-yard on Roaring Brook and a number of men were employed there, including Silvia. It was there that he became known for his abnormal strength and the story has been told of his carrying a heavy man, who had been injured, for half a mile without assistance.

When the plant was closed, he

returned to his farm and he worked the land and went out to day labor all about the community. On the trap scows, where the heavy work of driving the great spikes was all done by hand, his great strength and knowledge of the business made him a valuable man, always sought when such work was to be done.

The business of digging and shipping kaolin clay was in the mining of this clay in connection with a regular industry at that time and in the crude equipment employed for the laborious loading of vessels with huge

Unidentified farmer tills the soil of Seven Gates Farm around 1920. Today, Seven Gates Farm is a lush complex of fashionable estates. However, some pasture is leased out to sheep-grazing farmers who keep the meadows marginally farm productive. Stan Lair collection, courtesy of Mr. and Mrs. Eugene Baer.

clumsy wheelbarrows, few indeed could compete with Manuel Silvia.

During these years, while his family was growing up, he became acquainted and made a place for himself in the community. Always ready to help in sickness or time of need, offering the hospitality of his house to all who passed that way, Silvia was a man who was respected by his neighbors and generally popular with all who knew him.

His knowledge of the shoemaker's trade stood him in good stead during that time and because he repaired shoes for his own family, others began to bring work to him. Many men and women now living in distant parts of the country have had their shoes cobbled at "Manuel's" while they waited for them in the long kitchen of the old house and tried to learn a few words of Portuguese from the children or from Rita, his rosy-cheeked wife.

In his work about the farm Silvia showed familiarity with old fashioned methods that were strange to his younger neighbors. Lacking a tool for a job, he would employ another in a fashion remembered only by the older inhabitants. Thus it was when he had a field of grain to cut and thresh and, having no binder or cradle, he used the ancient sickle with good effect and probably is the last man in the country to have used this implement for such a purpose.

In carpentry, too, as he often made his own repairs on wagons and many other things about the farm, boys and men would often watch him hew a square timber from a round log. Such work had been a lost art with all but the oldest men for many years before that time.

After having been on the island of Martha's Vineyard for fifteen or

sixteen years, he felt a longing to return to his home in the Azores and departed with his family for a winter vacation. But unfortunately for him, he had become inured to the more robust climate of this country and the warmer and more moist weather of Saint George brought a serious illness upon him from which he did not fully recover until long after his return. Moreover, the more primitive methods of living as practiced there, no longer seemed homelike or desirable to him and his stay in the Azores was not the pleasant visit he had planned.

The time came when the older Cape Higgon residents, who had mined clay for many years, began to give up the

industry and opened no more new pits. The market for the product continued to be good and Mr. Silvia decided to try his hand in business for himself. His farm lay along the same valley where the clay had been dug for generations and, with his knowledge gained from working for others, he had no difficulty in locating the clay and equipping himself for the work of mining it out. In some of the pits he opened, Silvia did all the work below ground himself, removing a vessel load of clay from the pit. The amount of work involved in such an undertaking can scarcely be imagined by anyone unfamiliar with the process, and had he not been blessed with a wonderfully strong body and rugged health, he must have broken under the strain.

Those days passed also. The market for Vineyard clay was supplied from other sources. One by one the families moved away from Cape Higgon and Mr. Silvia's family, now grown to maturity, became scattered. Several years ago he and his wife left also, leaving the farm to return to the big estate, now much larger, where they spent the early years of their married life.

Here on Seven Gates Farm, Silvia is now (1930) employed. He does not have to work as hard as he did when younger and life is much more pleasant than during the early years, when the struggle in which he was engaged was almost too much for human strength.

(Reprinted with permission from the *Vineyard Gazette,* Inc. ©1930).

Bottom Left: Ruins of the old brick yard at Roaring Brook in Chilmark. Here, clay was mined for use in making red brick. *Above Left:* A group of workers at the Roaring Brook brick yard stand in front of their living quarters, referred to as the "Frenchmen's Boarding House." *Below:* An unidentified Portuguese family stand beside their living quarters on Seven Gates Farm, circa 1910. Photographs from the Stan Lair collection, courtesy of Mr. and Mrs. Eugene Baer.

Joseph Burgess of Oak Bluffs

Like a chapter from the life of one of the pioneers is the story of Joseph C. Burgess of Oak Bluffs. He is a tall, sparsely-built man, wiry and straight despite his seventy-seven years. His complexion is light and his features so typically Yankee that not until he speaks is his nationality betrayed. For he is a Portuguese, born just outside the city of Horta on the island of Fayal.

On the vine-covered hills of that gem of the Azores he spent his youth in tilling the farmlands with ox-teams, harvesting the fruits and grains and tending the flocks and herds. A self-sustaining race, those Portuguese farmers of his day produced nearly every need from their own soil.

He had little schooling. There were schools that were kept by day and night, but his days were devoted to toil and, when the night came, the guitars that tinkled in the orange groves called him and he joined the carefree

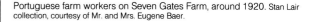

throng while the girls and boys danced beneath the moon and the gourds of sweet wine flowed freely.

So life went on until he was twenty-two years old. Recognized as a farmer, physically unfit for military service because of a clever trick he played upon the examining officers, he might have been there today, but for the curious working of fate. For there was a girl in the group which danced, who excelled all others in his eyes. But romance failed to blossom and he left his home for a foreign country.

Whaleships stopped at the islands to ship men and in the cities and large towns there were always to be found shipping agents who catalogued the names of those who desired to go to sea, seeking passage to America in that manner.

So Burgess entered his name and within a few days he found himself aboard a Provincetown schooner upon

which he had been shipped as one of the foremast hands. This schooner was outward bound on a year's cruise in the Atlantic Ocean. But fortune favored the craft and in eleven months' time she made her home port filled with sperm oil. Here Burgess was paid off with $15.50 for his work and what few clothes he had been obliged to buy from the ship's slop chest.

He had relatives in New Bedford and to that city he made his way, eventually finding the people he sought. Then he looked for employment, but these relatives insisted upon his buying better clothing, lending him the money for that purpose. So that, as he says, he started out in America in debt, without any trade and speaking no word of English.

His first job was obtained upon a Dartmouth farm, where he agreed to

work for six dollars a month and his board. Cheap as his labor was, his employer attempted to reduce his wages by one dollar at the end of the month. He next worked on a farm near Fall River, where he received $18 a month, a much better wage. So passed a year and he returned to New Bedford, to find that times were dull and work scarce.

Through the efforts of his relatives he learned of a position on Woodledge Farm in Oak Bluffs and so he arrived on Martha's Vineyard. He agreed to work on this farm for a year for $100 and his board and carried this agreement through to the end. Then, for a year, he worked on an estate in Vineyard Haven, where his wages were better.

In the meantime he had been learning English until he could converse intelligently, and his ambition prompted him to do

something more for himself. Accordingly, he bought a small piece of land in Oak Bluffs and planted it with garden vegetables. This garden he tended night and morning while working on various estates. His regular working day was of ten hours duration for which he received a dollar and a half.

He harvested his crops after these working hours and carried the produce through the village each night, often selling three or four dollars worth. Encouraged by these results, he purchased more land and took up truck gardening as a business. He raised acres of strawberries, onions and various other crops, clearing the woody growth in sections of his land until he had about seven acres of cultivated area. He paid for this, built a barn, purchased livestock, including horses, and, finally, a house. He drove a fast driving horse, owned a shining buggy, the smartest kind of a turnout for those times, and paid for all from the proceeds of his little farm.

But life seems lonely on the farm and he began to long for company, as he humorously remarks. The lady of his choice was finally located, but there were serious obstacles in the way of immediate marriage, for she was but ten years old. "I waited for nearly seven years for her." he says, "because I didn't want anyone else, and when she was sixteen and a half years old and I was thirty-four, we were married."

Regarding cost of labor and materials, it is interesting to note some of the bills he paid at this time. When he decided to build a house, he obtained lumber prices and sought out a carpenter to do the work, submitting plans for a six room house. These plans were drawn by Burgess. The carpenter agreed to build the house for $75 and to paint the house for $25 more.

So Burgess and his young wife went into housekeeping and the years that followed brought trials and hardships. Thirteen children were born to them, eleven of whom are still living and grown to maturity. "It was no trouble to get plenty of fuel to burn and enough to eat," says he, "but as the children grew older, we wanted them to be educated and as decently clothed as were other children. Those things cost money and we had to raise it. Twice I mortgaged the place up to $800 and all the time I was working on my land."

He could not work his farm in winter, so he turned at times to wood-chopping. His first venture was an agreement to chop one hundred cords of wood at $1 a cord. He tended his stock night and morning and, taking a little bread and coffee, went into the woods carrying two axes. "I used the heaviest axe in the morning when I felt freshest and when I began to get tired, took the lighter one. My regular day's work, if the weather did not interfere, was to chop and put up two cords of wood." Unless it rained very hard he never stopped working.

"We lived pretty hard during those days," he says, "and our house was not as comfortable either. Food was cheap and the island farms produced plenty of vegetables and meat and we had plenty of milk. But there were things that had to be bought. I remember keeping an account of the flour we used and it was thirteen barrels a year."

When the time came that some of the children were old enough to help on the farm, life became easier. The debts were paid and prosperity smiled once more.

Outside, the fields smile beneath the sun, heavy with crops, while the trees, planted long ago by the owner's hands, shade his door. He does not work his farm himself, but he still keeps his herd of cows. Gone is the horse and buggy, but in the garage are a couple of fine automobiles. It is a pleasant picture of life's eventide and the reward of a life of toil and devotion to duty, and also a tribute to the day and the people of that generation "when every rood of land sustained its man." (From *The Vineyard Gazette*, July 19, 1933)

Mary in the Lane

author unknown

More than a passing notice should be given to the brave, capable Portuguese women living on Martha's Vineyard, who were left widows with a family of three, four, five and six children, without owning a home and without money with which to pay for daily food and necessary clothing.

Perhaps the first to settle in Edgartown was the slender, little woman familiarly known as "Mary in the Lane." She came from the island of Fayal, Azores with two small children, a daughter and a son, in the year 1900.

Placing the children with some Portuguese friends who had left their home in Fayal for Martha's Vineyard previously, Mary went out daily seeking what work she could do in families. Usually this work consisted of laundry and cleaning or assisting in cooking.

By so doing she was able to care for her children without any other assistance, placed them in public school of the town, where they learned to speak English fluently and read and write in the language; always speaking with a good accent and also interpreting for their mother.

A few years passed. Mary acquired a small house and lot "in the Lane" and continued to earn enough to support herself and her children. She became persuaded by a man from her own race and home in Fayal, a man older by many years, to marry him. By him she had another daughter and, when the aged husband was no longer able to contribute to the family support, Mary sought laundry work which could be done at her home and continued to work in other homes by the hour.

The old man Enos sickened and died after a prolonged illness. Mary was able by her frugality and industry to keep her home, bring up her younger daughter, buy all the necessities of life, keep hens, and plant a vegetable garden, in addition to the laundry work in which she excels.

She is now over seventy years of age, still busy and earning her living. "I've worked, worked all my life," says Mary. "In the house, on the farm, in the fields, in the woods — see my head — just feel top of my head!"

We felt the top of Mary's head. We felt the ridges — long, hard ridges on the top of her head — deep and well-defined ridges made when she was but a young child.

"You know how come?" asked Mary. "No," we reply. "You see in my country poor peoples carry wood, stone, baskets of clothes, food, everything carry on head in Fayal.

Some rich peoples have donkey to take wood, but my peoples no have donkey. We use head. Used my head when small — so small — so little," says Mary in the Lane.

"Have you ever been home since you left the old country?" we asked. "Just one time I thought to go," says Mary, "but my father die, my mother die, my sister so poor. I send my pay-to-go moneys to help her. I stay home," says Mary in the Lane.

All honor to her and to her honesty, helpfulness and independence! She has raised a good son, two good daughters, all valued citizens and voters in the town of Edgartown on Martha's Vineyard.

Mary thinks, "shame for peoples no work for living and ask town to buy coal and food for them. I work, work. No ask town to help and I no very strong," says Mary in the Lane.

Mary Enos (left) in her garden on Pent Lane in Edgartown with her daughter, around 1938. Courtesy of her granddaughter, Jean M. Andrews of Edgartown.

The Portuguese in Fall River *(edited and abridged)*

by *Joseph J. Welch and Michael Regan*

An Azorean farmer, alongside his home in Santa Maria, takes time to pose with his hand-made tool and basket of fruit well at hand. Farming and gardening are age-old and beloved traditions that have been brought to this country by the Azorean.
Courtesy of Casa Da Saudade Library, New Bedford.

Farming

The true Portuguese farmer seems to have an innate love of flowers. Doubtless the beautiful flowers of his native Azores have helped to stimulate this aesthetic sense within him. When taking a trip through Fall River's farming suburbs, one cannot see even the smallest farmhouses without their well-kept dooryard plots of sweet peas, nasturtiums, lilacs or gladioli.

Well-kept vegetable gardens near the home of the Portuguese truck-farmer bespeak his frugality, his ability to get the most out of the smallest amounts of land. Often a fairly large family is supported rather comfortably on two or three acres. The work of the Portuguese farmer appears to be a family enterprise. About each farmhouse, one can see a number of youngsters, all busy with the work of the farm. Into the fields, too, go the mother, the father and in some cases the grandfather and grandmother to aid with the general farm work. It is not unusual to see an old grandfather, his eyes dim, his face seamed and lined, his back heavily stooped from years of toil in the Azores, working side by side with the youngest member of the family.

There is little time for rest and recreation for an industrious truck-farmer. He must work not only all day but often long into the night, marketing his produce. And the return is not at all in proportion to time, labor and money invested. To talk to one of these farmers is indeed a revelation. They complain bitterly (and not without cause) about the manner in which they are pressed on both sides — one by the mortgage-holder, with interest often running as high as eight percent and, on the other side, they are faced with falling market prices for their produce and unscrupulous middlemen who quote unfair prices on the farmer's goods. Crops are disposed of readily in Boston and Providence as well as in this city.

Dress

Universally speaking, Portuguese in Fall River have adopted the American mode of dress. Occasionally, however, one can see an elderly Portuguese woman with a long, black shawl, the ends of which are bedecked with tassels. These shawls are drawn tightly over the head and fastened under the chin by a brooch. Their dresses are usually black, reaching down to the tops of their heels.

Among the men in Fall River there is no appreciable difference between their dress and American dress except for the headpiece — the "carapuca," whose use is confined more to the rural districts, and the little knitted caps worn by some Portuguese in Fall River. This little headpiece is scarcely larger than a skull cap, fitting snugly over the head of the wearer. As a sort of decoration there is a little tassel at the top of the hat. It is said to be the kind of hat worn by fishermen in some sections of the Azores and is often seen worn by the Portuguese fishermen at Provincetown.

Customs

As to customs among the Portuguese in the rural sections surrounding Fall River, Christmas is celebrated as it is in the city. The day before Christmas, the Portuguese farmer kills the choicest pig in his pen for the Christmas celebration and invites his less opulent relatives, neighbors, and friends. Among all the Portuguese in America, their festival days — Christmas, New Year, Santo Christo, there is "open house," where unstinted hospitality is the rule. Relatives, neighbors, friends, acquaintances, even total strangers may call at a Portuguese home and receive a cordial welcome.

Religious Organizations

There are seven Roman Catholic churches in Fall River, the oldest being Santo Christo, which was founded in 1892. The first Portuguese church in the area was mission church which was established in 1876. Prior to that time, the religious needs of the Portuguese people were administered by a New Bedford priest who drove every Saturday night to Fall River and celebrated mass on Sunday.

The most well-known Portuguese clergyman, an assistant at Santo Christo parish, John B. DeValles, became a hero of the First World War. He was never long absent from the firing line. Repeatedly he was in mortal jeopardy in meeting the bodily and spiritual needs of his charges irrespective of their beliefs. He did not emerge unscathed to safety always. On one occasion he was wounded badly and though hospitalization was necessitated, the patriot could not be held back long from the scene of action.

Though he escaped death by gunfire, soon after the war he was stricken with disease. In the evening of March 12, 1920, he breathed for the last time. His body was taken from New Bedford to Fall River, to be received by a military pageant and borne to the cemetery of St. Patrick, there to be laid in a grave beside his mother. His possessions, including the medal and the French cross, were entrusted to a Boston council of the Knights of Columbus.

The first soldier from Fall River to lose his life on a French battlefield was Joseph Francis, whose father was a native of the Azores. In recognition of his sacrifice, as a tribute to his memory and an object lesson to the developing generation in fulfilling their bounden duty to the nation, in peace and war, as loyal sons and daughters by reason of birth — or by adoption through the medium of naturalization, a post of the Veterans of Foreign Wars was named for him.

Sports

The naturally sturdy, healthy body with which the average Portuguese has been endowed lends itself admirably not only to the gaining of a livelihood but also to athletic endeavors. The race has produced several outstanding professional athletes and some of the finer types of amateur sports-leaders have been of Portuguese origin.

Fall River is regarded today as the leading soccer city in America. At the present time, there is a Fall River team, the Ponta Delgadas, who are contending with a Boston team for the New England final championship in an effort to capture the Dowar trophy, the symbol of amateur soccer supremacy in America.

There have been several Portuguese boys from Fall River who have achieved national prominence in professional soccer. Foremost of these is William (Billy) Gonsalves. There are some soccer enthusiasts who say that Gonsalves is the greatest soccer player ever produced in America. He has often been styled "the Babe Ruth of Soccer." Young men of Portuguese extraction predominate in membership in the Boys' Club of Fall River which is devoted to physical improvement among boys and men of the city.

Fall River soccer great, Billy Gonsalves, is the "Babe Ruth" of local soccer legend. *Courtesy of the Fall River Herald News.*

A Legacy of Photographs

One of the finest legacies of the New Deal is the contribution made by an extraordinary group of photographers working for the Farm Security Administration (FSA) and the U.S. Office of War Information (US OWI). Originally hired by the Resettlement Administration (RA), whose aim was to help destitute farmers secure land, their job was to document the Depression on film, thus stirring public awareness and compassion while emphasizing the need for government aid. In 1937, the RA became the FSA and Director Rexford Tugwell appointed Roy Stryker in charge of photography. Stryker hired the best photographers he could find.

By 1942, the FSA budget dwindled and its objectives shifted to matters concerning war preparations. Meanwhile, Stryker moved to the Department of War Information, which had a larger budget. He took FSA photographers Jack Delano, John Collier and Gordon Parks with him. The new assignment was to show how America's farmers were preparing for war.

In telephone interviews, we talked with Jack Delano in Puerto Rico; with Mary Collier, wife of John Collier, in San Francisco; and with Louise Rosskam, widow of Edwin Rosskam, in New Jersey. Delano, Collier and Rosskam photographed Southeastern Massachusetts for FSA and US OWI and we have used their work, along with biographical notes, to illustrate the following section, "The Portuguese in New England," (and pages 3 through 7 of the Introduction).

"The FSA work was an extremely important experience for all of us," noted Louise Rosskam. "It was not like exhibiting your work in an art gallery or on a wall. This was the opening of America for everyone to see." (For readings on the FSA, see the Bibliography).

"During the whole eight years, I held on to a personal dream that inevitably got translated into black and white pictures. I wanted to do a pictorial encyclopedia of American agriculture." — Roy Stryker. *In This Proud Land.*

Left: "Mr. Antonio V. Possante, a Portuguese FSA client and apple grower. Has two children. Cultivates 27 acres which produce about 500 bushels of apples." Lowell. January 1941. *Right:* "Mrs. Richard Carter, a poultry farmer; she runs the poultry business of 1,000 hens while her husband drives a bulldozer at an army camp (Edwards) nearby." Middleboro, December 1940. FSA photographs and captions by Jack Delano.

The Portuguese-American Race:
early customs in New Bedford

by Stella Vera

In 1858, a young girl, eighteen years of age, came to New Bedford from the island of Pico to marry a young man, who had previously come on a whaling voyage. This woman related to her children that when she arrived in New Bedford there were only twelve Portuguese women.

The first Catholic baptismal register in New Bedford shows the birth of two Portuguese children, sisters, daughters of a Portuguese father and mother. One was born June 4, 1842 and the other was born April 2, 1846. They were both baptised on the same day in 1846.

The baptismal record was as follows:

Name:	John Leeschandry
Child of:	Ennis Leeschandry
and:	Mary Catharina
Born:	June 4, 1842
Was Baptised:	May 17, 1846
Sponsors:	Histula Ennis
	Mary Catharina

Name:	Lucia
Child of:	Ennis Leeschandry
and:	Mary Catharina
Born:	April 2, 1846
Was Baptised:	May 17, 1846
Sponsors:	Julia Cais

The surname "Inacio" is today translated to "Enos" and in that epoch must have been translated to "Ennis"; "Leeschandry" believed to be a translation of the name "Alexandre";

Julia and Catharina are Portuguese names.

In an interview with a lady, a daughter of Portuguese parents, born in this city in the year 1861, it was learned that when she was about nine years of age the houses were very cold, the furniture in the houses was very simple, no carpets, armchairs or sofas; wooden chairs and the rest of the furniture also wooden. Near the houses were wells of water for the principal uses of domestic life, for other uses of less importance, like the washing of clothes, large hogsheads were placed near the houses to catch the rain water. The houses were illuminated by kerosene lamps. Bathrooms were then not known, the "toilettes" were built some distance from the houses.

The dress was very modest. The hat and the gloves were then not in vogue on Sundays. In church calico dresses were the only kind worn. One Sunday in spring of the year 1868 appeared in Saint Mary's Church, a church which was then frequented by all the Portuguese, a Portuguese woman with a silk dress. For several weeks that was the topic of conversation. It was a real scandal. This woman was a native of Fayal and was the owner of a rooming house.

In the mills wages were from five to six dollars per week, with a twelve hour working day. The seamen on whalers did not have a certain wage.

They were unable to determine their earnings until after the voyage, as it depended upon the catch of whales.

In 1870 the Portuguese in New Bedford lived more abundantly and with more money than they had in the islands, deserving compensation for the hard work and for the severe climate. But they always maintained the same simple life, totally deprived of comfort.

In 1893, twenty-three years later, the whaling industry occupied a good number of Portuguese, but the principal occupation was in the cotton mills. Some of the houses were then heated by coal stoves and, as they were not well protected against the cold, doors and windows were well closed and well caulked during the winter and the cracks in the floors were covered with pieces of cloth. They now had running water in their homes, but continued to use the wells and the freshness and coolness of the water was appreciated. The bathrooms were still a privilege of the rich.

Carpets, sofas and armchairs were now being used in the homes, but of a mediocre quality, nothing luxurious. At some of the reunions in the churches a few silk dresses and hats were seen, but very few, still the calico dresses, the shawl and the mantillas predominated.

In 1902 the mode of living of Portuguese society represented only one important change, the dress of the

Portuguese ladies had suffered one complete transformation. The silk dress, the hat, the gloves, the coat had completely conquered the Portuguese feminine society. At the reunions and in the churches one would gather that they were in the midst of high society, abundantly rich and much superior to those who were seen in the best of society in our Azorean capitals.

In 1910 the pressing need for comfort began to show, the exigency of the bathroom or at least the "toilettes," the acquisition of good carpets, of good parlor, dining room and bedroom furniture. With the high salaries and business profits during the war period, that desire for comfort and luxury materialized.

At the same time that progress of comfort that took place in the houses noticeably transformed the mentality of the Portuguese people. Until 1910, it was generally their ambition to return to their native country; afterwards the feminine element, principally, had a fixed idea to become permanent residents.

In the last twenty-four years, the Portuguese have conquered all professions. Today we have artists in all the branches of profession, clerks in all the branches of commerce and industry, including the larger commercial houses and American banks, nurses, a profession that is considered very honorable in this country, teachers and professors, representatives in the legislature, proprietors, merchants, manufacturers, dentists, doctors, lawyers, judges. (Dr. Manuel C. Pereira, Vice-Consul of Portugal in Fall River, from an article written for "Os Portuguese em New Bedford," edited by the *Diario de Noticias,* New Bedford, Massachusetts)

Jack Delano made this photograph in January, 1941, along Potomska Street (now South Terminal) in New Bedford. The area was once affectionately referred to as the Portuguese Navy Yard. From there, local mariners plied a part-time trade harvesting seafood from the bay, or launched their "yachts" for summer sport.

Jack Delano told *Spinner*. "Our assignment was to photograph every conceivable subject related to Americana that caught our eyes. This was Roy Stryker's vision. That is why I covered textile mills, truck farmers, housing, ethnic groups and everything else that I could. In New England, I was told to do a lot of reading. I read *Flowering of New England* and met with Harold Ballou. The activities I covered, such as the potato festival in Maine, were up to me."

The Living Conditions of the Portuguese in New Bedford

by Elsie S. Moeller

1820 to 1870

It is believed that the migration of the old American families of New Bedford from Water Street to County Street may have begun sometime about 1818. The early whaling seamen's tavern's, remnants of which are still seen here and there, and their associations and reputations probably led to the changes in the residential sections.

Along South Street, so-called because it was the southernmost of the east and west streets, and Water, Wing and Howland Streets decade after decade the new arrival has fared. At first he was looking for temporary stopping places, or boarding houses, until the sure job was offered or until the whaleships went away on another voyage, and what more natural than to settle near the same boarding places. Also, at that time the old houses vacated by the families who could afford to keep them to rent, were the only places of abode for rent and, as to allowing foreigners en masse in any but the shore section of town, it would not have been allowed by any of the tight-laced old residents. If one or two found their way out to farm land, though marshy and undesirable in the section on Allen Street, towards the Dartmouth town line, it was only as "squatters" in the most miserable and straitened of circumstances. Tolerated here, also, only until the irate owner moved them on, or else because he himself was too indifferent in regards to the poor land (and there was plenty of it then) to bother whether they were there or not.

Above: "Bringing home some salvage fire wood in a slum area." *Above Right:* "Employees entering a textile mill." FSA photographs and captions by Jack Delano, New Bedford, January 1941. *Bottom Right:* "Family of Portuguese house painter who live in low income government housing project." US OWI photograph by John Collier, New Bedford, Spring 1942.

Photographers Jack Delano and John Collier were working as artists on the WPA Project when Roy Stryker discovered their work. Delano's stirring exhibition in Philadelphia of Pennsylvania coal miners, and Collier's stunning portfolio entitled "Activities of a Sheep Camp in New Mexico," won them the coveted FSA positions.

The first of the newcomers came from Fayal, probably before 1830, brought across as part of the whaling vessels' crews. Here they first set up their household goods and opened their little shops. The first shop, it is stated, having been set up here by a Portuguese at the corner of Howland Street, was that of Joseph Pedro, who, it is believed, before that had a store in the center.

That the shore sections, or lowland sections, to which the Portuguese were relegated to settle in were extremely undesirable at times, the following extract bears witness, and there were many of these floods before this one, in fact they were of quite common occurence. Especially in March and the month of the equinoctal storms, September:

"Water Street yesterday suffered from the worst flood it has experienced for a long term of years. The water entered stores and dwellings, doing a large amount of damage, and scores of cellars were flooded, many of them to a depth of more than four feet. The heavy rainfall and melting snow transformed the streets running east and west into rivers and early in the afternoon the water began to accumulate on Water Street, between Howland and Grinnell. The sewer became clogged with snow and dirt and the outlets were insufficient to allow the torrents that were being poured in to escape. Then the water began to flow out of the catch-basins and manholes until at five o'clock the entire square bounded by Howland, Grinnell, Front and First Streets was submerged to three feet. As the water rose the families who lived in the first stories of the houses in that section were driven from their homes. It invaded stores, and cellars were filled to the floors above. Hundreds of men, women and children found when they came home at night that they were unable to reach their homes and gathered at the street corners surveying the scene with rueful countenances. Several enterprising boatmen were on hand with improvised ferries to their homes for the modest fee of five cents. On the corners of the streets leading to

the flooded districts were displayed signs, 'boats to let.' At the corner of Howland and Water Streets the water was nearly 11½ feet deep.

"All who were not provided with rubber boots were taken across at this point on the boats by policemen and bystanders. Manuel Oliver, a shoemaker, was out. He will lose about $25.00. Manuel D. Rogers, grocery and provisions, was also invaded to the extent of about $200 damage. In the basement of a house that was flooded was a girl who was confined to her bed. She found herself floating around in not less than four feet of water. She was reached by men in a boat and taken to the upper story of the building. Groceries and supplies of scores of families, which were in the flooded cellars, were destroyed."

In moving their goods and chattels the good old method of the human being as a pack horse was resorted to, the women as well as and generally before the men and the children bringing up the rear, dragging a home-made cart with smaller things. Also the neighbors all lent a hand, to be reciprocated when they were in like circumstances, and maybe if some of a certain family's household goods were unusually large, someone found a horse and rickety wagon to transfer the necessities to the new home.

They did and do move often and have made considerable economic progress, as measured by the ownership of property, in every generation that has come to this country. But often sadly, it is a known fact, at the cost of the health and happiness of the entire family, the necessary money for moving and buying the property has been saved. But, particularly in the farm lands, it is well they have, for few enough men today are willing to struggle with New England climactic variableness and its farm land at its best.

The tenement, the regular two and three decker, as such was unknown in New Bedford until the 1890's and the houses that the Portuguese occupied in the beginning were the old large family dwellings vacated for a better and more stylish district. Many families living in such houses, the climate of New England being such as not to make the Portuguese feel at home, closed up more than half of what few rooms they had and stayed together in as few rooms as could be kept warm at low cost. When they built houses they were either

John Collier's wife, Mary Collier, told *Spinner*, "Working at FSA was John's basic education. Roy Stryker believed in the group process. John's assignment was to get the stories of families, not single pictures. Before shooting, he would become acquainted with people, sometimes even living with them. On the whole, New England was too green, too lush for John. He preferred the colors of New Mexico and California.

John Collier photographed what he called "workers at a linguica (Portuguese sausage) factory." The Lisbon Sausage Company on Rockdale Avenue, near Cove Road, was managed by Jose A. Amaral, shown feeding the linguica from the stuffer into its casing. His wife, Maria, is tying the ends of the casings. The older woman, below, peeling onions, is unidentified. US OWI photograph, Spring 1942.

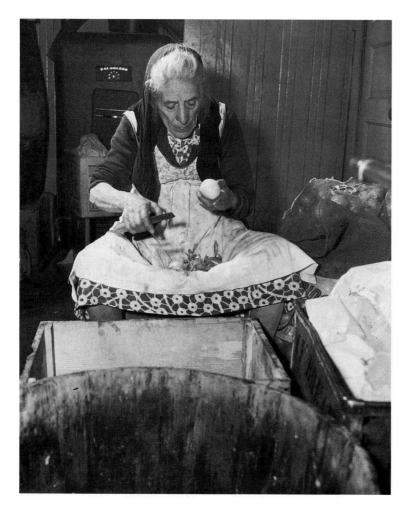

extremely small or merely shacks. Especially in cases where they "squatted," the walls were of the flimsiest construction: roofs of pieces of tin and, in the undrained districts, they had to be built up on high underpinnings. If not, the whole family were subjected to the damp floors and, of necessity, a sort of trench was dug around the house for drainage. For further protection in the winter, the sides were banked with straw, mixed with dirt.

There are no statistics available for these years to show the actual number of people in a home, but as the Portuguese habit was a child a year for the poor mother, it can be understood that the number was more rather than less and, of course, there was always the boarder, sometimes a man, sometimes a girl. This boarder was often a relative from the islands, whose family, as a whole, had not yet come to the states.

The Latin immigrant's conception of the sacredness and exclusiveness of the homes is not what it is in the Anglo-Saxon mind. They are not fastidious as to crowding. The man and wife occupy one bed and all the children, and maybe a boarder, a bed in the other corners of the same room. This may be abominable to our point of view, but it does not necessarily imply immorality on the part of the immigrant, to whom it is all a regular part of existence.

Between 1860 and 1870 the rent for four small rooms in a small house in the South Water Street district, with an outhouse in the back yard, which was the convenience even the best families boasted of in those days, was $2.50 a week. This was exorbitant when the weekly wages of the working man of that date are taken into

consideration, as he received $6.00 at the very most and generally $5.00 was the tops.

The foreigner who comes to these shores is not slow to adopt American ways of dress and living, but one of the last things he changes is his cuisine. The Portuguese still eat their best-loved dishes: linguica, chourico, chourico mouro and morselas, which has been anglicized to "morcella." When the Portuguese mariners first

landed from the whaleships they had to eat New England fare per force. What they got was dumplings, Indian meal and much chowder. Only when their families, and the few pioneer girls who came as brides, arrived were they able to have their own familiar dishes.

The families used to kill a pig once a year and, if prosperous, they killed two. This flesh, besides giving straight pork and ham, furnished the stuffing

for their linguica. If they were not well-to-do, they lived mostly on beans, plain New England beans, but cooked in the Portuguese way with other vegetables, such as cabbage, onions, and other greens, which is a very tasty dish when it has plenty of salt. They did well even to have beans, when their rent was $2.50 out of $6.00 a week. Before the linguica was made by commercial concerns the families used to build smoke houses in their own yards to cure the lengths, as the smoking was one of the most important factors in making it tasty. The following is a genuine recipe for making those dishes:

"After killing the pig the meat is divided into two groups. The fat meat is salted and the lean is cut into pieces about one cubic inch thick. This meat is put into clay or wooden tanks and spiced with garlic and salt. Some use wine, others use vinegar. Paprika is used as a means of coloring."

In the Azores and Madeira pepper is also used. After a day or two, this meat is filled into casings of the pig. The washing of the pig's intestines, the casings, is the job every girl, peasant or American immigrant, dislikes. The resulting product is linguica or chourico, according to the thickness and length and this, in turn, depends on the size of the casing. Linguica is made in longer pieces and chourico is made in short, thick pieces. If blood is added to the chourico, it is called chourico Mouro. Chourico Mouro was introduced by the Moors when they invaded Portugal. Another filling, called farinheira, is also common. It is made of corn flour, paprika and pieces of pork fat. It is smoked and becomes a light brown. Morselas are the big favorite, although they are not as common. They are made of fresh pig's blood, onion, parsley and plenty of pepper and, if desired, rice. They are cooked and become almost black and have a strong tempting smell. They do not keep more than a few days.

In the Azores they keep them in clay tanks filled with lard. This style of keeping was absolutely necessary because the peasants have to be self sufficient. This is so because it is impossible to transport things to some parts of the country, except on donkeys or mules. The linguica and chourico and other foods are smoked in the fireplaces or smoke houses and kept over the fireplace. After being kept some time it becomes as hard as leather. In America the casings are now imported from China.

The Portuguese had gardens in the 1860's and in all probability had them in the 1850's and 1840's. Whenever they have a chance to plant a seed of

any kind near their abodes they do so, for it is an instinct for this industrious home and earth loving soul to plant and grow things, perhaps because he loves them. He must also have his wine, which is harmless and so grows his grapes on his farm or on a trellis in the backyard in the city, which also forms a shady spot on a hot summer day.

Early Portuguese immigrants to parts of New England are said to have been peculiarly healthy with a low death rate, maybe because most of them were mariners in the prime and vigor of their early manhood. Certainly they included but a small proportion of those in the perilous periods of life, the very young and the very aged, being mostly in the healthy ages when the mortality is low. Until 1850 the population of Massachusetts was almost entirely American, but then, as the families of immigrants began to multiply, their numerous children formed a larger proportion of the people. Their children were of the perishable age group and most of them belonged to the poorer classes, whose improvident habits and straitened circumstances are most unfavorable to the development of sound constitutions and the maintenance of health in their children.

These causes were probably the fount of the consumption, which made such serious inroads upon their numbers in later years, but which was not helped, nor paid much attention to, until the beginning of the next century. However, as the treatment for tuberculosis in those early days, in even the best of families, was "tightly closed windows and large cups of hot water to drink," the lack of records concerning the disease among the

foreign elements in the town is no surprise.

Nor could smallpox be laid at the immigrant's door in the early years. "From 1840 until 1892, so far as appears from the records, and substantiated by several well-known citizens, New Bedford was comparatively free from visitation of the disease."

As to the celebrations, "the distractions of that day were few. There was no means of getting about. The pleasant places that are now reached by motor so easily were remote and inaccessible, except for the wealthy." Disporting on a sabbath was frowned upon. The psychological effects of healthy recreation were as unknown as croquet. No clubs had yet been formed and the Portuguese had to depend on himself and the sparse elements for his recreation. The Portuguese must be gay even if he is not cheerful, "for judging by their amusements in the islands, they are not a cheerful people, but their celebrations are gay. The dances and crowded balls, which are constantly occuring, the religious processions in the streets and the exciting church services, which the policy of the Church of Rome has accommodated to their tastes, indicate a necessity for stimulus, which a cheerful people seldom need, but which is necessary to produce gaiety. Certainly the native Americans of that date did not go in for gaiety very heavily and this may be part of the reason why at least one quarter of the Portuguese elected to spend their old age in the old country.

There were no records kept in New Bedford previous to 1891 to show whether the Portuguese voted religiously when he had the chance or not, but an elderly gentleman, who

was acquainted with some of the older residents, states that, to his mind, the first generation of Portuguese immigrants made wonderful residents. They were industrious, thrifty, righteous, peaceful and courteous neighbors, but they were in no hurry to either become citizens or vote. A great many of them returned to their native land, either yearly or when they considered they had saved enough money to live there comfortably for the rest of their lives.

He could not say much of the second generation, when it came along

about the 1880's and 1890's, but that it was then they began to figure in court for all sorts of misdemeanors, which the first generation had been innocent of. Yet the truer to their original make-up the aliens remain, the harder it is always for them to become assimilated if they make their abode here. For they remain a stranger in a strange land, sometimes all their lives, that is, to the casual American. Because their appearance is against them they are spotted at first sight as not belonging to the flock.

Far left: "Portuguese mother with pictures of her sons who are all in service." *Above:* "Portuguese girls manufacturing gas masks." US OWI photographs and captions by John Collier, New Bedford, Spring 1942.

The Living Conditions of the Portuguese on Cape Cod

by Elsie S. Moeller

Editors' Note: While Elsie Moeller's essay is intended to compliment the ability of the Portuguese people to assimilate into and revitalize Cape Cod's social and economic fabric, she reveals attitudes which sharply patronize and stereotype the "dark-skinned newcomer." We have published this essay, not for the insight into the human condition which it intended to give, but for the way it reacts to and interprets the infiltration of Cape Cod by these "foreigners."

1870-1900

Until 1895 ninety percent of the population of Cape Cod was native born of pure English stock, maintaining to a remarkable degree the quintessence of New England characteristics with the wide virtue of Americanism. But the most radical change since the beginning of the Cape history is in process, and it is coming about in such a silent inconspicuous way that even those it affects most vitally have as yet hardly realized it.

The time has come to hang another portrait on the walls of the picture gallery, that of a newcomer with physiognomy and complexion quite as different from the Anglo-Saxon as the Anglo-Saxon was from the aborigines.

Would you be surprised to know that, in a certain graduating class in a public school in the township of Falmouth, fifty of the children were Portuguese and but ten were American? Would you be surprised to know that there are Roman Catholic Churches in Barnstable where only Portuguese attend? One sixth of the population in Barnstable is foreign, in certain neighborhoods one half. What a change from the old days when a dark-skinned newcomer was a curiosity.

With the exception of Provincetown, Barnstable has probably the greatest number of Portuguese of any town on the Cape, their advent here being similar to their advent in many of the small towns where they have now firmly established themselves.

The newcomers are ususally a small group, say half a dozen men, who appeared in the press of the cranberry season, when their services are gratefully accepted. They find accommodation in some old shed or barn, where they live pleasantly enough, the sound of dancing and a crude guitar on a summer evening being the only thing which proclaims their presence. They buy milk from a nearby farmer and are punctilious in their payments. Once established they proceed to make themselves extremely useful. They pick strawberries, blueberries, cranberries, and beach-plums in due succession. In the winter they gather shell-fish, and in the spring they import a wife and children from Sao Miguel or Lisbon, buy some abandoned farm-house and move in. The land that has lain fallow for a decade is coaxed into fertility. Besides tending their garden patches and their houses they work all day like beavers. The man teams, fishes, goes out for a "day's work" and picks berries. A quick Portuguese can earn as much as three dollars a day in blueberry season. The wife goes out scrubbing or takes in washing. Every single child goes to the woods and picks berries like mad all summer and goes to school all winter. And presto! in half a dozen years the village, which was almost deserted, resounds with a voluble dialect. The school which boasted ten pupils has twenty five, more than half of them with unpronounceable three syllable names. Gradually the community, which surveyed the intruders with resentment succumbs to force of numbers. The Portuguese youth educated side by side with the Yankee maiden, falls in love with her, and marriage is the sequel.

It is largely a matter of numbers. Where there are few Portuguese as in neighborhoods in Bourne they have no social standing. The natives even refuse to pick berries on the bogs with them at cranberry time. But where they outnumber the original inhabitants, as in Provincetown, we get the other side of the shield. They become storekeepers; the girls go to normal school and attain a teacher's diploma and intermarriage follows quite naturally.

Thus, as the sons and daughters of the Cape have wandered inland, as their progenitors wandered seaward, to win fame and fortune, a comely and quiet race has humbly taken possession of the deserted houses and is patiently and with infinite persistence making the light but productive soil to blossom like the rose.

It may come as a surprise to the visitor when he is told that of the more than four thousand residents of the town's "year-round people" three-fourths are Portuguese seeking their livelihood in the fishery or indirectly from its earnings.

They are engaging people. I do not see how Provincetown can be very life-like to writers who treat the Portuguese as incidental. Cape Cod, of course, has a rich historical interest without them but the Cape today is very much with them and has been so since the last quarter of the 19th century when large numbers came to New England attracted by success stories of pretty much the same stamp that all fish stories bear.

"The family of Peter V. Andrews, a Portuguese FSA client. They run a seven acre vegetable farm. They have just bought the first cow they ever had, of which they are very proud. Mr. Andrews works as a day laborer at a nearby army camp." Falmouth, December 1940. FSA photograph and caption by Jack Delano.

Record of Interviews
with a Portuguese Fisherman

from notebook (unrevised) of Alice D. Kelley submitted Dec. 14, 1939

Editor's Note: From Alice Kelley's notebook we learn much about the process she employed in conducting her interviews and about standard

There are few of the old-time fish stores left in Provincetown; rough gray sheds on the harborfront where the men store their gear. Though these ramshackle ware rooms are seldom noticed by the visiting crowds, it is here that one must come to really to know the fishermen. Here, one must sit and talk, when the February sleet if falling, and the harbor is banging away at the bulkheads alongshore under a southeast blow.

In introducing them one must use their nicknames. For they have an odd custom of bestowing nicknames on one another not in a spirit of levity but in dead earnest. They practically forget their real names. Sometimes the sobriquets are not very delicate, but always they are highly descriptive, and once a man comes by his nickname, there is no escape.

Joe Flounder sits on a mackerel "kag" across from Tony Yellow and deals out the cards for a game of two-handed bisqua; while Tony leans over and pokes the pot-belly stove. There is fishing gear on the walls, in the corners on the floor, everywhere — strung on netcorks, stacks of anchors, buoys, oars, and hangings of crackly yellow oilskins.

Through the doorway you can see into the next room, where Big Billy is tarring nets. He looks like a god of darkness, hanging the room with shadows. In another corner old Peter Fayal is overhauling his gear — a tub of trawl-line on which he is replacing the lost "gangin" and his huge fingers twist and tie with incredible speed as he makes the new strings fast and fixes a hook to each. But he pauses now and then to reach for the bottle of prune whiskey and then spins a yarn for the boys.

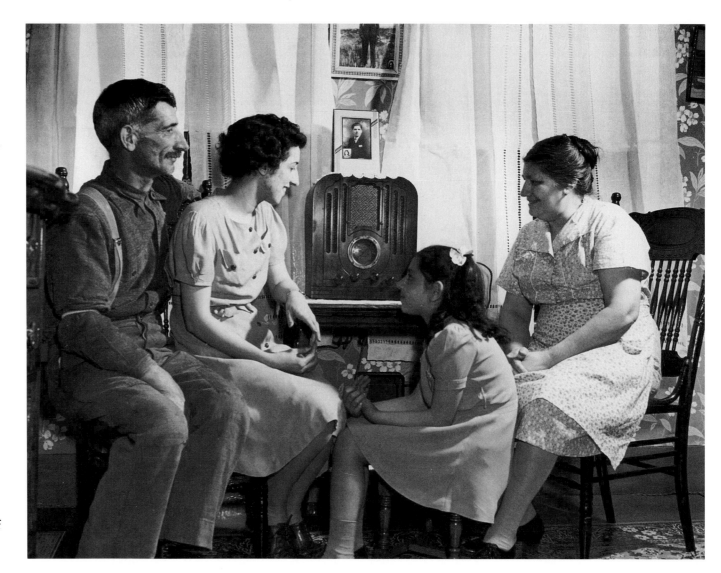

procedures used by all the writers. In diary-like form, Ms. Kelley reveals her own intimations, which seem patronizing and somewhat condescending. Yet, her honesty and directness provide a glimpse into the consciousness and methodology of the federal writer. From Kelley's notebook, unrevised, is the following excerpt which represents the first half of her conversation with one Portuguese fisherman.

Description and impression of living room . . . house of informant. Very much like American Cape Cod parlours of early nineteen hundreds. Apparently brought little from old country except tinsel pictures i.e. kind of mosaic made. I think of coloured mica. Mostly religious subjects . . . group photographs and some glass ware and vases. House immaculate. Must have acquired cleanliness from Yankees. On my one trip to the Azores beauty of country much obscured by filth in streets and houses. Temperature kept higher than average American house and less air admitted. Coffee invariably on stove . . . home made wine offered — almost never hard liquor. Men drink whiskey outside, if any. Women don't drink at all. Wife, Rosa, just come in from

Church. Still wears shawl over head except Sundays. Children speak Portuguese only with parents . . . all born in this country. Manuel is very glad to talk, but gets self conscious if any notes are taken. Shall have to make records immediately on leaving . . . Manuel owns this house but grudges taxes . . . most of them seem to feel that rent is legitimate expense but taxes are just a gift to government. Evidences of side lines in business. Rosa makes cakes and pies for sale, rents small apartment third floor of house. Manuel himself, between fishing trips runs his boat on excursions for tourist trade, rents himself out with buzz saw for fireplace wood, and has privately an interest in a package store down Cape.

Q: You were grown up when you came over here weren't you, Manuel?
A: I was nineteen. My old man come over and my mother and three of us.
Q: From Lisbon or the Azores? (**Note:** great rivalry between "Islanders" and Lisbon men. Lisbon considered superior. Cape Verde people called "Bravas" and generally have some negro blood.)
A: My mother's from Lisbon. She moved to the islands when she married my father. We come from — island of Gibraltar. (**Note:** must ask someone for correct name and locale his pronunciation peculiar and his ideas of geography vague.)

Q: The Captain (his father) was a fisherman, wasn't he?
A: Sure. We're all fishermen. My grandfather, too, in the islands. I wouldn't be anything else. I tell my wife sometimes the sea's my mistress. Makes her mad. She thinks I'm crazy.
Rosa: Don't talk that way to Miss Alice. You sound tough. (**Note:** I have been down here off and on since I was fourteen and am still "Meesh Alice" to the old timers who knew my people and knew me before my marriage.)
Manuel: I got to be tough. You can't be a fisherman and be soft. What is it you want to know about fishing?
A: It's a good life. You got to be strong and there used to be big money in it. Not no more though. Now the middleman he gets everything and they don't pay the prices anyhow. Sometimes you might as well throw away the catch.
Q: You do throw a lot of fish overboard sometimes don't you?
A: Sure. It don't keep forever. Give it away or throw it away if you can't sell it. I think it's like this, the government don't know the conditions of fishing. You make a big lot of money some seasons, then for a long time we're broke . . . we got to get good prices. There's a lot of things to think of, see? Like storms and then sometimes the fish don't run so good . . . there's good and bad seasons for fish just like crops to a farm. Ever think of that?

"There is, in this FSA collection, an attitude toward people. There is no attempt by a photographer to vindicate his subject, to be cute with him, to violate his privacy, or to do something to make a cliche. However they might have differed in skill and insight, our photographers had one thing in common, and that was a deep respect for human beings." — Roy Stryker, *In This Proud Land.*

Far Left: "Family of a Portuguese dory fisherman." *Left:* "Portuguese dory fisherman and his granddaughter." US OWI photographs ;by John Collier, Provincetown, Spring 1942.

Portuguese Fisherman:
an interview with Captain Joseph Captiva

by Alice D. Kelley
submitted February 15, 1939

Editor's Note: "Portuguese Fisherman," by Alice D. Kelley, is one of the many oral histories and research projects pertaining to ethnic and regional culture written by the federal writers. The version published here is the last of 10 drafts of Kelley's interviews with Provincetown fisherman Captain Joseph Captiva.

"I wouldn't never be happy without I had a boat under me."

Jeeze! I come near lose my boat. I just fix her up nice — new paint, clean her up, everything. Then I was going put in whole new engine. Well, I need some tar, so I get her in a bucket, heat up on fire, see? First thing I know, she catches — goes right up! My boy he shout. I grab the 'stinguisher and let her have it, but tar she burns terrible. I see I'm going lose my boat. I holler at the boy and the men. They won't go down. You can't blame 'em. The flames she's coming up. But she's my boat. She's all I got, so what could I do? I go down. I grab the tar bucket, throw her overboard, throw over some parts the engine, take blankets, stamp out the fire. Anyways, I save my boat. If she went, all my work gone —everything.

My hands she hurt preety bad, but I don't think she'll leave no scars. I been out fishing few days ago, but I wasn't no good. My hands she swole all up. Drive me crazy! Was a big catch and I couldn't do nothing. But I was glad get out in the boat again. I'll be out in 'nother week.

The boy's good fisherman. Portuguese boys, they do more like the old man. Some of 'em get these ideas to high school. Don't do them no good, 's I can see, but don't do them no harm neither. Lots these Americans they tell me their boys is in the city. Got jobs here, got jobs there. Me, I like have the boy on my boat. Teach him. Then I know where he is, what he's doing. The boat she'll be his. It's good for him know how to handle her.

clement e. daley 1988

I used to go out with my old man when I wasn't bigger than Jo. The old country, we was all fisherman, me and my brothers. My father fish, too. And his father. Some dragging, but mostly with hooks. That's about all they do back there. Fish, and maybe marketing and like that. I could work most as good as a man time I was fourteen. I come over here when I was nineteen. The way I come, we had folks over here. They write to my father, tell him

was good money over here. My old man come over and my mother and us four boys. Then we send for other people. That's how we all come.

On land the Portuguese and Americans don't always get on so good. But we fish together all right. It's different out in the boats. There's the same rules for everyone. The rules for a captain and crew are the same everywhere, and we all want the same things — a good catch and a good

market. We get on good on the sea.

They find out we're good fishermen. Anybody'll tell you they ain't no men can fish better than the Portuguese. We can always get jobs on the boats. I wouldn't want work on land all the time. Lots of men do when they get older, but not me. I wouldn't never be happy without I had a boat under me. I'm a good fisherman. Maybe I wouldn't do so good with a regular land job.

The Yankees they fish to get money enough to go ashore, run shops maybe, or do business. The Portuguese he don't like that. He fishes because he wants to. Because he don't want no boss. One time I try stay ashore couple years. I had a good job on a yacht. Good pay, the best of everything, but I didn't like it. Rather be independent. Not say this "yes sir" and "no sir" all the time. The Yankees they don't mind. They run stores, they work for bosses, and they don't care. But the Portuguese, he always a kind of a independent feller.

Of course the skippers are like bosses kinda, but it's not the same. And then you work you can be skipper yourself. I been captain now for a long time. My son, he'll be captain some day too.

I fish always on trawlers. It's hard work, but I don't never get tired. Makes a man hard, that kind of work. The trap boats, they get the bait. That ain't no work. Ain't fast enough for me. I like to fight. Fight wind and cold and weather. I don't feel the cold no more.

A while ago I come in from fishing. I come up on the dock, and Jeeze! I was dirty. Stand all night clean fish and it was dirty weather the whole trip after first day. Well, up on the dock the wind she was blowing like sixty. I take off my shirt, fill a bucket of water, and I give myself a good wash. Feels good! But they's some city folks come down on the dock and they couldn't get over it, how I stood there wash myself with no shirt and the wind blowing. Say, the wind's my friend — and the water. I feel at home. In a house I'm like a big bull. Jeeze! If I can't feel a boat under me, I want to die.

The Portuguese is great for giving nicknames to every one. More'n the Americans, I guess. The man over at cold storage, that's Bennie Regular. That ain't his name. That's his nickname. They call him that 'cause he's a regular fellow. They call him that since he was little. He's regular. They call me "Pulaski." That means peppy, full of life, full of fun. Then they was a whole family in town. We used to call them the "Baubas." Means dumb, kind of foolish. And they's Joe Portygee. That means he's all Portuguese. Just like in the old country.

Then they's my boy. They call him "Kak I." I dunno what that means. And young Morrie over there, he's "Fonda" on account of this Captain Fonda, told such big stories, and "Zorra," that means fox. Zorra's family got that name long time ago, like my family got "Captiva." Zorra's family was awful good fishermen, so where they live they call 'em "Fox of the sea."

Then they's a whole family they call 'em "Goddam." Jackie Goddam, Mamie Goddam, and like that. That's 'cause the old lady she couldn't speak English so good and she'd call the children when they was little, "You come here, goddam." "Don't you do that, goddam." So they call 'em the "Goddams."

Then they's lots ain't so nice. The Portuguese they make lots of jokes and they'll name a man because he acts this way or that way, goes this place or that, and sometimes the names they ain't so polite. They's one family, they used to call 'em the "Dirties." I guess the old woman she ain't such a good housekeeper or something. Anyways, that's what they call 'em. You ask, "Do you know Frankie, or Manuel, or

Above: "Manuel Zorra, known as one of the best fishermen on the Cape, who in spite of bad fishing conditions, still keeps himself going by running a small boat with a minimum of crew, frequently by himself." Provincetown, August 1940. FSA photograph and caption by Edwin Rosskam. *Right:* "Portuguese dory fishermen gossiping in front of their fishing shack, where they store their gear." Provincetown, Spring 1942. US OWI photograph and caption by John Collier.

Tony?" and they'll say, "You mean one of the "Dirties"?

They's names, too, for places. The Lisbons, we call 'em "Quail." That means rabbits. They's a real Portuguese family name, too, "Quail." But Lisbons is always called "Quail." And the people that comes from St. Michael's Island, we call 'em "Kikes."

Lots old country people changes their names over here. Say old country names is too hard to say. I think that's foolish. Anybody can learn say "Silva" or "Captiva" or "Cabral." Jeeze! They ain't so hard. Some the Perrys was Perrera, I guess. And here's these two brothers and they change the name, and now one's called Smith and the other Carter. That don't make no sense. Some the Roses was Rosario. But you wouldn't get me to change my name, Captiva. I guess not!

My great-grandfather he was Spanish, and he was took prisoner by the Moors. After two, three months he escape. He comes to Portugal and settle down in little village near Lisbon. He was young fellow, very handsome, good fisherman. He had scars from Moorish prison. He was brave and also he told big stories, how he escape and kill Moors and everything. So everybody they call him "Captiva." That means "prisoner." So that's the name we had since then. People say the Captivas got to be brave because of my great-grandfather.

When I tell the children, first they won't believe me. But now they do. First they laugh and say, "Some more stories!" The old country she's far away. And they think they know more than their old man.

It's the schools does it. They used to keep sending word home — have so much milk, so much orange juice. Must brush teeth. I never brush my

Photographer John Collier pursued his subject, the Portuguese of Provincetown, throughout the town. He went fishing, shopped, socialized and ate dinner with them. The photograph above, captioned "Portuguese housewife doing her shopping," is one of several taken with the family of fisherman John Russe (no names are provided for other family members) in the Spring of 1942.

John Collier, without having graduated from high school (he suffered from a nameless condition then, now called dyslexia), became full professor of anthropology at San Francisco State. Today, he teaches a course called, "The Photograph as Communication," at the San Francisco Art Institute.

teeth in the old country. Nobody did. And I got fine teeth. I send back word to the teacher once. I says, "Tell 'em I know them kids when they was little. Their fathers was fishermen just like me. They never had no orange juice and no quarts of milk." But they laugh. Say times is change. I guess so.

The schools is better over here. They wasn't no public schools where I come from . You pay fifty cents a month each child to a teacher and the one man he teach everything. The young people over here, they have a good time. Back home the old folks was strict. Young people was all the time running away. My kids they bring their friends home. That youngest girl of mine, she's always after me dance with her, go out places. Kids ain't afraid of the old folks no more. I think that's a good thing.

Look at the Fisherman's Ball. It's for the families. My wife was there and my girls. My girl, the youngest one, she likes make me dance with her. She says, "Don't be behind the times, pa." She's a great kid.

It's nice when the whole family goes out that way. That's the way in Portugal. The families make what we call fiesta together. It's not like here, the women out all day, the men out all night. Unless once in a while like Saturday nights the men they go out have a few drinks. Plenty people say the Portuguese don't care for their wives, 'cause they don't make much fuss. They care all right. Sure, they care. Only with us the man's the boss. Everything is for the man. Makes him feel big, I guess. If a woman she's a good wife, has children, keeps the house nice, she's all right. All the same, with us it's like with all the other countries. The woman she's boss in the house. She runs the house the way *she* wants, just so she has the meals right and takes care the children.

I think the Portuguese take more interest like in the children. Maybe it's only fishermen, they don't see them so often. The Americans they talk about the kids, but they don't stay around them so much. Sometimes Americans they'll say, "I shouldn't never have married. Just a worry." But the Portuguese he likes a good family.

This is a good season for fish. It's warm, that's why. When it comes cold and they's ice in the bay and like that, the fish they make for warmer waters. Have to chase them all over the place, but now they most jump into the boat.

It's dragging I do. We drag with big nets along the bottom. I don't go out nights much no more, but I got accommodations on my boat so's eight men can sleep on board. Eight men. She's a sloop. That's one mast. But they ain't no sailing now. My new engine she's beautiful. Raises my profit. Used to cost ten, twelve dollars a day to take the boat out. Now costs only two, three. Much better engine.

I got a good crew, too. Me, I'm captain. Then I got engineer, and a cook. And my boy, he fishes. but we only stay out a day or two. Used to go to Banks every year. It's just a habit some fishermen's got. They got to go to the Banks every year. That trip to the Banks, it was awful. Stay away six months, work night and day, and then after that you've made three, four hundred dollars, 'Taint worth it. They's just as good fish near home, and not so hard work.

Of course, scalloping, that's different. That's terrible work, too. Out weeks and dragging with big heavy steel nets. But there's big money to it. Big money. But it's awful work.

"I had a pretty good hunch that the pictures that were ignored then were what would prove most valuable in the end. You can't have a perspective when history is your bedfellow. All you have is a hunch. So I'd tell the photographers, look for the significant detail. The kinds of things that a scholar a hundred years from now is going to wonder about." — Roy Stryker, *In This Proud Land.*

Right: "Portuguese grocer," inside Anybody's Market. *Below:* "Market in the Portuguese fishermen's district." US OWI photographs by John Collier, Provincetown, Spring 1942.

Have to be strong like a horse to stand it.

I don't never get scared. I don't know nothing else, only fishing and the sea. I never think about drowning any more 'n you think about danger in the streets. Sure, the women worries, I guess. They used to get down on the beach and yell and pray when there was storms and the boats was late out, but the womens always worrying about something, anyways.

My wife now, she worries sometimes about the boy. I tell her he's better off to sea than running around with all these wild crowds. Ain't drowned yet, nor I ain't drowned yet. She wouldn't really want me to come ashore. Her people was fishing folks too. She knows I wouldn't be no good on land.

My boat can hold twenty-five thousand pound. We don't often get that much. Sometimes we do, though. One time we went out seven thirty, eight o'clock at night. Nine o'clock we come back in — full. Twenty-five thousand pound this silver perch. Made a thousand dollar that one night. We fish on shares. I get most because the boat she's mine, all the men take their share.

We go out nights when we hear the fish she's running good. That's a funny thing. We don't have no regular plan, where we go, but no boat never goes alone. We start out, try all the places where we know fish comes sometimes. Then when we come back, one boat comes up. The Cap says, "You had good catch?" If I say, "Yes," then likely he'll say, "Jeeze, I didn't get nothing. I'm coming with you to-morrow." Or if I didn't do so good, next day I go out with a crowd's got a good catch.

We start about three, four in the morning. It's dark, and boy is it cold!

Well, and then we got outside the harbor, not far — couple hours, maybe — and start fishing. It's get light then and they's coffee on the stove. Everybody feels good. I got a beautiful stove on my boat. We cook chowder, oyster stew, make coffee —everything. And plenty of room.

We don't get so tired unless by night we've worked hard. Then maybe we want stretch ourselves, have a little fun. But we don't mind getting up early. People don't need so much sleep 's they think. Look at me. Been fishing thirty years. Sometimes up two, three nights. I always start early mornings. But when I get home, I don't want to go to bed. Maybe have a little nap, then work around the house, or go out and see my friends. Have a little drink maybe down to Mac's, have some friends in for supper and a glass of ale. Once I'm off the boat, I want a change.

If I couldn't fry fish and make chowder, I'd have starved plenty of times. The Yankees they generally puts salt pork in it. But we use the olive oil. Roll the fish up in flour. Then put your oil in the pan. Let it get real hot, smoking. And don't keep turning the fish, Leave it cook one side till she's brown's a pork chop. We make galvanized pork, like this. Take a good pork roast or chops and all day you dip 'em in sauce made with vinegar and garlic and real hot peppers, then you cook 'em like always. Fried fish and galvanized pork — that's real Portuguese.

We made the Cape. We built it up. We're the Portuguese pilgrims. Us and the American fisherman. We make Gloucester too. I was up there a couple years. I fished all over, out of Chatham, out of Gloucester, everywhere. When first come here there wasn't nothing, but sand and a few houses and docks and boats. We used dry the codfish out on the Dunes. They'd be pretty near miles of it spread out. The whole place stunk.

They was fishermen all up and down the Cape. The old whalers went out then. Captain Avila down here, he found a chunk of ambergris once. And fishing off the Grand Banks was a gold mine. You'd get so much you couldn't load it all. Times you'd be up two, three night cleaning, up to your knees in it and half frozen.

Then the artists they come down. They must have painted a hundred miles of nets and boats and docks. And then the writers heard about it, and the summer people. But we started it. Even now they'll ask you to take them out in the boats and they ask questions. Fishing seems exciting to them.

It's a good life. You got to be strong, and there used to be big money in it. Not no more, though. Now the middleman he gets everything and they don't pay the prices anyhow. Sometimes you might as well throw away the catch. It don't keep forever. Give it away or throw it away if you can't sell it. I think it's like this, the government don't know the conditions of fishing. We make a big lot money some seasons, then for a long time we're broke. We got get good prices. Then they's credit. We used get credit eight months, a year maybe. Now it's tough to get three months. Money's scarce, they say, but I don't know. They's plenty for mortgage houses, for

Left: "Aboard the *Frances and Marion,* a Portuguese drag trawler, fishing for cod. Dinner aboard." Captain John Russe is the man at center. *Above:* "Aboard the *Frances and Marion.* Homeward bound from the banks, the drag nets are hoisted aloft today." US OWI photographs by John Collier, Provincetown, April 1942.

projects, for new playground. People don't appreciate the fisherman.

You won't find many nowadays got much of anything saved. We most of us belong to one of these burial insurance societies. But the widows of most of us wouldn't have much if we went. That's why a man's foolish not to buy a house if he can, even if he has to have a pretty big mortgage. And that's why it's good to own your own boat. The Portuguese aren't as good for business as the Yankee fisherman.

Pretty soon we got to go down the Cape settle some business. The draggers and the seiners, they're in together like. Now the cold storage's got worried. They use the weirs — like traps — and they trawl. And they don't want us in shore get the silver perch. Last time we have a fight about this, they agree we go three miles out summers. But winters we fish everywheres. That's why they don't like us. There's no reason we should go outside winters. The weirs ain't out winters. Summer's different.

But we won't have no trouble. We'll all go up to Boston. Whole bunch of us. They got to have silver perch. Perch's about the only fish they can make money on. It costs three cents a pound freeze the fish, and maybe it's cheap fish, gets only one, two cents a pound. Like that they don't make no money. But they's plenty of fish. They claims we take all the fish. But that ain't so. They just want it all. And it don't make sense we should go outside winters when they ain't fishing.

We don't mind going up to Boston. I guess not. Last time we hired us two buses. Sing all the way, stop have a little drink now and then. Had a *good* time. And we win, so coming back we felt fine. Was a nice trip. I guess we'll have a good one this time.

Above left: "A Portuguese (Cape Verdean) who came to this country more than 40 years ago and worked as a fisherman and railroad worker. After a paralytic stroke he opened his home to tourists, *below* and *right,* and now derives most of his income from this source." Truro, August 1940. FSA photographs and captions by Edwin Rosskam.

Edwin Rosskam began as a painter, living in Europe, then moving to Tahiti. Later, in the U.S., Stryker hired Rosskam as an FSA editor after seeing a book Rosskam edited using FSA file photographs. Louise Rosskam, also a photographer, worked with Edwin. She told *Spinner* that he journeyed to Cape Cod on his own and brought the pictures back with him to his Washington job as file editor.

Living in New England

illustrations by Stephen Cook

Editor's Note: Another book idea buried in oblivion was that of a volume entitled, "Living in New England," to consist of left-over material from the American Guide Series, representing the six New England states. Conceived as "a new type of literature," the book would describe the economic and social life of the people in New England, with special emphasis on the working and farming populations. The bent in these works seems to be on the independence and character of the proletarian New Englander.

The "Tiverton Fisherman" is one brief entry taken from this large collection. Through the dialect of Captain Nat, we get a vivid sense of the climate, working environment and salty character of the Tiverton waterfront.

Tiverton Fisherman *an adventure with Captain Nat*

Author Unknown   submitted 1938-39

The warm August sun sent heat waves dancing along the old dock while the water lapped against the wooden piles creating an atmosphere of mid-summer serenity. Fishing boats entered the harbor one by one. Soon the waterfront was alive with activity as the morning's catch was landed. The butter fish and squiteaque were quickly bailed out of the wells into the waiting barrels. After being iced and covered they were rolled onto the truck, which was to take the load direct to the New York market at Fulton Street. That business over, the fishermen turned to cleaning their boats, greasing the motors and the other things that must be done to make ready for the next day's run. This work was left to the crew while the captains talked of luck and prices.

Captain Nat, seeing his last barrel tagged and checked, lighted a cigar and settled down on a pile of rope to have a "draw and a spit." Turning to a young lady who had been watching the morning's work with great interest, he called, "Good morning, Effy. Do you still want to know why I'm a fisherman and not a farmer, or a lawyer, or a doctor like your dad? Sit down, child, and your old Uncle Nat will talk to you.

"Fishing seems to be in the blood around these parts and I was born a fisherman just as were my father and grand-father before me. For generations we've sailed out of Tiverton, fair weather and foul. Hail, rain, snow or blow we'd be out in it, beating down the wind or up with the tide. We're slow to take up with anything new but appreciate improvements when finally adopted. You take my old boat the *Mitzpah* — she was a likely a craft as ever caught a breeze. Noank built she was, and able. She'd beat any of the fleet to the traps and back. That meant getting the best prices for your catch as it does today. She went by sail alone and when power came in Dad put in a Lathrop but kept the mast in her just in case. But the mast was in the way when it came to the bridges. In those days the Stone Bridge and Railroad Bridge both worked by hand, which, if the tide was wrong, meant an hour's delay between

the two of them. So one day when Dad was in Fall River, we boys sawed off the mast. Dad shook his head when he saw his sloop dismantled, and said that we'd managed to ruin his boat. Later he had to agree that it was an improvement and that he liked it.

"But there wasn't much said any further about it cause we Yankees don't talk much unless we see the point in so doing. Maybe that's why folks call us queer, and sot, even cold-hearted. Now when it comes to talking with strangers, we can't see why we should answer all their fool questions.

They'd be just as wise after we'd lallygagged to 'em all day as they were before. Most strangers seem to be awful shaller, and if there is any one thing a fisherman hates it's shoal water.

"Tell me, sis, have you ever been out where the water is deep — tall and green we call it — had your boat rollin' scuppers under? Now that's what you mought call living, with the old ground swell rollin' you 'round and the for'ard end of your boat looking you in the face every time she starts to climb. Never seen much of it, hey. Well suppose you've had lots of book l'arnin, tho, being's how your Dad's such a big doctor. Shucks I can remember your grandsir plain as day, a boat builder he wor and no better man ever swung an adze. Allus 'lowed his son'd be a doctor and so he is. I had a bit of schooling in my time. Was mighty good at figgers and took my Latin and navigation easy enough. Got what I could right in that old academy yonder. Had lots o' teachers, men an women too, but for downright larnin Miss Peace could help a fellar no end. A lady, too! Oh, yes! Twas her uncle as

discovered the Columbia River — real Yankee fisherman, by thunder. Tell ye, gal, some great men's come from this old port.

"It does look like a sleepy old place now but a place changes more than the people born in it. Take my mother's folks now — old whaling aristocracy. Regular old sea dogs. Sailing in those days — maybe round the Horn to China, beating up and down the Pacific searching for whales, they'd be gone sometimes two and three years at a stretch. One time they'd be on the African coast, then beat away down around Cape o' Good Hope and over to Indo-China then up the China coast toward Bering Strait and back down the Pacific. Now sometime you get your cousin Lucy to show you the old whalin' letters and they'll give you some idea of why we Yankees are so proud of our sea history. Take your cousin Hatty — she's prouder of her father's sextant and sea chest than she is of that new hundred thousand dollar house o' hers over there on the neck. Purty house too as I ever see, but she told me settin' right where you be this minute

she hadn't drawn a happy breath in thirty years. You see, they went out West and struck oil, got rich as all get out, but whalin' blood can't rest happy on a western prairie, so Hatty's back now where she can breathe the clean sweet smell of the old Atlantic.

The Eel Catch

"What's that you say? You'd like to go out in the sloop with me to pull trap? Well now, sho — as soon as the tide is right today we're setting seine for eels, but we only use a skiff instead of a power boat because the set is to be made just up the beach a ways, but you're welcome to come if you care to. It won't take long to make a set — about an hour — according to the catch.

"The boys are putting the seine on the rack now. The seine does look like a pile of hay, but its on that rack systematical enough, as you'll find when they start to let it run.

"If the tide's about ready to drop then it's time to set, as the eels come out with the falling tide. John is on the beach holding one running line, Sam rows the skiff and I'll pay the line out (about three hundred and twenty feet), then Harry starts throwing the seine over, or just letting it run. As Sam rows the boat, the lead line sinks and the cork line floats. She's like a big tennis net with a long bag in the middle and as Sam rows he makes a half circle of the net and she looks like a little coral atoll we've seen in Bermuda. The seine is seven hundred and fifty feet from tip to tip so you see she's no play toy.

"Back at the beach we give the other line to Jim. Now with both lines on the beach we pull on these and haul the seine in. She picks up everything on the bottom as we drag her ashore. We'll gradually close the net and keep hauling until she's on the beach. The arms come first; then when the twine

is finer, that's the bunt and in the middle is the bag of still finer twine. When the boys bring the ends of the net together the fish will run back into the bag.

"Look up the beach there! Every woman and child and dog in the colony is down to help, too. The women folks tell me that it's great sport for them to haul on the lines. The kids get in the way mostly, and the dogs bark at the crabs we throw into the beach. Altogether it's nearly as much fun as a three-ring circus.

"Keep a hauling, boys! Keep the lead lines down, and the corks floating. If we haul too fast we pull her under and the eels will go over the top. Keep your fingers out of the twine or you'll tear it. Haul on the ropes — that will pull her in. Here comes the bag, so cross the lead lines over the mouth and we'll have her ashore in a jiffy. Yes ma'am she's loaded! Got to be something in her after you've dragged

her in over more than five hundred feet of the river bottom. Plenty of culch! That's where the eels are, tho, under the cabbage and kelp. Throw out the sea weed, then we can see the eels. There they are! Roll the twine and see their golden bellies. We've a mess this time. Bail 'em out boys into the eel car. A nice catch.

"All we want is the eels. You folks help yourselves to the mixed stuff.

"Ready, boys? Guess you've got all the fish and eels out of her by now. Is the car covered so they can't get out? All right. Haul in the running lines, shake the culch out of the seine, load her onto the rack ready for another set."

"So, miss, you think it takes a long time to haul that line into the skiff. 'Tis a bit, three hundred and twenty feet on each arm, and with the seven hundred and fifty foot seine, it is quite a piece of gear. It costs a pretty penny to go fishing and do it right. Each season has its own expense.

"Well, there are about two hundred and fifty pounds and they'll have time for two more sets before the tide falls off. These eels will all be shipped to New York. That's the best live eel market.

"Now I must go back to the dock and talk to Leander about a mug up. Do you want to come aboard the schooner and find out what a good Lee is? Guess we'll find something in the galley worth stopping for.

"Smells good. Has to be good. A fisherman eats only the best and plenty of it. There's a big pot of tea, plenty of cold meats, quantities of doughnuts, stuffed cookies, layer cake, pies — three kinds — all good stuff, so sit right down and have a mug up."

We Work on the WPA

Editor's Note: These interviews with Captain Joe Antone of New Bedford were made as part of a series of personal profiles of WPA workers. The collection was penned, "We Work on the WPA" and its purpose, presumably, was to illustrate how the WPA served as a salvation for America's proud workers. It would provide the public with an intimate look at the personalities who worked the WPA, while demonstrating the benevolence of a project which put useful people to work for the public good.

The two interviews employ different techniques on the part of the writer (one being more rudimentary in the oral history style than the other) and paint a profile of a man characteristic of many men who sailed in New Bedford's renowned whaling fleet — the Cape Verdean whaler.

Whaling ships and other vessels lie at anchor in the Brava harbor, Cape Verde Island, circa 1900. Courtesy of the New Bedford Free Public Library.

Captain Joe Antone, *Cape Verdean seaman*

by Nellie Coombs   *submitted August 6, 1939*

This is the story of Captain Joe Antone as he dictated it to me from notes of his own. He's trying to write the story of his life sometime before he dies.

Interview #1

According to my birth certificate, I was born at St. Antone, Cape Verde Islands, January 6, 1876. I entered school at the age of six. I was no doubt educated in the Roman Catholic religion by my parents and teachers who were strict Roman Catholics. I left school at the age of 15.

After leaving school, I was sent by my father on an errand. At that time, travel was done on a mule or horseback and I knew my trip would take a whole day and night. As I was descending a mountain, my gaze fell upon the ocean. There was a square-rigged vessel passing by with all her sails set, bound south'ard. Somehow, as I gazed at that schooner, a feeling welled within me, and before I knew what was happening, I felt myself yearning for life at sea. Knowing that I was building castles in the air, I thought it best to continue my journey for night would soon be falling. So I continued and found my sister waiting for me. After greeting each other, she insisted upon my staying a few days at least before returning home.

Before long she noticed how miserable I was, but never asked the reason. Later I retired but could not sleep. My mind kept wandering back to the sailing vessel which I had seen go by. After what seemed an eternity, I fell asleep and before long I was dreaming of a windjammer and I was one of the sailors. Oh, how real everything seemed. So you can imagine my disappointment when I awoke and found it was only a dream.

The following morning I dressed slowly, even though it was a cold November morning. As I gazed out of the window, I noticed a small sailing vessel had entered the harbor, and I made up my mind not to return to my father's house. I engaged myself on this little vessel to cross the channel to St. Vincent, Cape Verde.

I arrived next morning. We went in and anchored. Could it be true my dreams were coming true?

After taking in the scenery in the city, I took a boat which was going out in the harbor, to look over all the vessels that I saw there when I was coming in. I saw a large sail coming in from the north which entered and anchored in the harbor of Port Grandee. This sailing vessel was the American whaling schooner *Agate,* which sailed from New Bedford, Mass. October 16, 1891, bound for the Cape Verde Islands, and commanded by Captain J. G. Winslow of Provincetown. It was coming to the Cape Verde Islands to pick a whaling

Left: The bark *Greyhound.* Arthur F. Packard photograph, courtesy of T.M. Holcombe. *Right:* Cutting in a whale. Courtesy of the New Bedford Whaling Musuem.

The Cape Verdean whaleman, who arrived in America in the early 1800s, parted the waters for all other Crioulos to follow. Originally farmers in a drought-stricken land, the whalemen boarded American vessels simply to gain passage to the New World. Eventually, these farmers-turned-whalers became expert seamen. Their reputations as skilled whalemen attracted hundreds of whaling captains to the islands to sign them on as crew. Also, because of the poverty of their homeland, they were a source of cheap labor for a struggling New Bedford whalefishery.

Immigration from Cape Verde intensified as these whalemen settled in New Bedford and sent for their families. As the city's Cape Verdean community grew, New Bedford's reputation, especially on the islands of Brava and Fogo, became the subject of everyday conversation. People shared the news of relatives and close friends who had made the passage. New Bedford became the "Ellis Island" for Cape Verdeans. Over 18,000 islanders passed through the port of New Bedford between 1900 and 1920.

By the turn of the 20th century, many Cape Verdeans bought and reconditioned old whaling ships and sailed their own people to New Bedford. Voyages aboard these packet ships sometimes took two months. Once they settled in the area, Cape Verdean men found work on the New Bedford docks, where today they constitute the majority of the city's longshoremen; women were often employed as domestics or worked in textile mills alongside other immigrants; and entire families labored as pickers on the cranberry bogs, where they became the backbone of the industry's workforce. Today, Cape Verdean neighborhoods are close-knit and culturally unique communities, with individuals involved in all aspects of the large community. Caption by Ronald Barboza.

crew. Included in the skeleton crew which had sailed her over, were a Portuguese 3rd mate, Lebanon Rodrigues, and three Portuguese seamen, Frank Pina, John Rodriques and Julio Diniz. The new recruits taken on at the Cape Verdes were Joe Antone (myself), Miguel Sylvia, Antonio Santos, Antone D. Cala, Jose John Manhana, Antone Imbabo and Teles Banco.

I shipped aboard this whaler and cruised around South Africa for a while and caught some whales. After a while we went to St. Helena. I arrived at St. Helena on September 15, 1892. We found a big fleet of American whalers lying at anchor in the harbor. The fleet was as follows: barks *Greyhound, Morning Star, Platino, Sunbeam, Petrel* and *Bertha;* brig *Rose Becker,* and schooner *Clara L. Sparks,* all from New Bedford, Mass.

There was also lying at anchor a big three-masted schooner from New Bedford, the *Lottie Beard,* taking in the oil from the whalers to transport to New Bedford.

I was paid off before the American consul, James B. Griffin, and shipped again for another voyage. I went out to the whaling grounds and cruised around for a while and came back to St. Helena, March, 1893. I shipped as seaman from St. Helena, March 25, 1893, on the whaling bark *Greyhound* for 150 lay. I went down to South Atlantic for a year. I came back to St. Helena and was discharged April 1, 1894. I shipped as seaman on the bark *Morning Star,* 160 lay, from St. Helena, April 10, 1894, bound for the United States.

I arrived in New Bedford, June 27, 1894, and that ended my slavery on the American whalers. That's what it was — slavery. How do you think those ship owners built their fine mansions on the hill? We seamen worked and slaved for nothing while the owners got rich. My lay on that voyage was 160, which meant my share on the voyage was at the rate of one barrel in every 160 barrels. If I needed anything when we were at sea, I had to buy it from the ship's slopchest. They charged ten dollars for a pair of overalls, and two dollars for just one pound of tobacco.

It was because of such conditions the whalers had to come to the Islands to get a crew. The American seamen wouldn't ship on them because of the conditions, and the young fellows found they could make out better in the mills.

I stayed around New Bedford for a while, but after becoming acquainted with the American people and their ways, I thought I would try coastwise vessels and I shipped and sailed out of New Bedford and back again on these coastwise vessels. I was paid off at the end of each trip and sometimes before the end of the trip. We would have our bags ready before entering the harbor and once we were coming in by Butler's Flat Light and there was a ship lying there waiting for her crew. I yelled over to her and signed up before I had reached shore and been paid off.

After I got tired of coastwise service, I shipped on a fishing vessel belonging to Kelly and Sons, Fairhaven, Mass. I fished for cod off Block Island for a while and then down the Sound for pollock and after two summers of fishing, I made up my mind to go into the revenue service. On October 27, 1903, I shipped as seaman aboard the *USS Dexter,* U.S. Revenue Service, under command of Captain Hand. I served 15 months and was discharged.

February 3, 1904, I enlisted as seaman in the United States Navy. I was sent to join the South Atlantic Squadron, commanded by Admiral Sigsby. I served 4 years and at the end of my service received my honorable discharge from the U.S. Navy February 1908, while aboard the *USS Constellation*. This ship is now at Newport.

During my service in the Navy, I took a course in ocean navigation and succeeded in passing the examination before the U.S. Steamboard Inspection service for a license to navigate sailing vessels over 700 gross tons, and also an examination for a license to navigate steam and motor vessels for all the waters of the oceans.

For the next four years, Captain Joe served on a number of vessels engaged in coastwise shipping.

"On April 5, 1912, I was appointed commander of the steamer *Fortune*, bound from New York to the Cape Verde Islands. Ten days after we left New York, the wireless operator reported to me that he had heard an SOS from the British steamship *Titanic*, which had struck an iceberg and was sinking. I was only two hundred miles south of her, but before we had a chance to answer her SOS, other vessels were heading to her that were nearer, so I continued on my way.

Above: Captain Benjamin Cleveland (left) and Cape Verdean crew of the Brig *Daisy.* By the early 1900s, virtually the entire crew of every New Bedford whaler was Cape Verdean. *Right:* The schooner *Margarett* fits out for another voyage. Her final voyage was as a would-be packet ship in 1925 with Joe Antone (a.k.a. Manuel T. Chantre) as captain and part-owner. After being ripped apart during a storm on her way to Cape Verde, she limped into Brava and was scrapped shortly thereafter. Arthur F. Packard photographs, courtesy of T.M. Holcombe.

Captain Joe continued his career in the merchant marine until January 17, 1917, when he enlisted in the U.S. Navy. He resigned June 30, 1918. From October 1, 1919 until October, 1923, he served on various vessels.

"On October, 1923, I was appointed navigating officer on the schooner *Blossom,* of Cleveland, Ohio. It belonged to the Cleveland Museum and was being sent around the world on a scientific expedition. This voyage was written up and appeared in the July 1927 issue of the *National Geographic* Magazine as "Sindbads of Science."

On Saturday, November 10, 1923, we weighed anchor from New London, Conn., and set sail across the Atlantic Ocean. I was the only man on board who knew anything about the sea. The crew was made up of college men.

We were sailing along the night of November 16th, with one of the crew at the wheel. I was below in my cabin. Suddenly a great mountain of water appeared in the distance and came rolling toward the ship. The man at the wheel got scared and ran away and hid, which meant there was no one at the wheel. Unguided, the vessel swung around and the mountain wave hit her broadside. I cannot understand why she did not go way over. Somehow I managed to get to the wheel and braced myself and gradually brought her around.

As captain of the vessel, it was my job to assign each member of the crew to certain stations and to hand out the work they were to do. There was a Harvard man on board whose job it was to clean out the two toilets every day. But he wouldn't do it. Finally I

had to say to him, 'Because I'm a Cape Verde you do not want to obey me. What you or I am on shore does not matter here. As long as I am the captain, the crew has to do what I say. If you refuse to do so, then I shall have to turn you over to the consul to be placed in jail for breaking the maritime law.' The man cleaned the toilets the rest of the voyage but when we reached the Cape Verdes, he quit and went to England.

I stayed with the ship for a number of cruises and then I resigned. I was a bit too honest for some of the stuff they were doing on the side.

On October 27, 1925, Joe Antone cleared New Bedford on the schooner *Margarett*, bound for the Cape Verdes. This boat was owned by him. From his logbook is the following entry:

"Scraps from Logbook"
"Sat. Oct. 31, 1925. The day comes in with high northerly winds. Cloudy with rain. Wind increasing with a gale force from northeast. Sea running high as mountains. Vessel laboring very hard. At noon we lay in lat. 39.47 north, long. 67.30 west of Greenwich. Later in the day lost jibs and foresails. About 2:30 PM lost main trissail. The storm center passed over the ship. 3 PM sea smashed all the boats. Everything above deck washed away and some of it washed back again. Seas breaking over ship. 4 PM lost rudder.
"November 1, 1925. Gale moderating. Crew working to clear up the decks and rig up a jury rudder. We sailed under this jury rig 53 days and nights, covering a distance of 3800 miles and made the port of St. Antone, Cape Verdes."

Captain Joe had other troubles on the voyage, not the least of which was an attempted mutiny on the part of his first mate. He had to let his ship go in the Cape Verdes for want of money to repair it. After that, he sailed until 1933, when he quit the sea. He was taken to Newport to the hospital and nearly died of pneumonia. From then until last year, when he went to work for WPA, he was unemployed.

Interview #2

You don't need to wind up Captain Joe Antone to make him talk. You don't need to put a nickel in him either. All you do is shove him in your car, drive him out to the wilds of North Dartmouth, ease him into a comfortable chair beneath a pear tree and then take the plugs out of both your ears. He'll talk all right, and you need a dictaphone to take it all in because he thinks nothing of setting you down in Buenos Aires and just as you're becoming accustomed to the climate, he's yelling at you from 'way over in Lisbon. Or else he's in Bermuda and the next minute he's over in New Orleans, berating the white man there because they class him as a negro and he isn't a negro. He's a Cape Verdean and why do people have to be so stupid.

Why you want the story of my life? I gave it to you once. I gave it to you from my birth certificate until I saw you last fall. You want that again, you go read up what I gave you. My life's just the same now as it was then, only I'm a little older.
I'm sixty-three years old. Did you know that? I'm sixty-three years old,

and oh, how I wish I was thirty years younger. If I could have what's in my head now and be thirty years younger, there's a lot of things I'd do different. I used to go out for four to six months and come back with eight and ten thousand dollars. Where that money now? I dunno. I was damn fool.

I don't know where my money go. I never drink; I never smoke. But it all go somewhere. Now I'm on WPA. When I was in Brazil, I used to know lot of people. Nice people. I used to know a lady doctor there. I used to be very friendly with that lady doctor. I wonder what she say to me now if she knew I'm on WPA.

My wife used to get mad sometime. She say I got a girl in every port. I tell her she's crazy. She make me sick. I always behave myself. I just had a lot of friends, that's all. My wife has a terrible temper. It's so bad she has headaches and it's just because she has that temper. She's gone down to Horseneck Beach today with all her people. No, I wasn't going anyhow. I don't fit in the corners with her people.

I wish I could go back to the sea. When I get out on my ship, everything's peaceful. It's nice out here at your home. It's just like being at sea on a day like this. When it's quiet like this, the only thing you hear is the flapping of the sails. I used to follow the shade of the sails all 'round the boat. Never wore much clothes on a sailing ship. When it was too hot, we'd plug up the holes in the scuppers, fill the deck about a foot and a half of water and then wade around in it barefoot. That was the life.

Now I don't have time to enjoy anything. Now we have to work Fridays, I don't have time to make ships models at home. We get out at

CHAS. W. MORGAN
A typical whaling-ship
Now enshrined at Col. E. H. R. Greene's estate, So. Dartmouth

Built in New Bedford, 1841   313 Gross tons   298 Net tons   105.6 ft. Length   27.7 ft. Beam   17.6 ft. Depth   Ship rig.

Crafting model ships was encouraged by both the WPA Arts Project and the Toy Project. This illustration by Richard B. Noble is one of several in which he combines pencil, ink and watercolor and uses real string in the rigging. In the collection of the New Bedford Free Public Library.

half past two and when I get home it's so hot and I'm too tired. Saturdays and Sundays I can't do anything. The kids bother me too much.

My boy who lives at the north end is a cabinet maker. He want to use my tools so the other day he told me why didn't I move my bench and tools up to his house and I could work there week ends and nobody would bother me. I think I do that.

You saw that model I showed you in that store window. I made that. Now I got three orders for ships models but I don't know when I can do them. Maybe next winter when it's not so hot I'll feel more like it when I get out of work. I don't have to worry about them laying me off. I'm a veteran.

But I'm getting so sick of all these investigations. Did you know they investigated me to find out what happened to those models I made for WPA? There were some fellows who they fired from WPA and they put a complaint in about the ships models the mayor and Mr. Francis and Dr. Rousseau got that I made on WPA. They were trying to get back at the mayor and Mr. Francis because they were fired.

A young lawyer fellow came down to me and asked me what happened to the models I built. I told him I didn't build no models. All I did was repair them, paint them and rig them. He told me not to get technical with him. He wanted to know what happened to

the models. So I told him the mayor had a model of a clipper ship I repaired and rigged, and I told him Mr. Francis had a model of the *Morgan*. I told him I didn't know what happened to the other models. Someone told me Dr. Rousseau had one but I didn't know.

Then the lawyer made me go with him down to the mayor's office and made me identify the ships in the mayor's private office. It was one I made. Then he made me go to Mr. Francis' office and asked me if that model of the *Morgan* was mine and I tell him it was. Then he took me to Dr. Rousseau's office and showed me the model and I told him it was mine. Then he took me over to the Hotel Harvey and asked me if a model there was mine and I was mad. I told him if he'd open his eyes he could see that model was at least sixty years old and I'd been on the Toy Project only nine months.

Then he asked me about a letter the mayor wrote me and he said he had to see it. I showed it to him, but the mayor was smart. All he said was thank me for the work I'd done for him. I told the lawyer I'd worked for the mayor in his campaign last December and the mayor was thanking me for it. Then he showed me a letter from the Legion. The boys at the Legion made a mistake. They thanked me for a model I made for them but I never made no model for them. I know how they got that model. Last Christmas when they took out the toys for the kids, they took one of my models along and left it at the Legion headquarters. That's how the Legion got it.

Those fellows were trying to get something on the mayor and Mr. Francis, but they were too smart for

them. I know the mayor had his model at his home but they heard about the investigation, so they brought them to the city hall. They put them on public display, so nobody could say anything about them. Now they tell me not to make any more ship models until thing cools off. I don't care. After all, I'm supposed to be working on toys.

Sometimes I sick of the whole business. Sometime I think I wish there was a war. Then I could go back to sea where I belong. And I think pretty soon we'll have that war. Now England and France have sent men to Moscow to talk military alliance. I think Russia will be crazy to sign anything with England unless they do it on equal terms. I don't trust that Chamberlain.

They say England's a democracy, but nobody gets anywhere in the government unless he's a nobleman. In this country they say we're a democracy, but nobody gets anything here unless he belongs to the sixty families. I don't call that democracy.

Sometime I think people are just plain stupid. They vote those fellows in down in Washington and now look what happens. Every time President Roosevelt wants to do something for the poor people, they won't let him. What do you make of that? We made that fellow up in Boston sit down the other week. I took some of the petitions around and I got sixty names. That made those Republicans change their mind a bit.

Would I like to go to sea again. Give me a good windjammer and I go anywhere. I don't like steam. I got papers for steam too but I don't like that jerking. Just give me a good windjammer and I'd like to go sailing down to South America again. Then I'd be happy.

Editors' Note: The Federal Writers'Project produced several booklets featuring devastation and disaster. In this area, most notably, was a picture booklet entitled "The New England Hurricane." While the WPA was hard at work reconstructing and cleaning up from the damage, the writers and photographers were also at work making a documentation. This interview with Frank Hurd, like many others, may or may not give an exact representation of the event so described; but it does characterize the trauma and destruction that affected so many people in New England, September 21, 1938.

The Hurricane of 1938
interview with Frank Hurd

by Warren E. Thomson

Somewhere between four and five o'clock on the day of the hurricane, we were playing cards in my cottage at Winsegansett Heights, on Sconticut Neck in Fairhaven. There were four of us: Lillian Morton, Herbert Simmons, Mabel Simmons, that's Herbie's wife, and me. Charley Fernandes and Lena

Arden were in the cottage south of us, right next door.

Well, Lena came in and asked us to help her bring her boat up on the beach, because the tide was coming up so high that she was afraid that it'd wash away. That tide was so high that, by the time we pulled the boat up beside the cottages, there was water pouring over the retaining wall in front of my cottage. It never got there before. I didn't know how high it might come, so I ran for my car. I wanted to run it up the road onto high land, figuring I'd walk back to the cottage and carry my things out, if the water came up inside. The road runs along beside the water, but behind the cottages for a while, then turns up the hill.

Well, just before I got to the turn (I'd say it's about fifty yards from my cottage) the water was up to the car doors. The motor stalled. I tried to open the door and couldn't, the water was pushing so hard. And fast! I could see it coming up, just the few seconds I watched. I tell you I was scared! I braced myself and pushed with my feet hard and the door opened a little, enough for me to squeeze through, anyway. I fought my way out. There was water up to my neck then. I swam for the bluff, about fifty yards away, and made it.

There was a terrible sight in front of me when I turned around. The water was over the top of my car by then. It was coming so fast. That was the whole trouble: everything happened so quickly, you didn't have a chance. People have told me since that it was all our fault, said we fiddled around too long, but that's not so. We didn't have any real warning, you know, and nobody believed that the water would come so high so quickly. We'd never seen anything like it before, except in the newsreels. Anyway, it was awful.

Water was high up on the cottages and rising. The three that had been with me were climbing up on a roof. Mr. DuBois was there, too. He lived in the cottage next to mine, not Charley's

but the one on the other side. Lena and Charley were walking towards them on top of a wall. Even with that, the water was up to their necks. A fence floated along in front of Lena. She grabbed it and shoved it over to Charley, but he didn't put out a hand. Lena told me later he must have had a heart attack, because he turned blue in the face and sort of slumped down. Lena couldn't reach him. A wave came along right then and washed them both off the wall. It washed her right on top of the Greek's garage, but Charley disappeared.

By that time waves were breaking over the cottages. Sometime just about then, (I'm not sure, everything happened so much at once) the roof that Lillian and the others were on split, right down the middle. DuBois was on one half, my crowd was on the other. Both pieces went floating off fast. Drifting wreckage kept hitting them. They were almost awash. I could see pieces of wood hit Herbie in the leg, but he hung on. Lena was screaming her head off on the garage. Afterwards she told us she was trying to tell us about Charley, but then we thought she was yelling for help. We'd seen Charley anyway. We threw her a rope and hauled her off, up on the bluff where we were. There were quite a few of us there. I don't remember who. One of them was a priest, I think.

Finally the tide started down. Fifteen minutes more and even the bluff would have been under, but it started down, went fast, too. Pretty soon we were able to look for the others. Lillian, Mabel and Herbie were found about eleven o'clock. They were all right, except that wreckage had banged them considerably. I guess they were pretty well shot from the strain,

too. I wasn't there. A fellow had taken me home by then. All I had on was my underwear and a blanket wrapped around me. I had to take off my clothes to swim, you see. DuBois was found drowned the next day, I think. They didn't find Charley for a couple of days afterwards. He'd died from the heart attack.

I never want to see anything like it again. It was awful while it lasted and it's just as bad now. You can't imagine what it was like, unless you were there. I hope to God I never see it happen again.

Left: "What once was our home at Sconticut Neck." October 10, 1938. *Above:* Crescent Beach, Mattapoisett. October 3, 1938. WPA photographs and caption from the National Archives.

A Lexicon of Trade Jargon

Fishing Industry

by Elsie S. Moeller
submitted July 13, 1938

Information gathered from A. J. Tavares Shell Fisheries, Cove Rd., New Bedford; Mr. Albert Cook Church, employee at Pierce and Kilburn shipyard; *The Gam* by Charles Henry Robbins, Ochs & Co. Publishers, Boston, 1899; and from a captain on the State Pier in New Bedford.

Ash Breeze: When it is calm weather and a man is rowing a dory with a pair of ash oars.

Beach Comber: The worst insult you can give an able sailor.

"Bit Thick Aloft": When a man is stupid.

Broken Trip: When a vessel returns with only a few fish.

Bugs: Lobsters under the legal limit.

"Douse His Kites": Take in sail.

"Drop Your Ballast": Drop what heavy article you are carrying.

Fog Breeze: When the wind is blowing about 20 miles an hour in foggy weather.

Gallied: Applied to school or single fish which dart aimlessly about when frightened.

Lily: The detachable barb on the end of a swordfish spear or harpoon. When a fish is struck, the pole is withdrawn, leaving the lily attached to line embedded in the fish.

"Make A Beer": Instead of earn some money or earn a living or on a trip.

Mud: Thick Fog.

"Mug Up": Time to eat.

Oiled Up: When one has considerable liquor aboard.

Poop: A wave is said to "poop" the ship when it lifts her by the stern and rushes her forward.

Puddler: A captain who fishes on grounds where there are no fish.

Slick: A oily spot on the water. Generally indicates fish feeding; the oil coming from menhaden which serve as food for many varieties of fish.

Twine Man: Man who mends nets expertly.

Trash: Any fish that accumulates in seines, nets or trawls that is useless for food or bait.

Water Haul: To fail to catch the school with the purse seine.

Wharf Rats: Urchins who play about the wharves and have to be watched to prevent petty pilfering.

Whole-sail Breeze: One in which the four lower sails can be carried and no more.

Editor's Note: "A Lexicon of Trade Jargon" included terms from rope, rubber, shoe, textile, fishing and other industries. State administrator Muriel E. Hawks wrote Roy Bradford in March, 1938, that the collection of jargon from the textile industry should be "living slang, not technical terms, obtained in conversation with employees of the mills and especially with persons in the offices of the unions."

Silk Weaving

by Julia L. Keane
submitted July 13, 1938

Information from Mr. J. Goldfarb and Mr. H. Lawton of the Gilt Edge Silk Mill, Kempton St., New Bedford. Interview with Mr. R. J. Clark, office manager of National Silk Spinning Co., 79 Brook St., New Bedford, revealed that only technical terms are used in the plant and these are the same as for cotton spinning.

Caterpillar: The loose end or broken warp end that weaves up into the goods in a zig-zag manner.

Railroad Tracks: Streaky goods and uneven yarn causing marks in the goods.

Shiners: stretched synthetic yarn.

Snow Ball: a bunch of yarn and fuzz which is caused by a broken end being mashed up between a reed and a harness.

Star Marks: broken fillers in the goods caused by breaks in the filling yarn chafed by a sand roller.

Rubber Industry

Author and sources of information unknown

Artist or Painter: A cementer.

Death Watch: The shift that works from 11:00 P.M. to 7:00 A.M.

Dog Watch: The shift that works from 3:00 P.M. to 11:00 P.M.

Drip catcher: Steam fitter.

Jackass: One who uses a two wheel hand truck.

Manager: Male employee who comes to work late, or all dressed up.

Mechanic: A worker who is always trying to fix his machine when there is nothing wrong with it.

Office Girl: A worker who is often late to work.

Police Hound: Efficiency expert.

Shoemaker: A crude, inefficient, unskilled workman in the rubber fabrics and hard rubber plants. (Not in the footwear factories.)

Sparks: Electrician.

Stockholder: One who takes extraordinary interest in his work.

Ticket Killer: One who brings about the danger of an increase "ticket" by working too fast and finishing the day's work too early.

Tin Knocker: Tinsmith.

Wood Butcher: Carpenter.

Wrecking Crew: Steam fitting crew.

Shoe Industry

Author and sources of information unknown

Airedales: Suede shoes with a lot of hair.

Bat: Cheap shoe.

Blacksmith: a crude, incompetent craftsman.

Bootblacks: The ironers in the finishing and packing departments; resented by the ironers.

Crispin: an old-time shoe worker.

Dead Horse: Unfinished work for which a piece worker has been paid before completion.

Dutchman: Wedge inserted between the lifts of the shoe to correct foot posture.

Fat Ankle: An old lady's high shoe.

Irish Kid: Patent leather.

Knifer: One who carries tales about his fellow workmen.

Minister: A boy who catches soles as they drop from a cutting machine sorting rights and lefts as they fall and putting them into boxes.

Tack Chewer: A laster who works with a mouth full of tacks, the tongue serving as third hand to present the tacks to him head foremost.

Toad Stabber: A cutter's knife (term used only in Marblehead, MA)

Trips: Bad leather.

Wrecker: Cobbler.

Rope Manufacturing

By Julia L. Keane submitted July 13, 1938

Information from Mr. Arthur F. Bowler, manager, Lambeth Rope Co., Tarkiln Hill Rd., New Bedford; and from the superintendent of New Bedford Cordage Co., Court St., New Bedford.

Beer: indicates a certain number of ends of certain size of yarn, and number of ends vary with the size of yarn to make bundles of identical size. This term was brought to the works by early English workers and is difficult to explain, but is understood easily by the workers. Upon inquiry, informant stated there are now only two real Lancashire men in the plant.

Forming Twist: the first twist put into a strand of rope or cord.

Laying a Rope, or Topping: forming twist in each strand and the three strands brought together.

Lieceing: running a liece string over and under the ends of warp threads, across the warp and back, to keep the threads in place.

Liece Rod: takes the place of the liece string when the warp is placed on the loom.

Rope Top: a cone shaped block of wood with the point cut off with grooves for each strand of rope —used in laying a rope.

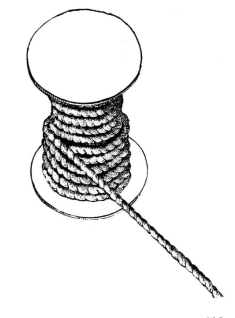

The Woman Behind the Counter

by Marsha L. McCabe

"*For in imagination I had gone into a shop; it was laid with black and white paving; it was hung, astonishingly beautifully, with coloured ribbons. Mary Carmichael might well have a look at that in passing, I thought, for it is a sight that would lend itself to the pen as fittingly as any snowy peak or rocky gorge in the Andes. And there is the girl behind the counter too — I would as soon have her true history as the hundred and fiftieth life of Napoleon or seventieth study of Keats and his use of Miltonic inversion which old Professor Z and his like are now inditing.*"

Virginia Woolf
A Room of One's Own

No one knew where the two strange children came from. No one could account for their sudden, nervous arrival. They seemed to blow out of the wind like dustballs and land randomly in the classroom. Everyone stopped work. The room filled with staring eyes. Someone laughed.

The two small girls inched forward — past the crayoned cornfields, past the stacked books, up to the front desk. Their lunch bags shook.

Miss Tripp looked up from her attendance sheets. "What are your names?" she asked matter-of-factly.

Names? They were not prepared for the question. They glanced anxiously at each other and said nothing. They didn't know.

Miss Tripp thought they didn't hear. She tried again. "Where are you from?"

From? They couldn't say. They looked around the room and found safety nowhere, not in the laughing faces of the pupils nor in the searching eyes of the teacher.

Opp. page: In front of the old schoolhouse on Horseneck Road, Miss Louisa Chace's seventh grade class poses on a September day in 1907. Present are (left to right): Front row, George Dewey Lake, Mabelle Dolores Smith, Lawrence Ascar White, Esther Agnes Silveira, Leah Elizabeth Allen, Leon Whitfield and William James Smith; middle row, Elvira Oakley White and Althea Brownell Gardner; back row, Herman Thomas Tripp, Samuel W. Lake, Lucy Maria Gifford, Amie Josephine cummings, Carrie Silveira, Mary Culler Smith and Sarah Silveira. Courtesy of the Silveira family. *Left:* View from the Wesley House shows Lake Anthony, now Oak Bluffs harbor, as it looked around the turn of the century. Stan Lair collection, courtesy of Mr. and Mrs. Eugene Baer.

Perhaps they're mutes, Miss Tripp thought, studying their scrubbed, frightened faces. Someone had taken the trouble to dress these children properly. Someone had aimed them in the direction of the **school**. She would give it one more try. "**Who are your families?**"

The children said nothing. Miss Tripp threw up her hands in defeat. "What ails these children?" she cried.

The sisters clung to each other. Why did this lady talk so funny? Was she trying to make the other children laugh? What was school and why did father send them here? When they started out this morning, they had words for everything. But now, all the words seemed wrong.

School. Their first day of school. They had run laughing, unsuspecting, over the windswept roads to the schoolhouse. Carrie, who was seven, had waited a full year for her sister, Mary, to turn six so they could walk together. But father hadn't told them what a curious place school was. In his quiet, brooding way, he said only — they must go now and "learn something."

They learned something astonishing: that other people spoke a language they had not heard before. On that lost September day in 1900, when the two sisters left their community on Martha's Vineyard and entered Cottage City school less than a mile away, they were children of the Azores. Their American world was Portuguese.

An excited pupil ran up and whispered something in Miss Tripp's ear. The teacher's face brightened, softened. But, of course. She should have known. They could not speak English. "Sit down," she said, pointing to two empty seats. Relieved, the children joined their classmates and waited to see what would happen next.

Carrie and Mary knew with wrenching certainty their six and seven years of living did not apply here. The bright, happy chatter of their past was, as if, swept away; these new faces and voices were rushing in to fill the empty spaces. How quickly their world had changed! They would never be their parent's children in quite the same way again.

After school, Carrie and Mary scrambled home to their island on an island, to their people, Portuguese seamen who followed the whales from the Azores to America and stayed on. The immigrants settled in Martha's Vineyard, a wayward corner of Massachusetts, cast adrift in the Atlantic, five miles from the mainland. The island was primarily inhabited by independent Yankees. The Portuguese newcomers, who fished and farmed as their fathers had done in the Azores, were largely hidden to them.

Carrie's father, Manuel, was a small farmer who grew vegetables on the family's quarter-acre plot. Every inch of land was turned into lush garden, where things grew deep or poked out of the ground or climbed to reach the sun. Carrie stepped from stark Vineyard winters into a jungle of vines and stalks — orange and yellow salads, right there for the picking. Throughout summer and fall, Manuel took his vegetables to market and pocketed his small profits. Someday they would move on to bigger and better gardens.

In contrast, Carrie's mother, Carolina, restricted her gaze to the matters at hand, five children under seven, who pressed around her and forced her to concentrate on detail. She would not allow her vision to wander outside the immediate boundaries for other reasons as well. Beyond the house and yard was an alien world watching her.

In this close, strict Portuguese community in Cottage City (renamed Oak Bluffs in 1907), the women spent their days keeping house and tending infants. When new infants arrived, older siblings took care of the growing toddlers. Most of the women's work was done inside the shingled cottages in hard New England winters and in wet foggy summers. Children were both seen and heard as they played around outdoors, though they were forbidden to play in dirt. Dirty children made dirty houses.

Within the prescribed boundaries, they grew up. Though the boys were free to be good Portuguese boys, the girls were bound by more rigid rules that emigrated with their parents from their homeland. Strangers, whom Carrie was forbidden to talk to, were shadows on the edge of her life, as elusive as the thick fogs that hung over the island but nevertheless a part of the odd landscape of things. She was never near enough to hear their dissident Yankee speech or search their fair, weatherbeaten faces for warnings. Steps and porches and backyards defined Carrie's world until the day she entered Cottage City School.

On rare occasions when Carolina and the children appeared in public, they took precautions. Carolina set the tone as they huddled together, eyes lowered, voices hushed, in order not to arouse the suspicion of strangers. Forbidden places were everywhere along the route. The children were not allowed in public buildings nor even in shops, which Carrie had begun taking a keen interest in. Bakery shops. Dry goods shops. How she wanted to go in one! But even to ask permission would be a violation of the rules, the unspoken rules beyond the spoken ones. They were not to go in shops. That was that. Their mother wouldn't let them.

Since Carrie could not see a shop for herself, she conjured up her own dream-shop and stocked it with straw hats and hard candy and canary birds in cages. Children and dogs were welcome in Carrie's shop — a secret shop of abundance and disorder,

qualities forbidden to obedient daughters except in the dark places of the mind.

Yet Carrie knew her father had been a disobedient son, for she carried around his history with a certain troubled pride. Father had done worse than go into a shop. As a boy, he had run 6,000 miles away from home, had left the Azores without permission or a suitcase. He had crossed oceans, longitudes, continents, streets. He did all this for his children, he told them shamelessly.

"But I wasn't even born," Carrie laughed, thinking, if father could break the rules in so grand and glorious a way, might I, just once, break one small rule? Might I go into a shop? But the words caught in her throat.

No, she could not. She would be punished. They would stop loving her. Obedient daughters, disobedient sons.

***

Carrie's father, Manuel Rosa Silveira, at 18, left his homeland of Pico, forever, an island too small to contain the dreams of an adventurous youth. The Azorean archipelago rises out of the Atlantic, midway between the Old World and the New — mountains in the sea, a curious mixture of luxuriant flower and volcanic rock. Though the eight other islands opted for flowers, Pico settled for rock. As Manuel grew up, he began to feel his life defined by a stark geography that would leave him an impoverished farmer, as his father was, as his grandfather had been before him.

Like most island boys, Manuel had dropped out of school in the eighth grade. One of seven children, he followed the ancient patterns, watching over the goats on the rocky hillsides and tending the vineyards in the pastures below. The black cone of Pico stood watch over his life, spewing a gloom, a solitude over his boy-spirits. The burden of being the oldest son fell heavily on Manuel.

Oldest sons are obligated sons in the large, tightly-knit Portuguese Azorean families. As future patriarch, Manuel had the responsibility of seeing that things continued as they had for centuries. He was expected to support his aging parents, be a work model for his brothers and a protector to his sisters. But in his late teens, Manuel's loyalty to his family began to waver in the face of powerful voices within, urging him to break away, go off somewhere, try himself out. There was not enough world for him in Pico.

In the summer of his nineteenth year, freedom and responsibility crashed head-on in Manuel, and freedom won an easy, uneasy victory on a black night in Magdalena Harbor. A North American whaling ship had stopped there to replenish supplies and crew. It would soon leave for America. From the moment he saw it, Manuel knew it was waiting there for him. For him! Oh, he had heard tales of other island boys who had climbed aboard ships in the night and disappeared forever.

Manuel knew just what to do. When they were well out to sea, he would come out of hiding and surrender to the captain. And so it went. He carried out his plan.

When they were too far out at sea to turn back, Manuel, the stowaway, surrendered to the captain. The Yankee captain inspected him as if he were a piece of meat, for stowaways were no less commodities than whales, an important source of energy to the whaling trade. Manuel was put to work immediately. In time, the captain was grateful to have aboard the willing, spirited boy from the Azores.

In the months that followed, Manuel learned English from his shipmates, a hardy multi-lingual crew, mainly from the Portuguese Islands, St. Helena and the Hawaiian Islands. He also learned the hard and bloody work of whaling. In time, he became skilled and deadly with the harpoon, learned to cut up and boil down the blubber, turning great whales into oil for fuel and perfumes, crafting bone into jewelry. But the excitement and danger of killing whales climaxed early for the boy, Manuel, who became a man at sea. In time, the bad smell of whaling permeated his clothes, worked into his skin, and slid down to his very soul. But there was no way off this boat. He discovered he had joined the crew in the half-way mark of an around-the-world voyage. There were two years to go.

Moving off the coast of Africa, through the West Indies and into Hawaii, cris-crossing the equator, moving restlessly from winter to summer, from the Atlantic to the Pacific, Manuel no longer made geographic or seasonal distinctions. Oceans flowed into each other. Seasons disappeared altogether. There was only an endless succession of days and nights and, somewhere at the end, the dream of a new world, waiting.

When they disembarked in New Bedford, Massachusetts, the captain handed Manuel a ten-dollar bill, the only pay he would receive for a two year whaling voyage. New Bedford! The once major whaling port in North America glittered in the noonday sun and filled Manuel with hope. Never had he seen such elegant houses as those on County Street, owned by entrepreneurs whose fortunes came from the sea and the backs of Azorean boys like Manuel.

During the first week, Manuel ate little and slept in crowded rooming houses while he prowled the streets in search of work. Hope quickly turned to despair. There were no jobs here for a man from the Azores whose skill was harpooning whales. Nor were there friends or relatives to turn to for help. Clutching what was left of his money, aching with hunger and despair, Manuel saw the great whaling ship, the Charles W. Morgan, in New Bedford harbor waiting to sign on a crew. He did not want to return to sea but he felt his body move toward the boat. He felt his shaking hand sign the paper. Manuel stayed with the Morgan for four years.

After six years as a whaler, Manuel began to see himself in a surprising new way. All this time he thought he did not want to be a farmer like his father and his grandfather. But now he longed to put down roots, longed to buy some land and watch it grow. This new turn his life had taken became an obsession.

When he disembarked in New Bedford once more, Manuel planned to stay on whatever grim terms the new land demanded. He promptly found work in a rubber works in Warren, Rhode Island, and gradually made his way back to that place where he would spend much of his life — the southeast corner of Massachusetts. Here in New Bedford, Dartmouth, Westport and Fall River, he scrambled to survive as a hired farm hand, hustling from job to job. Hunger went

Manuel Silveira spent several years as a whaler aboard the Charles W. Morgan. The Morgan (center background) is shown here drying her sails while receiving provisions. An old man sits calmly before the Charles L. Jeffrey, unmindful of activity on New Bedford's waterfront. Arthur F. Packard photograph, circa 1918, courtesy of T. M. Holcombe.

Manuel Rosa Da Silveira, born in Pico, the Azores, taught Carrie "never to be ashamed of her background." Courtesy of the Silveira family.

with him for he earned little as a migrant. But he did what the poor must do to survive, snatching eggs from hen houses and swallowing the insides whole, searching the fields for overlooked, overripe vegetables and filling his pockets. Out of this lean and hungry beginning, he began to have a dream.

Someday he would farm his own land, land so rich it would fill root cellars and pantries and tables. He would need a wife, of course, to help him with the gathering and preserving. And they would need children to share in the harvest. Someday these children would go to school and "learn something."

A New Bedford priest suggested it was time for Manuel to meet a nice young girl. Manuel agreed. He began looking.

***

Carolina Amelia was born in the Azores on Fayal, an island as bright with flowers and green hills as Pico was somber with black rocks and craters. Early Flemish and later Portuguese settlers turned this round island bowl into a rambling farm where sheep and cattle grazed on the hillsides and small scattered villages prospered. Pico rose dramatically in the distance less than five miles away but this, and most everything else, was out of reach to Carolina whose 21 years of life tottered between bleak and desperate.

Her parents had died when she was an infant and Carolina was sent to an orphanage — a storage place for children who are put up for adoption when they are old enough to work. Carolina went without schooling, without holidays or celebrations, without any of the loving detail that turns children into loving adults.

When she was 12, she was adopted by the Alves family and renamed Carolina Amelia Alves, the new servant girl. She had moved from joyless orphanage to cruel household where she spent her teenage years toiling. If she failed to obey the Alves' continuous sharp commands, she was berated and slapped. Her feelings, never allowed expression, would remain locked inside her, forever buried, even when life grew considerably brighter. And so it would. While running errands around town for the Alves, she was able to make a few friends who would one day help her change her life.

When she was 21 and still a housemaid, an exciting, terrifying letter arrived from abroad. Two friends had left the Azores and settled in a land called New Bedford. Carolina knew only vaguely of America and she stared at the letter, full of words like "opportunity" and "wages," words she had never connected with her own impoverished life. The two friends promised her money for passage and a job if she would join them. Since Carolina was no longer bound to the Alves, she decided to take the risk. Thirty days later she arrived in the port of New Bedford.

From her arrival, Carolina was fearful and defiant of the new land, surrounded as she was by strangers and strange ways. She quickly found work as a domestic in a New Bedford household, a job she kept for five years. Because her employers insisted, she learned American cooking but otherwise she resisted American ways. Never before had she been paid for working — she liked being paid —and she saved what little she could for a future that seemed blurred and worrisome. She did not try to learn English, nor would she ever.

Though Manuel Silveira and Carolina Alves had lived five miles apart in the Azores, they would meet for the first time 6,000 miles from their homeland in a New Bedford living room. After a brief courtship, Carolina Amelia Alves became Carolina Amelia Silveira in St. John the Baptist church in New Bedford. They began married life on Martha's Vineyard, an island unlike those mountainous islands of their birth but strangely like them too, wind-tossed and desolate, alone and exposed. Five of their seven children would be born here. Their first child, Caroline Silveira, was born on April 20, 1893.

***

Carrie and her sister Mary were odd but interesting arrivals to their classmates in the island school. Most of the Yankee children were accepting. If on occasion someone caught Carrie's eye and called out "daigo" or "guinea," there being no other words for Portuguese children, Carrie paid no attention. She had entered a world of infinite possibility. Within weeks, she could read and write English; she could also outtalk her classmates. Her mind sharpened and sparkled like cut glass.

As fall turned into winter, Carrie arrived home from school increasingly

tainted with the language and manners of an alien culture. Carolina eyed her with suspicion and tried to cure her the only way she knew. "Speak properly, Carrie," she would say. "Speak in Portuguese." Other times, she would say, "Carrie, sit still. You're always running around like a wild thing." Carrie tried to obey but obedience was most difficult when her mother turned away from her questions. "I don't have time for questions," she would say.

Carrie persisted. "Did you know the sun is a star and all the stars are suns?" she asked her mother one day. "There's work to be done around here," she told Carrie. "I don't have time for such talk. Nor do you." Carolina would sometimes twist Carrie's ear, as the Alves had once done to her. Stung, Carrie tried again to be the daughter she was supposed to be. But the tension grew.

Manuel Silveira and Caroline Amelia Alves pose for their wedding photograph on June 13, 1892. Their first child, Carrie, was born a year later. Courtesy of the Silveira family.

Carolina's deepest fears were coming true. The dreaded stranger was no longer outside the house; the stranger was becoming her own daughter. Carrie seemed to be growing according to a plan of her own, at odds with Carolina's plan. The Lord knew, Carolina had planted good seed. But from the ground came dandelions and gangly sunflowers and wild roses whose petals blew like confetti over the yards and into the public places, out of control.

For her part, Carrie understood, without anyone saying, that good daughters were silent, obedient daughters. Her tireless efforts to be good collided with her own passionate, spirited nature. She suspected she had an ally in Manuel but he kept his feelings to himself. Caught between the old country and the new world, between wanting approval and disappointing, Carrie began to see her universe as irrevocably fragmented. Carrie's outward vision and her mother's inward pull, the tension and ambiguity of the relationship, would last a lifetime.

***

Tucked away where farms meet the sea, east of Providence and south of Boston is a lost, wet piece of Massachusetts far enough removed from the powerful centers to be nearly forgotten by the rest of the state. People use Southeastern Massachusetts to pass through on their way to Cape Cod, without ever seeing the tangled beauty of beach and dune hidden off the main route.

Over the years, the original township of Dartmouth would become five towns with boundaries and identities of their own. New Bedford, Dartmouth, Fairhaven, Westport and Acushnet flow in and out of each other, like the sea that shapes and unites them. The weather here favors bare feet or high boots, and the overwhelming fact of life for the inhabitants is water, the ocean at the edge of their lives, the ocean shaping the land, carving out delightful bays and inlets, harbors and wild places, and shaping many a livelihood as well. Here in this neglected, enchanted place, this swampy backwater, Carrie would spend most of her life.

Manuel was restless and knew it was time to move on. Just as the Azores were too small for the boy, so was Martha's Vineyard too restrictive, too contained for the man. When Carrie was nine, the family moved to Dartmouth, where land was plentiful and ran wild for 22 miles along the sea.

They temporarily leased a farm on Fisher Road and in the off-season Manuel searched for land they might call their own. The old dream had glittered and receded before him for over ten years now. After two years, the family put their money down on a 50 acre farm on Hix Bridge Road in the neighboring town of Westport. Manuel could not believe their good fortune. They were now people of property.

Manuel, Carolina, and their five children settled into a rambling eight-room house on land where hayfields grew wild and ancient stone walls set off rocky pastures. For years, the land had been allowed to go its own way but Manuel would set it right. He arranged and rearranged it in his mind, his eager eyes turning stubble into lush vegetable gardens, hay into feed, encroaching woods into wood for the wood stove. He saw the pastures full of cows fat with milk and he could see eggs, already scrambled, spilling from the coops.

The family went to work at once, for weeks, months, to turn the unruly piece of land into a productive farm. Now it was a matter of survival. Carrie, at 11, eagerly helped with the haying, the milking, the multitude of farm chores. She loved farming but as the oldest daughter, she was often called indoors to do the house work. She watched enviously as Mary and Sarah became the regular milkers of 28 dairy cows.

Eventually, six hired hands worked alongside Manuel, immigrants, from the Cape Verde Islands off the coast of Africa, where Portuguese settlers and native Africans mixed and married. Like Manuel, they made their way to New Bedford on whaling ships, then found work on farms or on the cranberry bogs. Remembering his own hungry beginnings, Manuel tried to pay them decently but he would never be a rich farmer. Each day was a struggle to expand his little markets. Soon he began buying extra milk from Westport Point to service the overflow. Carrie, at 12, became responsible for the night milk run, which allowed Manuel to go to bed early and rise at 1 a.m.

Sitting tall among empty ten gallon pails, wrapped in horseblankets, Carrie, and often Mary, clopped along the narrow winding roads to Westport Point. Their cart, pulled by two old horses, broke the silence with rattles and clanks that kept up for eight miles. In the half-light of summer, the trip was an adventure. But in winter, when night began early on these lonely roads, the girls were filled with fear. Conversations beginning with a certain brave cheer rapidly slid into despair.

"Do you hear a strange noise up ahead?" Mary would ask, peering into the blackness. "Do you see anything suspicious?"

"Nonsense," Carrie would say — And then a pause. "You mean like a man who escaped from jail?" Her words fascinated and repelled her. Even in the daytime, jail was the worst place she could think of. The thought of meeting an escapee from the New Bedford jail around the next bend, reached her in a place beyond terror.

"No, I mean just a really bad man with an axe," Mary would say matter-of-factly.

They rode on in stunned silence until they reached the Point. Here they unloaded the empty pails and filled up with fresh milk before setting off for home. In time, Carrie invented a nightly ritual that helped them ward off the unspeakable dangers awaiting them. They sang merrily at the tops of their voices, sang loud enough to make the cows jump and the sleeping insects dance. Their songs also kept them from detailing the exact dangers likely to extinguish them before they reached safety in the warm glow of the kerosene lamp in the window.

Manuel's day began at 1 a.m. for his new milk customers lived in the city, in New Bedford's South End. They were textile workers whose 16 hour days began shortly after his. Immigration was at its peak and New Bedford was reeling from change. Whaling had made New Bedford, for a time, the richest city in the world. Just as the oceans began running out of whales, the demand for whale oil was over. New Bedford never really felt the loss, for money once invested in whaling ships found a new source of wealth in textiles.

Manuel and Carrie, their wagon filled with milk from their Westport farm, travel to the city to sell the milk in New Bedford's populous, south end tenement district. Illustration by Clement E. Daley, 1988.

clemente daley 1988

Overnight, textile mills sprung up north and south of Boston, in Lawrence and Lowell, Fall River and New Bedford. Long cavernous buildings in brick and granite were built along the riverfront. New Bedford welcomed the new industry and made room in the North and South End for the surge of new people who would live and labor there. Block upon block of three-decker wooden tenements packed the neighborhoods near the mills. The air grew heavy with cotton dust.

Immigrants from Portugal, the Azores, and the Cape Verde Islands poured into the mills to become the pickers and carders, warpers and weavers, spinners and spoolers. Manuel met them before the early shift, his cart heaped with milk and vegetables from his Westport farm. In return for country goods, he received city goods including lard, flour, and cocoa.

At home, Carrie walked the rural roads to the sixth and seventh grades. Children of all sizes trickled out of the nearby farms and filled the one-room schoolhouse on Horse Neck Road, the girls in dresses and bobbed hair, the long-haired boys in knickers. Carrie no longer felt different from her classmates. She swung easily back and forth between cultures, speaking only English in school, switching to a sparse Portuguese when she was home. She asked teachers for opinions on subjects nowhere in her books. They said that facts, not opinions, were important. Nevertheless, opinions were still interesting to Carrie.

Carrie found no mention of the Azores in her books. She listened raptly when her father described Pico, the dark brooding island of his youth, and Fayal, her mother's island of flowers and sun. She asked questions about war and history and people who made history books. She asked her mother why their neighbor, Mrs. Howland, died in childbirth. Carolina said only the Lord knew.

When she reached the eighth grade, Carrie had gone beyond many of the children around her, who dropped out of school and out of her life to struggle on farms and in steamy mills. As the only eighth grader in the area, she needed to combine with a handful of other eighth graders at the Head of Westport. But the school was far from home and there was no way for her to get there. Manuel determined to solve the problem. The sun would rise; Carrie would go to school. He approached Mr. Pilkington, the mail carrier, with a request.

"Could you deliver Carrie at the Head along with the mail?" Manuel asked him. "And pick her up on your way back?"

Mr. Pilkington thought this an odd request but he was willing to try. The timing worked and, for a year, Carrie came and went as smoothly as a letter. Buried in mail bags, her feet often hanging in mid-air, she learned the intricacies of the mail business. Mr. Pilkington, who had a passion for bad weather, carried binoculars to assess the state of the sky. He issued warnings at every stop.

"Well, Carrie, do you see a nor' easter coming up there in the sou' west sky?"

Carrie looked. "I'm not really sure," she mumbled, not wanting to disappoint him.

"I think we're in for a dandy!" He spoke of the pull of the moon on the tides and he described the low pressure zones that would move in and consume them before the day was out. Carrie listened eagerly to everything he said.

Manuel kept watch over his children's education; Carolina watched uneasily from a distance. Manuel often asked them to read aloud so he might assess their progress. Having taught himself to read and write English, Manuel believed that whatever was written was true. He wished people would not be so careless with the truth, especially in New Bedford where old, casually discarded newspapers and magazines clogged the gutters. During his milk rounds, he gathered up piles of old papers and took them home to his children. They could not afford to buy such luxuries.

"They are gifts," he would say. "Read them."

Manuel also took his reading personally. Newspapers were full of bad news that cried out for the intercession of the Almighty. The family prayer hour, a full hour after dinner every evening, was devoted to people caught in disasters, even though word arrived in papers where fates were sealed long ago. Earthquakes, shipwrecks, hurricanes and tornados took the prayer hour into overtime. Carrie often tried to beat Manuel to the news and send out early warnings. "Mary. Sarah. Hide these. There's been a hurricane."

"Where?" they would ask.

"It doesn't matter where. Just hide them."

They pushed them under the sofa and prayed Manuel wouldn't see. A hurricane anywhere in the world called for an hour and a half of prayer, more than a mere tornado. Since every autumn in Westport, hurricanes were a real and terrifying possibility, Manuel believed in taking precautions.

Mr. Pilkington, mailman with a passion for bad weather, delivers Carrie to school at Head of Westport. Illustration by Clement E. Daley, 1988.

clement e. daley 1988

145

At 13, Carrie was short and quick. Her dark hair curled tight in the sea air and her bright, dark eyes were always full of questions. Willful and argumentative, she was not her mother's daughter. Nevertheless, she kept to Carolina's strict rules as she raced through the days to get the farm work done, the homework done, the housework done.

Romance was real to Carrie but had little to do with boys. On occasion, she looked for love stories in the magazines her father brought home but boys touched her life only at the edges. They sat next to her in school; they were rowdy at recess. That was all she knew about boys. Real romance was with nature. She could spend hours lost in the ebb and flow of the tides, or run through hayfields like a young colt, or try to write a poem about a cumulus cloud. (She had learned about the clouds from Mr. Pilkington.)

The accident occurred mid-summer of Carrie's thirteenth year. The family would always refer to it vaguely as "Carrie's accident," without supplying details or assigning blame. It was Carrie's accident, it happened, that was all.

She was running in the field, alone, when she heard the men mowing in the distance. How dare they begin the haying without her! She would catch up with them, she decided, and she ran to meet them, making trails through rows of dusty straw, unseen and unseeing — alighting like a grass-hopper, flicking off again and disappearing. Suddenly, the great blade of the mower came out of a sunny afternoon and sought her with a

Left: Carrie at her confirmation. Courtesy of the Silveira family. *Right:* One of New Bedford's early immigrant neighborhoods and commercial centers was on South Water Street, between Howland Street (right) and Walnut Street. This view, looking north, was taken around 1910. Courtesy of the *Standard-Times.*

violence. She remembered the blaze of the sun in the heat of the afternoon and the first violent jolt like fire searing her insides before plunging her into darkness. The men saw the child hurtle skyward, fall back to the ground. Her right foot lay beside her. Horrified, they rushed for help.

Weeks passed. People around her wept. Carrie smiled from her bed and wriggled her leg, wrapped in white from the knee down. She was defiant. So she had lost her foot. "Can't you see? I'm still the same as I've always been. I'm still Carrie." This she would tell her visitors.

In response, her visitors went to the next room to weep where she couldn't hear them. As soon as the doctor agreed, she was up and on crutches, which became extensions of herself. Soon she was hobbling about doing the old chores. She resumed the milk runs. She played tag as she always had with the younger children. When strangers stared at her bandaged foot, she'd say, "Oh, don't pay any attention to that. It's not a problem for me. Is it for you?"

In the fall, Carrie was ready for high school. Since there was no high school in Westport, she would have to live in

Dartmouth and attend the Russells Mills School. Boarding was not unusual among school children and Manuel made arrangements for her to live with the Lawton family. The cost was two dollars a week. Since school was as necessary as planting a garden, Manuel never hesitated. Manuel had not gone beyond the eighth grade and having a child in high school was a matter of personal pride. It called for sacrifice and celebration.

Three years later, Manuel and Carolina stood proudly in the Russells Mills School and watched Carrie graduate. She walked without crutches to receive her certificate for Carrie had a new foot. In the last two years of high school, she could no longer ignore the recurring, throbbing pain that shot down her right leg and set her ankle on fire. A Portuguese shoemaker took her measurements and a German immigrant designed her a foot made of cork and sponges. Carrie thought it was splendid.

Ever since Carrie's accident, Carolina brooded and worried about her daughter's future. Carrie would not be able to do a stand-up job. Since most women's work involved standing, what was Carrie to do? College would never come up; it was too far outside the family's experience ever to arise as a possibility for Carrie. But there was never any question about work. People worked. Daughters as well as sons worked; this was the order of things. How else was one to live? In her last two summers of high school, Carolina apprenticed Carrie to a local dressmaker, hoping there was a future here.

Carrie did not like sewing. She understood this promptly and decisively but she made an effort to do the job. Sewing was too small and private, too fussy. Needles and threads never had opinions, never argued. She could not bear to spend her life in a side-room when all the action was on center stage. Oh, she had finally glimpsed the action, for the apprenticeship offered one delicious pleasure. Carrie was instructed to go into the New Bedford shops and pick up material and sewing supplies.

Shops! They were full of wonderful things, just as she'd always suspected. She could wander up and down the aisles, run her fingers over cottons and corduroys. She could watch people prance and shuffle about. Real shops were as wonderful to her as the dream-shops conjured up by that lost, wistful child on Martha's Vineyard.

The world was an awesome place, this glittery, disorderly world of New Bedford. Carrie liked the city, she liked the fishing boats and fine buildings. She liked the diverse collection of people with their odd manners and strange tongues. She wanted to be out among the people. Carrie Silveira wanted to be a shop girl. And she would do it standing up.

***

The two travelers, Manuel and Carrie, rose like ghosts out of the morning fog and disappeared over the hills, reappearing later along lower Hix Bridge Road. The wagon was heavy with milk, the father, hunched and silent over the reins, the daughter beside him, lost in the desolation of the hour. Every morning, for a week now, Carrie made the trip with Manuel into New Bedford where she hoped to find work. They rose at 1 a.m., a time when the world seemed so indifferent, Carrie could feel her future tremble. That bright, imagined future seemed suddenly threatened by the new reality. Finding sales work would not be easy after all.

Here, on the road, Carrie began to understand Manuel's burden for the first time. For years, he had carted the milk at this unhappy hour over 15 miles of back-breaking, heart-wrenching country roads, hauled it through the early winters and wet springs, through summer fogs that blew in off the ocean and threatened

to erase him from the landscape. But nothing kept the intrepid Manuel from getting to the city. No surly weather or creeping virus, no unlucky ambush kept him from selling his milk. All this, Carrie thought, so his children could eat.

When they arrived in New Bedford at 3 a.m., Carrie tried to keep herself warm in the cart while Manuel made his rounds. It was much too early to look for a job. Instead, she imagined the lives of all the people who lived behind the doors where Manuel made his deliveries. So many seemed poor. She sat back and watched the city wake up. By 6 a.m., the South End buzzed with activity.

Milk wagons, much like their own, rattled and passed. Carts, heaped with summer fruits, clopped by. Crowds of workers, some shouting greetings in Portuguese and French, streamed into the mills. Bakeries and butcher stores opened. Curtains parted in the dry goods shops. Doors were unlocked, windows wiped, sidewalks swept. The day opened.

Carrie approached yet another proprietor of a South End shop. "I'm interested in getting a job here," she said, as if this were the only store in the world she would settle for. She could not remember how many stores she had gone to. Each shopkeeper examined her as if she were new merchandise when she filled out the application forms.

"Do you have any experience, Miss Silveira?"

She had faced the question before. They all asked this one first, as if to get right down to her shortcomings. "I'm just out of high school," she answered rather proudly at first, "but I'm a fast learner." The approach met with kindly frowns she interpreted as rejections; they would certainly take her if she had experience. By mid-week, she understood that her inexperience kept her from any hope of getting sales work. She did not understand city ways. She couldn't get the job without the experience and she couldn't get the experience without the job. What was a person to do?

"Excuse me," she said loudly and with new resolution to the man behind the counter in Harry's Dry Goods. She knew by his worried, preoccupied look he was the owner. "I'm interested in applying for a job here."

"Huh? Oh." The man looked down at Carrie as he would a child, for she seemed small to him. "Have you any experience?"

"Yes," Carrie said quickly, pulling her eyes away from his and finding safety in a heap of nightwear. "I've had experience at Tallman's. I'm good with customers, can run a cash register, anything." She blushed and thought perhaps she ought not to go too far. She ought to say she'd had experience and leave it at that. She waited breathlessly.

"Tallman's, you say. That's fine experience. It happens that I need a girl. Eight dollars a week is all I can afford. You can begin tomorrow."

"Yes," said Carrie, trying not to appear too eager. "Oh, yes!" Outside, the world already looked different.

Carrie's passport photo taken when she was 26. Courtesy of the Silveira family.

True, she had not done the honorable thing — She had lied to get a job. But worse, she was too excited to be ashamed. "I've got a job at Harry's Dry Goods," she cried, climbing in beside Manuel. "I'm going to earn eight dollars a week."

Manuel gave her a quick retreating smile. She would have to live in New Bedford now. She would be the first to leave the family.

That night, whenever Carrie closed her eyes, the redoubtable Harry appeared, pecking away at a cash register. This was her fear — the cash register would certainly scream the news of her woeful inexperience into the trusting ears of Harry.

Carrie arrived promptly at Harry's next day, her hair pulled back in a bun so no one would mistake her for a school girl, wearing her best and only dress.

"Look over the stock first," Harry said kindly. "I'll take care of the customers for now."

Carrie was relieved. The shop smelled of fresh cottons and old attics; sawdust covered the wooden floors. All around her nightgowns, underwear, sheets, pillowcases, socks and more socks rose in unfriendly piles. They were the enemy. They could not leave the store without the benign consent of the cash register.

Carrie examined the stock with one anxious eye while the other anxious eye watched Harry. Harry knew the secret of the cash register. Whenever he rung up an item, Carrie was there behind him, her frantic eyes following

his fingers over the keyboard. All morning long Harry felt her eyes on him. He wondered if his new sales girl might be too intense for dry goods.

When Carrie swung around, she collided with some socks that dangled from the hands of a customer. Would she take them? Of course, she would. She accepted the woman's dime and moved toward the cash register, slowly, as if acting out the final scene of an ignoble play. So this was how it would end! Over socks. Harry watched.

Carrie pressed the zero, the eight, the tabulator. The drawer flew open as it was supposed to. She deposited the dime and drew two pennies change. The socks could leave the store! She gave Harry a ho-hum look as if to say — anyone who has rung up so adeptly at Tallman's ought to be able to handle Harry's.

Carrie's hasty transition from school girl to sales girl, farm to city, parents to boss left her with little time to reflect on where she was. Overnight, the center of her world had shifted and relocated; she was a participant in life in an awesome new way. She was there in the crowd in a place called New Bedford, Massachusetts, in 1911, in a shop called Harry's. She was at the center of life.

Harry's Dry Goods turned out to be

a leisurely, family-centered store, small enough to allow her to become experienced before Harry discovered otherwise. Her days focused on the particular: how to handle a customer, where to pile the granny gowns, what price to put on a pair of knickers.

Since there were no regular hours (store hours occurred whenever customers came in), Carrie's day began at 7 a.m. and extended well into the night. No matter what the hours, often longer than the hours of a mill worker, her pay remained at eight dollars. Every Saturday, late in the afternoon, the piercing whistles of a dozen mills shouted all over the South End, announcing the end of another work week. Workers crowded into the stores with their week's wages and bought what they needed, usually paying something down and charging the rest. Bills were not mailed, for Harry, the bill collector, made house calls. Every week he collected a quarter, a half dollar, sometimes a dollar from as many as 300 customers.

Whenever Harry was out about town, Carrie minded the store. She began learning every aspect of the retail business. Harry was secretly pleased with his new sales girl for she was an indefatigable worker and had a way with customers. He especially admired the way she handled the cash register.

Carrie moved into an apartment over the dry goods store, sharing it with Ella, a fortune teller, who had approached Carrie as a likely roommate. Ella needed someone who could pay half the rent, for fortune-telling had its peaks and drops like everything else. Carrie quickly learned

that fortune tellers worked odd hours, whenever anyone appeared at the door with fifty cents. Many an evening, while Carrie read books, Ella read palms in the small, sparsely furnished living room.

Madame Ella, as she called herself, was consistent. She gave out only bad fortunes. Her specialty was disaster in its many variations. Her customers learned that their closest relatives spread scurrilous stories about them. They were warned to watch their spouses and never trust their friends. Customers never questioned the all-knowing Ella but left to seek revenge on the string of traitors surrounding them.

After listening to a week of this, Carrie could stand it no longer. A woman had just left in tears and anger, after thanking Ella profusely for the news that her husband was a sniveling cheat. "What you're doing isn't right!" Carrie shouted. "You ought not to bring such misery to people."

Ella's painted eyebrows leaped to her forehead, she reeled with anger. "Oh, look who's talking, Miss Goody-Good," she cried, flying about the room. "Well, I know for a fact that you've been stealing from Harry's Dry Goods."

Enraged, Carrie lunged at Ella. Having made contact, she did not know what to do next. She tweaked Ella's ear so hard, Ella squealed. (Carrie had learned this from Carolina, who had learned it from the Alves.) Ella was taken aback and forced ever after to change her habits. When Carrie was around, she softened the

This South Water Street scene, looking south near Division Street, is one block south of Harry's Dry Goods, Carrie's first place of employ. Courtesy of the *Standard-Times*, circa 1940.

bad news. She also began meeting her customers in the streets. Sometimes she arranged for confrontations between the wounded parties to take place outside the apartment window where she could part the curtains and watch.

As for Carrie, the action was on So. Water Street, in the pageant of people who stopped at Harry's and asked for help with dry goods. After two years at Harry's, his brother, Joe, who owned a larger store on So. Water Street, asked Carrie if she would work for him for ten dollars a week. Ten dollars? Indeed, Carrie would.

She decided to leave Harry with a clear conscience. "There's something you should know," she told him on her last day, "something I simply must tell you."

Harry looked at her in that worried, preoccupied way she understood was total absorption. "When I came here to work I didn't really have any experience. I lied. I had to have the job." Carrie grew hot with the shame and ecstasy of confession. She waited for forgiveness.

"I don't believe that for a moment," Harry said without hesitation. "And I don't think an exemplary salesgirl like you should go around saying things that aren't true. It's just not becoming."

Carrie left confused. Later, she remembered he had said something wonderful. She was an exemplary salesgirl. She liked the sound of it.

***

Carrie's move from Harry's Dry Goods to Levine's Department Store was a move from the common world of cottons into the more luxurious world of silver teapots and fur coats. But Levine's sold everything, right down to socks and infants wear. A sales force of seven, including four men and three women worked full-time on the floor.

The boss, Joe Levine, could neither read nor write but he nevertheless tended lovingly to 5,000 accounts. When he loaned money to his Portuguese customers, a frequent occurrence, both sides committed the obligation to memory without benefit of notes. For they, too, could neither read nor write. Carrie found her high school education useful at Levine's.

Joe Levine originally hired Carrie to do the accounting and she intended to. But accounting, like sewing, was a back-room job. She would have to talk her boss into putting her up-front.

She met him in the office. She looked up at him. He looked down at her. "My place is on the floor with the customers," she told him. "The customers are the most important part of a store. You're wasting me back here. If there's one thing in life I'm good at, it's customers. I'm good at helping them find what they came for. Selling, you know, is an art."

She believed it. She believed her work was no less valuable than the construction worker, the artist, the scientist. Her work was with people, to help them find what they came for. Carrie could not believe her new confidence. The act of saying these words out loud to a boss seemed quite astonishing to her.

Joe put her on the floor at once. Within weeks, she was his number one saleswoman. A fascinating mix of people walked the streets of New Bedford and Carrie came to know their habits. French customers insisted on having French saleswomen and said so in spirited French. If Polish shoppers couldn't get a Pole to wait on them, they walked right out of the store. Portuguese customers, however, would settle for anybody. They were always delighted with Carrie who spoke to them in their own language.

Carrie worked alongside Millie, the French woman, and they communicated in English. Since the store stayed open at the whim of customers, who often went strolling or to a show first, Carrie and Millie often put in seventy to eighty hours a week together.

Meanwhile, back in Westport, Manuel struggled to keep up the farm. One by one, the children left for work in the city. A year after Carrie left, Mary and Sarah took jobs in the textile mills, earning sixteen dollars a week as spoolers and winders. Veronica, the youngest, would soon go to Boston University.

Manuel could no longer manage a 50 acre farm, and his reason for doing so was gone. There were no more children to feed. Manuel's journey, begun on a black night on a whaling ship sailing from the Azores, was nearly over. He was a man of property, yes, but the dream needed children in order to have meaning. Manuel's work was done. He sold the Westport farm and he and Carolina bought a 4½ acre farm in Dartmouth on the Apponogansett River.

Carrie had worked for two years at Levine's when Mr. Kaplan, the owner of a still larger store on Water Street, made her an offer. Would she work for him for twelve dollars a week?

Eight dollars at Harry's, ten dollars at Levine's, now twelve dollars at Kaplan's was beyond Carrie's wildest expectations. Kaplan's, in the South End across from Bums Park, was another step up for Carrie.

The atmosphere was relaxed at Kaplan's, which always smelled of new merchandise and home cooking. Mr. Gilmore, the barber, cooked kale soup in the barbershop next door. The spicy smells of linguica and cabbage passed through the walls and into the noses of everyone who shopped in Kaplan's. Customers could see Mr. Gilmore stirring his soup through the adjoining window. He allowed them to watch, then drew the curtain and ate in splendid isolation. Mouths watered and went hungry. People spent money in Kaplan's with a vengeance. Kale soup was wonderful for business.

***

Overnight, the gaiety and ambience of New Bedford paled. In 1918, in New England and much of the country, a strange virus fell upon the people and weakened them. Many died. Even the air seemed to turn yellow. The swine flu was relentless. It found people wherever they were and struck suddenly. It entered churches and stores, whipped through crowds, reached into houses and workplaces; it assaulted people as they walked along the streets. Death entered and emptied houses. When space was needed to house the growing number of caskets, barns were opened and turned into morgues. On occasion, some presumed corpses sat up in their coffins.

Mr. Kaplan collapsed one day in the store and Carrie watched helplessly as he was carried out. The next day, at his request, Carrie took over the business. First she was given power of attorney to make out checks to wholesalers. She also supervised the workers and kept the accounts. As the buyer, she took the bus to Boston and discovered bustling Washington and Kneeland Streets. On Sundays, she knocked on doors, same as Mr.

Typical of the style of storefront businesses and dwellings along South Water Street are these establishments on the east side of the street, looking north near Delano Street. Courtesy of the *Standard-Times*, circa 1940.

Kaplan, and collected on the bills. She worked constantly and would not allow herself to let up.

Business was good at Kaplan's. People were buying black suits and dresses for funerals. Portuguese families, by custom, gave away the dead person's clothes and also bought a complete new outfit for someone needy.

The day Mr. Kaplan returned to work, Carrie collapsed with the flu. The illness hit hard. In the Dartmouth farmhouse, Carolina took charge as Carrie lay flat on her back, eyes closed, and waited for a reprieve. The merest glance at walls and ceilings made her head spin. Neuritis seeped into her chest. Only the radio offered any kind of solace. Mr. Kaplan visited faithfully every other day, assuring her with every visit that she was getting better. Seven weeks later the deadly virus left her and she returned to work.

The swine flu epidemic lasted for two years and turned New Bedford into a somber, cautious city in need of healing. Though the deadly germ left as easily as it had come, the healing would go on for years.

Carrie worked busily at Kaplan's for ten years. Her sister, Sarah, weary from twelve years of work as a spooler in the mills, became an employee at Kaplan's and worked alongside Carrie for two years. The sisters got along well. Meanwhile, Carrie began noticing how very many customers asked for wedding gowns. Carrie suggested to Mr. Kaplan that he invest in a few. Mr. Kaplan did. He did not, however, buy enough to suit Carrie.

***

Sometimes Carrie and Sarah played with the idea of owning their own bridal shop. The game began as a pleasant way to shorten the bus ride home from work. At first, the thought of having a bridal shop was so visually exciting, they were swept away by the color and feel of it. But, in truth, Carrie knew every aspect of the retail business and these were good times for weddings. The game took a more serious tone when words like capital and prime location slipped into the conversation. Later, when the sisters began arguing about who would do the window display and who would sweep up the sequins, the shop became real. But only when it was given a name did it become their own. An absolutely necessary addition to So. Water Street.

The discussion began in January and ended in June.

"South Water Street Bridal Shop," Sarah said.

"No," Carrie replied, "there's no pep to it. How about Blushing Bride?"

"No," Sarah said. "How about Silveira's Bridal Gowns?"

"That's boring," said Carrie.

They went on like this for months, then decided to ask their younger sister, Veronica, for advice. She was a student at Boston University and would certainly know more than they.

Veronica thought a moment. "How about The Cupid Shoppe?"

Carrie and Sarah liked the sound of it — The Cupid Shoppe. Thus resolved, the sisters set about to make the little bridal shop come true.

They worked fast. A $5,000 loan from Merchants Bank, using Manuel's and Carolina's Dartmouth property as collateral, enabled them to rent a store at 946 So. Water Street, next to Ed's Electric, for nine dollars a week. They ordered twenty-five wedding gowns and twenty-five bridesmaids gowns, hired two dressmakers, and The Cupid Shoppe, the only bridal shop in New Bedford, opened in February, 1928.

Business boomed. Prospective brides flowed into the shop, blushing about what they had come for. Sleeveless gowns from New York and Boston turned out to be inappropriate for New Bedford's Catholic brides. In the first few weeks, the dressmakers were busy making long sleeves. Sarah decorated the crowns of the wedding veils, the most important part of the outfit, with beads, ribbons, and orange blossoms.

Left: At the Cupid Shoppe, dresses (vestidos) are $5.00 and up, veils $1.00 and up. *Right:* The window of the Cupid Shoppe is all dressed up for a wedding and a ball. Here you will find the frock "for every vivid hour," according to the window advertisement. Courtesy of the Silveira family.

In 1928, when all brides planned to be married forever, they nevertheless engaged in ritual to bring them luck. While Carrie was busy fitting the gowns to the brides, the young women were full of chatter. Polish brides confided they would wear a bit of wedding greenery from a good luck plant they had growing at home in a jar. Portuguese brides would not allow their fiances to see their wedding gowns. If the prospective bridegroom came into the shop, he would enter with his mother and father, followed by the bride and her parents. It was not considered proper for the engaged pair to walk together until after their marriage. Other customers would not select their outfits on Friday, a bad luck day.

Brides had a habit, Carrie noticed, of asking for gowns four sizes smaller than they. When she tried to convince them to buy the proper size, they wouldn't. Carrie began pulling tags so new brides couldn't see what size they were wearing, an arrangement that worked for both parties.

Many brides made special appointments so the shop would be open only to them. Carrie did the fitting, then turned the sewing over to the dressmakers. Though Carrie was invited to most of the weddings, she had to say "no" and mind the shop. However, she delivered the bridal gowns personally, and people stared to see this small person carrying ruffles and puffs through the streets of New Bedford. In the bridal homes, she would be offered wine and return to The Cupid Shoppe a little nippy.

"Miss Carrie," as she was known, became the confidante of happy, vaguely troubled young women whose futures shook with insecurity. Carrie's future looked more promising than ever. She had become a formidable business woman in a town where everyone, suddenly, seemed to be getting married. She and Sarah were happier than they'd ever been. Then Sarah herself became a bride and was married in a gown from The Cupid Shoppe.

Though Sarah continued working in the shop, the greater burden of owning a business fell on Carrie. Sarah had household responsibilities now. For Carrie, the weeks settled into long demanding hours and rigid schedules. At midnight on Mondays, Carrie washed the linoleum floor so Sarah would find the shop clean the next morning. Tuesday was the day Carrie traveled to Boston to buy gowns.

Twice a year now, every spring and fall, Carrie had begun taking the bus to New York on buying trips. The unruly glamour of the textile district buzzed in her mind for weeks later. Never had life seemed larger than when she was in that city! After all, she was a farmer's daughter from obscure Westport buying wedding gowns in New York City. The idea tickled her.

There was never any time for Carrie to become a bride herself. Working 80 hours a week left her with little time for romance. Time was not the only problem, however. Though Carrie was in her mid-thirties, Manuel and Carolina still insisted on meeting and approving every date she had. As a result, Carrie had fewer and fewer dates, for she was not willing to pay the price. On occasion, when she dated a man her parents did not know about, she could hear their reprimands in her mind. In the end, she remained the obedient daughter and gave up the idea of ever marrying.

But she was her own person in the wedding business, the one in control. Here Manuel could not intrude, nor could Harry, nor could Joe Levine nor Mr. Kaplan nor could anybody. Carrie had moments of pure ecstasy. Then in April, soon after they opened, the great textile strike shook the little bridal shop to its foundations and left the owners battered.

***

The strike had been brewing in the hearts and minds of the workers for a long time now. Long hours, short pay and bad air were a way of life for the workers, who were mostly Portuguese immigrants. But the final humiliation for the 30,000 people who worked in the mills occurred the day after Easter, April 9, 1928, when the owners of the twenty-seven major mills in New Bedford and Dartmouth announced a ten-percent wage cut.

For a decade now, the workers had experienced speed-ups, stretch-outs, lay-offs and wage cuts, resulting in average earnings of $1037 a year (or half the government estimate for a minimum health and decency budget). Since the owners' profits the previous year had exceeded 2.5 million, the ten percent pay cut was the final indecency. The city smoldered with angry workers.

Three days after the announcement, the seven craft unions that made up the Textile Council voted to go on strike. They agreed to wait until Monday, however, in order to give the mill owners time to back down. When the owners stood firm, the workers made good their threat. On Monday, both union members and unorganized workers walked off the job.

Thus began the six month war between owners and workers, a war Carrie watched with trepidation from her bridal shop on So. Water St. Her sympathy was with the workers, for they were her customers — immigrants who could not speak English and had no one to speak for them. But sympathy aside, her economic fate was tied to theirs.

The wedding business fell off immediately. Prospective brides who had already purchased gowns could no longer pay their weekly bills. Those who were planning marriage postponed their weddings. At first, Carrie gave back the deposits and took the losses. But later, she could no longer meet wholesale bills and therefore could not return the deposits, an unhappy situation for Carrie.

The summer of '28 in New Bedford was like no other summer. Bakers and fishermen donated bread and the day's catch but hunger was a fact for many. People lugged food pails through the streets — soup had become everyone's main course. Steps and porches were crowded with idle workers; mobs prowled the streets. Fear and anger were everywhere.

The war heightened in mid-summer when the mill owners announced the mills would open on July 9th. Expecting the worst, Mayor Ashley called in the National Guard as well as 150 police from surrounding towns. The day of the scheduled opening, they stood guard, pistols and rifles ready, when 20,000 workers marched peacefully through the streets. Though the march took place without incident, the National Guard stayed on and became a formidable presence, sometimes bringing more fear than it warded off. At night, Carrie could hear the sound of hoofbeats clopping up and down the streets, coming and going, coming and going. The sound of violence in those hoofbeats took over the night and left Carrie fearing what would come next.

In the first cold days of September, butchers, grocers and landlords faced bankruptcy from extending credit over the past six months. The strike ended abruptly when the Textile Council agreed to a five percent pay cut. Immediately, the mills began moving south, an exodus that coincided with the beginning of the Great Depression. But for the workers in New Bedford, the Depression was a continuation of what they had already endured.

The wedding business never recovered from the wounds inflicted by the strike and the retreat of the textile mills. Nevertheless, Carrie stayed in business for ten years. During these years, she watched the vibrance of the South End flicker and dim. Against a wall of mute mills, where doors were closed and machinery stopped, businesses came and went quickly. Here and there,

shops seemed boarded up permanently, as if no one could imagine doing business there. Through the years of the Depression, Carrie held on in the wedding business but, in the end, working 90 hours a week was too high a price for staying open. It was time to get out.

These were not good times at home either. Manuel was ill and would never again get out of bed. The family pulled together. Over the years, Carrie had paid off all but $500 of her original $5,000 loan. Now she secured a new loan that cleared the old debt and enabled her parents to catch up on two years of back taxes and make some necessary house repairs. Veronica, who had graduated from Boston University, was now teaching in Westport. She began sending money home just as Carrie and Sarah had aided her when she was a student.

Carrie's bridal shop came in on the eve of the textile strike. It went out in the great hurricane of '38.

Far left: The bread line at the Washington Club on South First Street during the 1928 strike extended from the club house to Brock Avenue each Tuesday, Thursday and Saturday. The Club would give out 2,000 to 2,500 loaves of bread and 250 gallons of soup to the 3,000 children in line on this day. From the Ashley scrapbooks at the New Bedford Free Public Library. *Left:* Carrie performs alterations and fittings on a would-be bride at her South Water Street shop. Courtesy of the Silveira family.

155

The 1938 Hurricane moved ten rooms of the Silveira house into the house's basement, creating a watery grave for furniture and belongings. The house was rebuilt into a single-story cottage. Illustration by Clement E. Daley

On the wet gray afternoon of September 21, 1938, Carrie sat hunched over copies of old Civil Service exams in the New Bedford Free Public Library. The bridal shop, closed and boarded, loomed in her mind like an ill-fated wedding. Now 45 and starting over, she did not know whether to enter her name on a Civil Service list or go back into the retail world as a saleswoman.

Though she was comfortably indoors, walled in by a thousand books, her concentration was disturbed by the look and feel of the day. There was a strangeness out there that she could not define; she felt it as she walked through the hot thin air along Pleasant Street, the weight of a leaden sky pressing down on her.

New England weather always announces its intentions clearly but this day seemed to be hanging there uncertainly. At the center was an eerie quiet, a stillness, made all the more ominous by the dark wet sky hanging low over the city, as if waiting to make a decision.

As Carrie glanced uneasily toward the window, a gray drizzle fell from the darkening sky. Then she heard an eerie whine, a crying in the wind. The strange wind grew so strong, so fast, it

was out of control before anyone knew what was happening. It slammed into the city and blew the region into submission.

The hurricane of '38 was not supposed to hit New Bedford. Right up to the moment it hit the city, the forecasters promised it wouldn't. But unknown to Carrie and the forecasters, communications were already wiped out along the path of the hurricane so there were no warnings of the intensity of the storm about to conquer them. The hurricane had swept northward from Cape Hatteras, North Carolina, racing 600 miles in 12 hours, slamming into the New Jersey shore, Long Island, Connecticut, Rhode Island and now bearing down on the coast of Massachusetts, on New Bedford, and sending Carrie, who sat

in the library, to the window to see what it was all about.

She could not believe what she saw. At that moment, the big chimney of the Standard-Times building crumbled and fell to the pavement below. "My God, My God," she cried, thinking only that she had to get home. As she ran from the library into the streets, two large windows from the nearby cooperative bank crashed to the sidewalk. She picked her way through pieces of glass as she ran to the Padanaram bus stop.

The city had come to an abrupt halt and the last bus had made its run. Carrie began running wildly along Pleasant and up Union Streets. The wind, now blasting at 80 m.p.h., pushed and pulled her around as if she

were a rag doll. She stumbled, fell, got up, went on. The world had gone mad! The weather was relentless, as if the gods had decided to cast revenge on her homeland — this lost, wet corner of Massachusetts, this enchanted place that tourists bypassed on their way to Cape Cod — and punishment would be swift and horrible. It was unreal, it was not happening and, at the same time, she could see it happening.

In the harbor, the tides rose ominously. Boats split and sank or were tossed upon the beaches. Carrie could hear the angry ocean at the edges of her life and feared it would roll up Union Street and sweep her out to sea. She tried to run faster. Just then, a car making its way through the rising water pulled up beside her. "Get in," cried Mr. Goldrick, a neighbor.

Midway along Dartmouth Street, the car sputtered and stopped. They abandoned it and parted. Carrie picked her way along Dartmouth Street where great elm trees fell like toothpicks and lay in her path. She crawled over the trees, as if this were the natural order of things, and kept going. All around her, chimneys had toppled, porches crumbled, windows were broken, trees leveled, poles were down, wires tangled, lights were out, cars abandoned, and she moved through this shattered world as a stranger seeing the place for the first time.

What would she find at home? How were her mother and sister bearing up? In her mind's eye, she saw her house floating down the Apponagansett River with them in it. No! It couldn't happen. As Carrie neared the Dartmouth Town Hall, she saw a crowd gathered. A familiar voice called out to her, "Carrie, you can't get home. They sent a boat out to get your mother and sister." Yes, it was happening.

Moments later, Carrie saw her sister Frances paddling down the street in a row boat. A stunned old woman sat in the back of the boat, her face racked with shock and grief. Carolina had resisted leaving until the last moment.

In the eye of the hurricane, she had run around straightening up the house. After clearing the kitchen sink, she smoothed the bedspreads, folded the towels, rearranged a bureau drawer and insisted she wasn't going anywhere. Finally, they pulled her from her home — the final indignity — and sent her out into a world of strangers. Meanwhile, the crowd at Town Hall drifted, floated, sank into the dank basement of the structure and waited for calm. There were no lights.

That night, the evacuees were dispersed to nearby homes and a reluctant Yankee household was asked to take in Carrie, Carolina and Frances. Though the house was roomy with many bedrooms, they were shunted to a single room with one bed. No supper was offered. Carolina, weak and ailing, lay on the bed and prayed in Portuguese while Carrie and Frances spent a sleepless night on the floor. The house, except for the loss of electricity, was untouched by the hurricane. Without lights, they could not find the bathroom and the night seemed to go on forever. Little did they know their ordeal was just beginning. For the next nine months, they would live in temporary housing while their once-large house was fashioned into a cottage.

Had Carolina seen the devastation at home, her heart would have broken. Carrie and Frances kept her from the truth, never allowed her to know that the house had crumbled like a doll house. Ten rooms had toppled into the flooded basement. Had Carolina stayed behind, she would have fallen with the stuffed couches, the maple dining table, the sewing machine and drowned as they had, lying in a watery grave on the ocean floor of their basement.

Their yard was full of boats. The yachts in Padanaram Harbor had gone wild, wind and tides breaking them from their moorings and sending them into streets and yards. The owners built boat frames and asked if they could leave them there until spring. The following summer the Silveira's moved into their new home, carved from the upper story of their old house and moved to a new location on Elm Street. The cost was $1800. Forever after, they referred to the new house as their "Cape Cod cottage."

Carrie went briefly back into the retail business. Then the war that changed the world also changed Carrie's life.

***

New Bedford and its large Portuguese population heard the news from circulars which mysteriously inundated the city. Notices appeared in church pews, behind apples in the grocery stores, and in the help-wanted section of the newspapers. Patriotic Portuguese-American citizens were needed to work in the censorship department in New York City. Carrie read the notices indifferently, for they had little to do with her. And yet . . .

Over the years, Carrie had kept up her Portuguese, always remembering Manuel's words: "Never be ashamed of your background, Carrie." Carrie was not ashamed, she was proud, and she buried herself in Portuguese magazines and newspapers while riding to and from work on city buses for over 20 years. Still, the idea of being a translator was too exotic, too out of the ordinary to apply to her. And yet . . .

On an ordinary day in the fall of '42, a day that promised nothing in particular, Carrie had the morning off from her job as a saleswoman at Silverstein's. She was dashing from the telephone office to the electric company, frantically paying bills, when on a whim, she flew into the Duff building in New Bedford where testers were giving oral exams in reading.

Carrie easily read the sample letter for the tester.

"OK, let's go get fingerprinted and photographed," the tester said, rising and nearly knocking Carrie to the floor. "You have to be in New York by Monday. Report to the Morgan Annex on 34th Street." Carrie was stunned. "But I don't know what to tell my boss," was all she could say.

"We'll send over an FBI man to explain," said the tester. "If your boss is patriotic," he'll let you go. He dismissed Carrie abruptly and turned to the next person in line.

Shaken to the core, Carrie stumbled back to work, determined not to reveal, for at least a few minutes, what she had done. Already it was too late. She could see by the look on Mr. Silverstein's face that he was not pleased by the swiftness of events. The FBI had already been in the store checking on her character. How could she have done this? She burst into tears at the mess she had made of her life. Mr. Silverstein reluctantly agreed to give her her vacation money that afternoon and she was free to go.

On Sunday, Carrie packed and unpacked. She sat and paced; she said goodbye, then said, no, she wasn't leaving. Finally she boarded a bus in Providence and sped off to New York City.

For all her uncertainty, she knew exactly where to go. In the Catholic Digest, she had read that a sister of the Polish Immaculate Conception Church had bought a building on 44th Street and used it as a residence for women. She made her way to this place, St. Joseph's Home in Hell's kitchen, near the piers.

Feeling like an uninvited guest, Carrie stood awkwardly on the steps of St. Joseph's with her suitcases and rang the bell. Sister Celine greeted her with smiles and said she was welcome. A room was waiting for her and breakfast would be served at seven o'clock. It seemed an auspicious beginning for Carrie.

From the moment she arrived in New York, something unusual and wonderful began happening to Carrie. Here in 1942, with the world at war around her, Carrie found peace. She had left behind the restrictions of parents, church and town; she was her own person for the first time in her life. Here in New York, there was no one to tell her to be home early or caution her about strangers. Above all, there was no one to disapprove of her. She began listening to herself, to the voice that was trying to make itself heard. The city opened itself up to her like a book she had been meaning to read. She would read it all, page by

page, word by word, until she finally had to put it down in exhaustion.

Her days at the censorship bureau began at a crowded, noisy table piled high with letters — personal letters, business letters, postcards, letters scrawled on torn sheets. The letters embarrassed her. Reading other people's personal mail was not her idea of a noble occupation. Many letters were to and from New Bedford, and she often found herself reading the personal mail of people she knew. For this, she received $67 a week, the most she had ever earned.

In her two years on the job, Carrie never found a spy. But next to her, an American teacher of the Portuguese language, found a spy in every letter. Carrie also worked alongside many Brazilians who inspected letters from Portugal, then forwarded them back to Brazil.

The mail revealed to Carrie what she had often sensed but never experienced firsthand — America's prejudice against dark skin. When Brazilian businessmen came to the United States as a group, she learned that those with darker skins were sent to Virginia and those with lighter skins were allowed to remain in Washington. The problem was brought closer to home when her brother, in a Navy uniform, was turned out of a Washington hotel because his skin was declared too dark.

Carrie was profoundly shaken by the incident. How could such a thing happen? It stayed with her the next day and the next. She began carrying around the burden of it like a great weight in the soul. For her brother,

the rejection was a single event, troubling enough by itself. But how must it be for people of color who experienced rejection as a way of life? As time went on, the incident touched her ever more personally. Her brother's rejection was everyone's rejection. It was the rejection of herself.

Her appreciation of city life was not dampened by her inner confusion. New York was an event to which she was personally invited and every night was an invitation out. She went to lectures at Carnegie Hall, plays on Broadway, radio shows on 52nd and 50th Streets. She joined the Portuguese Club and every Saturday

Carrie's days at the censorship bureau in New York during World War II began at a crowded, noisy desk piled high with letters written in Portuguese. Her job was to translate the letters into English. Courtesy of the Silveira family.

night ate dinner there with a growing list of new friends. She even discovered that New Yorkers were small town people who knew only their own part of town. And here in New York, for the first time in her life, Carrrie discovered politics. She was 49.

This new direction was no accident. It stemmed directly from her new awareness of discrimination. Though Carrie had always been fiercely patriotic, her brother's experience in a Washington hotel changed her focus. It left her standing in a place she had never been before: outside of American society waiting to get back in. She began to feel an affinity for that raggedy band of others who shared the outside with her. In time, her new awareness would become a complete change in consciousness. For now, it led her to an interracial house in Harlem called Friendship House.

Friendship House was run by an unlikely person, a Russian baroness. Prior to the Russian Revolution, Baroness DeHueck lived on a palatial estate maintained by 700 servants and agricultural laborers. Deprived of her wealth by the revolution, the Baroness did the unexpected: She went to New York and became a revolutionary, American style.

Here at Friendship House, Carrie met Miss Grant, an elderly blind black woman who introduced Carrie to politics. Miss Grant lived on 96th Street where Carrie went once a week to read to her. In turn, Miss Grant began to teach Carrie a new way of seeing.

The road from Friendship House and the vision of Miss Grant led Carrie to

On the back side of a June, 1947 snapshot taken on the roof of St. Joseph's Home on West 44th Street, where Carrie lived, a scribbled note reads: ". . . was I ever big? Shame on me." With Carrie (left) is Miss Mullin and Miss Reed. Courtesy of the Silveira family.

the Xavier Labor School on 16th Street. Here, a new Carrie began to grow out of the old one, a participant, not just an observer. Oh, she had always thought she was there in the center of things, but was she? A daughter of immigrant parents, she had heard the great whaling tales from her father and followed the sweet-sad journey of her mother from Fayal to America. From the sidelines, she had watched New Bedford industrialize, had seen the mills open, had witnessed the strike of '28. She had experienced being an employee and an employer, but had she made a difference? She thought not. She had watched the world from a safe distance, watched and waited to see how things would

turn out. In a Washington hotel, things had not turned out very well.

Carrie took the plunge into a new life. Three nights a week she began attending classes on labor ethics, taught by two activist priests, Father Philip Carey and Father John Corridan. She watched these involved priests take their religion outside of their churches and into the streets and workplaces of the poor. She watched them act on their beliefs.

She also watched her classmates, the ones who sat next to her in the labor ethics course, do likewise. Outside of the classroom, they were movers, marching with the telephone girls to

form a union, tying up the stock market telephones. They took a stand with Father Corridan on the waterfront in support of the longshoremen. They believed people should take charge of their own lives and, if enough people worked together, change would come.

Carrie had never thought about things this way. As an employee and an employer, she had always struggled alone. Though she had seen the textile strikers joining together in common cause, their struggle was not her struggle. Or was it? Here were these good Catholic priests who believed that people would win the ultimate struggle if they worked together to win the smaller ones. "Sin is by omission as well as commission," Father Carey told her. "Speak up. If you see injustice, speak up." His words shot through her like electricity. She did not know what to do with so much knowledge.

***

The news from home was both shocking and expected. Carrie had been in New York for two years when she received word that Carolina had suffered a stroke and was dying. She rushed back to New Bedford and stayed by her bedside for two weeks. Carolina died shortly after. The year was 1944.

After the funeral, on the bus to New York, Carrie was overcome with images of Carolina. She had been a fiercely loyal mother, overprotective, yes, but always on Carrie's side, wanting the best for her. All the tension and irresolution of the relationship pressed in on her. Meanwhile, Carrie had other decisions to make, too. The job at the censorship bureau would be coming to an end soon. Where should she make her life? Was she a New Yorker at heart? Could she go home again?

For the moment, Carrie's involvement in so many activities weighted the scales in favor of staying in New York. She was still attending classes in labor ethics, a commitment that would last for five years. She was still involved in Friendship House and the Portuguese Club. At this time, she moved to a room on 44th Street and hoped she could find work in her old occupation, the retail trade.

A sketch made by one of Carrie's friends and given to her, focuses on the section of New York, 63 Vesey Street, where Carrie worked in the censorship bureau. Courtesy of the Silveira family.

She was quickly hired at Arnold Constable on 41st Street. Though she preferred sales, she won their hearts when they discovered she'd had a decade of experience as a fitter. Here she became the supervisor of five tailors and 25 dressmakers. The tailors feared Carrie because she was so exact and they sometimes gave her a needle and thread to finish off the work herself. Her best known customer was Mrs. Roosevelt; Carrie often got samples from the dresses she ordered.

This was a time of change for the retail stores and not the best time for Carrie to return to sales. The larger department stores were beginning to build in the suburbs. Though she now earned $65 a week, there could be no hope of raises for the sales people. On such a salary, Carrie would always have to live in a room. Returning to New Bedford meant she could live in a house. Her sisters, Mary and Frances, who were living in their parent's house on Elm Street in Dartmouth, invited Carrie to live with them. Carrie stayed in New York, working at Arnold Constable's for five more years, then returned to the New Bedford area in 1952 to live with her sisters in their "Cape Cod cottage."

Carrie resumed her work in downtown New Bedford as a saleswoman at Silverstein's. Much of the work was heavy work, lifting and hauling stock from one floor to another. Though the working hours were finally set and regulated, she was back to earning $35 a week and working six days a week.

After 3½ years at Silverstein's, feeling the need to earn more money, she moved to a new job at Hutchinson's on Pleasant Street where she sold toys, books, and supplies. The store was divided into departments and sales people were not allowed to wait on people in other departments. She never liked the new arrangement but otherwise things were going well for Carrie. From a starting wage of $40, in 5½ years she worked her way up to $60. Everything changed, however, when Mr. Hutchinson's son took over the business and hired younger people. Many older people were laid off.

At 68, Carrie, the exemplary saleswoman with 30 years of experience in the retail business and ten years experience running her own business lost her job. She was stunned. She began making the rounds of every retail store in New Bedford. As she was turned down, store by store, she remembered how she felt so long ago when she rode in on the milk wagon with Manuel. But this time there was a difference.

Potential employers looked her over closely and shook their heads. No one asked, as they did when she was 17, "Do you have any experience, Miss Silveira?" Obviously, she had too much experience. She was out-of-date, too old in their eyes, to be a saleswoman. Oh, the irony of it. She had too much experience! What was a person with all that experience supposed to do for the rest of her life?

In the end, there was only one way to live, job or no job. "Always be dressed and ready to go," said Carrie. So Carrie was "dressed and gone" in the many years still ahead. She became "the babysitter" of Padanaram Village. She was a passionate advocate of jobs for senior citizens and covered their activities in the Dartmouth *Chronicle* and the *Standard-Times* of New Bedford. She was a charter member of St. Mary's Guild and a leader in church activities. She immersed herself in courses at the "Institute of Health and Long Life" at Southeastern Massachusetts University. She traveled to Boston with "Fair Share" and lobbied for lower utility rates for consumers. She joined the NAACP and the Nuclear Freeze groups.

She kept up her reading in the "Great Books" club and was a frequent caller on radio station WBSM's "Open Line" talk show, outspoken in her opinions on behalf of the sick, the old, the poor, the forgotten and people of color. She became a Dartmouth

dispatcher of food and transportation for shut-ins and, for many years, she and Frances took their turns at home, nursing their sister Mary through a long illness. Carrie never lost the faith, never lost her vision of people acting together to make change.

***

Carrie died in January '87 at the age of 93. According to her obituary, in the *Standard-Times* of New Bedford, Carrie was the daughter of Manuel and Carolina Silveira. No mention was made of that black night in Magdalena Harbor when Manuel became a stowaway on a North American whaling ship, of his struggle to acquire land and make it grow, or of his early morning trips by horse wagon from his dairy farm in Westport to New Bedford's South End where he sold milk to the textile workers.

There was no mention that this Portuguese immigrant picked up old newspapers from city gutters in order to teach his children to read English, no mention of his courtship of Carolina and of her lifelong struggle of being a stranger in a strange land.

As for Carrie, her years "behind the counter" on So. Water Street were forgotten. No mention of her first job at Harry's was made or of the smell of kale soup wafting into Kaplan's from the barber shop next door. There was no celebration of her bridal shop —

The Cupid Shoppe — and no regret for the day her house drowned in the '38 hurricane. Her New York years were not described, nor was her return to New Bedford to a larger life.

In her obituary, Carrie's life was described in one sentence: She was a former retail worker in New Bedford.

***

Carrie, at around 90 years old, stands in front of her home on Elm Street in South Dartmouth. Her sister, Mrs. Veronica Russell said, "She seemed to enjoy every little detail of life." Photograph by Candida Martin, circa 1980, courtesy of the Silveira family.

On the Fall River Line

interview with Ray Connors

by Jane Strillchuk

Ray Conners was one of the head pursers on the Fall River Line for 14 years. After graduating from B.M.C. Durfee High School, Mr. Conners' brother offered him a job on the Commonwealth. Mr. Conners reminisced about his adventures on the Fall River Line with us.

The Line was started in 1847 by the New Haven Railroad Company. It consisted of several ships like the Commonwealth, the Priscilla, and the Plymouth. "No one will ever replace that Line —nowhere, no how!" states Mr. Conners.

Silverware, furnitures, lifesavers, and models of the ships of the Fall River Line are on display at the Marine Museum in Fall River. We are more than grateful to John Gossen, Curator of the Marine Museum, for allowing us to have access to the museum. And to Ray Conners, we thank you for giving us your time and sharing with us the part of your life that you spent on the Line.

The following is an edited transcription of the interview with Mr. Conners.

Far left: Steamer *Commonwealth,* New York bound, around 1930. *Center:* Ray Connors and his mates share some cheer aboard the *Commonwealth.* Left to right, front row: unknown; Raymond Connors, Assistant Purser; Captain William McDonald; Dan Shay, Steward. Back row: Saloon Deck Watchman; Front Clerk; Dining Room Cashier; Front Clerk; former Fall River Fire Chief MacDonald, bartender; unknown. *Below:* Cover of Fall River Line promotional magazine. Photographs courtesy of the Marine Museum of Fall River.

"All's Aboard that's goin' Aboard, All's Ashore that's goin' Ashore!" There was always a great crowd to see the boats off to say goodbye. It was a good life.

The passengers' social class was from the highest to the lowest; we had some of the finest society people travel on those boats. All the aristocrats from Newport, Rhode Island would use those boats from New York to Newport. We even had the Vanderbilts

There were also some working-class people traveling on the Line. The Fall River Line was very accommodating to businessmen because it was a place where one could travel and yet get a good night's sleep. Businessmen from Boston would travel on the Sunday night trip, and would get to New York on Monday morning. They would stay in New York for the week and return on the Friday night boat. By Saturday, they would be back in Fall River, and by noon-time, they would be back home in Boston.

Every Friday night, a stockbroker named Sasselberg would come on the boat and would give me a ten dollar tip. I would make forty-two dollars a week, but with this guy's generosity, it would be fifty-two dollars. We got friendly and he would invite me to his big house in Edgartown on the end of Martha's Vineyard. Unfortunately, I never went. When he came on board he would always have a stack of new ten dollar bills about two inches thick.

One night he said he had a big surprise for me. He told me to meet him in his ten dollar stateroom on the boat. "A surprise," I thought. "What could he possibly give me?' 'An armful of diamonds?' 'Eighteen wrist watches?' 'What?' " I went to his room that night to receive my "big surprise."

Main Lounge, Steamer *Commonwealth*. Courtesy of the Fall River Historical Society.

In his bed was a new born baby. It was his two week old son. The big surprise was to show me his baby. He was so happy about this big surprise — he had to let everybody know. Of course, I had to laugh.

The passengers' prices would vary depending on their accommodations. The prices were $2.25, $3.00, $7.50, and $10.50. It was only $4.44 from Fall River to New York, and for 72 cents you could have taken a beautiful hour and a half ride to Newport from Fall River. The $2.25 and $3.00 bedrooms were small, but they were nice, not like a cheap hotel. The porters kept the rooms very clean. Only the ten dollar bedrooms had a shower and a big bed and couch. The passengers traveling in the less expensive rooms would have to share a community bathroom, but it was a luxurious bathroom. Nothing was cheap on the Fall River Line.

The Route of the Fall River Line was from Fall River to Newport, and then New York. We had boats that would go from Providence to New York and that was called the Providence Line. In the summer there would be boats running from New Bedford to New York. That trip would take care of all the people from Cape Cod and the Islands. One summer I requested a transfer to the New Bedford Line. What a summer! It was a terrific summer! We'd go down to Oak Bluff's and Nantucket when we had the time.

Coming out of our pier in the Hudson River, New York during the fall and winter was the most beautiful sight you could ever see. All the lights were shining from the towers and the big tall buildings as we were coming

out. The tug boats around us would light up like fire bugs at night. The big battleships up on the docks of the Navy yard looked like mountains as we turned into the East River. You could also see the Battery — a famous park on the edge of New York where they would film movies. It was the most beautiful sight you would ever wish to see in this country, I think.

It would take twelve hours from New York to Newport. The boat would leave New York at five o'clock p.m. and would only arrive in Newport at quarter to five in the morning. It was a good ride — a quiet one.

Every morning when we docked in Fall River there would be three limousines waiting on the pier. They were owned by a fellow named Clancy. They were not taxis; they were big Buick limousines. It would cost 50 cents to go from the boat to uptown; three dollars to go to Newport; and eight dollars to go to Boston from Fall River, if you missed your train. Those limousines were always polished; they were beautiful!

Once in a while there would be a suicide. Think they would just jump overboard? No! There were funny suicides! I remember coming out of Long Island one night and seeing a girl sitting on the edge of the railing of a lifeboat. She was going to jump into Long Island Sound and drown herself. I went over to her and tried to talk her out of it. I slid over the railing and sat in the life boat right next to her.

"Don't come near me! Don't come near me," she said. I lost about eight pounds from sweating. After a while, I had enough nerve and got my arms around her. I got her back into the lifeboat and onto the deck.

I carried her down to the stateroom, and there was her chaperon with two other girls who were drunk. By this time I was ready to die myself. I went over to the chaperon and hit her in the face — I had to wake her up.

"What's the matter, what's the matter!" "This girl tried to drown herself," I said. "So let her drown herself. She tried to jump out a window in the hotel."

The next morning when we got to Fall River, the three girls and the chaperon were waiting for me with the captain. They had told him about my saving the girl's life and I had to go to Boston for a suitable reward.

We got on the train in Fall River and went to Boston. A nice car met us in Boston, and drove us to Somerville. The girl that tried to commit suicide had a beautiful home. She called up her husband and said, "Charlie, I got despondent last night and you know why. An officer from the Fall River Line saved my life. Now I want you to get him something to remember us by. We'll be here waiting for you."

Everything was rosy then — they were all kissing me. I was all set! Then suddenly, everything changed. She had gone upstairs to her bedroom and within seconds came running back down. She got on the telephone to get hold of Charlie.

"Charlie, you son of a bitch, you had that same woman in our room last night. Don't you come near this house

Steamer *Commonwealth* rounding the Battery, New York City, 1924. Courtesy of the Marine Museum of Fall River.

because we're gonna have a party and we don't want to be disturbed!"

The other two girls kept staring at me. One of them came over and told me that we were going to have a party. All I could think of was how the hell I was going to get myself out of this one. So I talked with them for a while, I told them of my friends who worked in a broker's office in downtown Somerville. I tried to

convince the girls that these guys would help our party — we would have enough partners to dance. One of the girls said, "I'll go with you downtown."

"You can't, these guys are married. They wouldn't want — uh — girls looking for them."

I finally got out of the house and grabbed the first cab I could find to

South Station in Boston. I went home on a train. When I walked on the quarter deck of the boat, the captain asked me, "Hey, how'd ya make out, Ray? What'd ya get?"

"What did I get? I wasted the whole day and two dollars and twenty cents for cab fare from Somerville to Boston!"

One night out of New York, the head waiter said to me, "Purser, see that lady at the table over there? I guess she hasn't eaten here before, because after we served the finger bowls and the after dinner mints, she took the mints and put them in the finger bowl and stirred it up and drank it!" She didn't know what it was.

We had famous chefs from down South, all of them were black; these chefs were real southern gentlemen. We had a good crew; everyone seemed to get along very well. I never remember a fight or any disorder among the staff.

There was a big mystery one time on the Fall River Line. It all turned out to be a phony suicide. This guy left his door locked; his bed unslept in, and his clothes hanging on the hooks. On the upper bunk in his room, he left three envelopes: one addressed to his wife, another to his boss, and one to "To whom it may concern." In front of each one of them he left a half dollar.

The porter sent for me; and I read the note "To whom it may concern." I opened it and read:

Sorry, I have to do this. Things haven't been going right. I haven't been feeling well, and I decided to end it all.

After reporting the note, people kept on asking me, "Are you sure that man was on your boat?" All I know was that he was a passenger on my boat that night. The police and everybody kept on looking for the guy for two months and then stopped bothering us. He just walked on the boat and left the letters, his clothes, and locked the door to his room. He left the boat without telling anyone while we were docked in the harbor. The police found the suicidal guy a year later in Chicago. He just wanted his wife to collect on the insurance.

We had some wonderful parties — society parties. Universities would hire the boats to go down to Harvard from New York, or Harvard would hire the boat from Fall River to go to New York to play Princeton. You could hire the boats to go to certain places, but you had to pay for all the expenses. You would have to pay for a great deal of stuff, but it was fun.

We ran little horse race games on the deck. The horse race game consisted of a long platform with six lines on it with horses about as big as a single hand. A beautiful girl would toss the dice around and would usually get two or three sixes. Then you'd move the horses on the platform. Everybody would bet on it. That was a good game!

Far left: Curious passengers come out on deck to observe the *Commonwealth* under tow. Courtesy of the Marine Museum of Fall River. *Center:* Unidentified chef aboard the *Commonwealth*. Courtesy of the Fall River Historical Society. *Below:* Upperdeck corridor on the *Commonwealth*. Courtesy of the Fall River Historical Society.

There were a lot of nice wedding parties. We would raise hell! Sometimes we would have one of the seamen scoop up a live fish and fill the honeymooners' bathtub up with water and put the fish to swim in there. When the newlyweds wanted to take a nice bath before anything happened, there would be a big fish floating up and down in their bathtub. They would come screaming to me.

"A fish," I would say, "How the hell could a big fish climb into your bathtub?"

If the honeymooners had a small room with no bathroom, we would take the fire hose and get the water to hit their porthole. The water coming from a fire hose hitting their windows would give the effect that there was a storm outside. The poor newlyweds would think the boat was sinking, and sinking!

Remember that fella named Sasselberg? Well, when the stock market crashed in 1929, he lost his money and his house in Edgartown. But somehow or another he retained

Left and above: Dancing and romancing aboard the *Commonwealth. Right center:* A neighbor's view of the *Commonwealth* berthed at Fall River Line Pier. Taken by Casey Roberts in December 1933. *Far right:* Dockside in Fall River. Photographs courtesy of the Marine Museum of Fall River.

the garage (it wasn't part of the deal on the sale of the house). So for one summer, I missed him.

The next summer he started coming on the boat. He would have a little lunch bag with him with a sandwich in it. Instead of having a ten dollar room, he would have a two dollar and a quarter room. I would invite him to dinner because he had been so good to me. I was trying to repay him for all the nice things he had done. The funny thing was that a couple of years later he made a comeback and built another house in Edgartown.

During the depression fellas would come down to the pier in Fall River that I knew and went to high school with. They would say, "Ray, I haven't been able to get a job. If I could only get to New York; I know I can get a job." I'd look around to see if anybody was looking, then I would say, "Get in there. I'll get you a place to sleep." We did have a hole; they call it a hole but it was a bunkroom. It was a place where you could sleep for free. "Go ahead have a sleep!" The only thing was that after about ten or twelve days, down they'd be to see me in New York at the boat. "Didn't get the job,

if I could only get home, my mother's cooking, I miss my mother's cooking." "Get in there." That happened alot.

Another interesting incident happened one time from New York to Long Island. "Here's our father's ashes. He always wanted his ashes spread across the Long Island Sound. Would you do that for us?" One lady asked the captain. Naturally, our captain agreed. The ashes were in a small box sealed with lead.

I mentioned that we should put on a little ceremony for this guy's ashes. There was no prayer books on the boat, so we had to use a black notebook. After dinner we held the ceremony.

We had the hardest job just to open the box because it was sealed with lead. We finally got it open and we started putting a nice act on for the passengers. The captain got up on the deck and had the black notebook in his hands as though he was a monsignor. I told the captain when I gave him the signal to start praying for the ashes. I started throwing the ashes in the Sound. Then suddenly, the wind changed and all the ashes went flying in my face, my hair, and my clothes. A

month later, I could still feel and smell the ashes on me. The ashes stuck in my skin and only vasoline could get it out. I thought, the guy's toe is over here, the legs over there. I could feel it for a whole month.

My assistant purser was named Gerald, a German name. When World War II started, the bugger disappeared. I used to hear from him from time to time and in the back of my mind I thought he was a German

Far left: Standing by the controls, looking toward port side, are Mr. MacQueen and Mr. Sullivan (background). Taken aboard the *Commonwealth* in June 1935. Courtesy of the Fall River Historical Society. *Above:* In the pilot house of the *Commonwealth* are Messrs. Brayley, Simmoni and Rectur. Courtesy of the Marine Museum of Fall River. *Right:* View from the Mount Hope Bridge bids the *Commonwealth* goodbye as she leaves Fall River for the last time, under tow, in 1937. Courtesy of the Marine Museum of Fall River.

spy. He always had a camera with him, no matter where we went. He was always taking pictures: Navy yards, Newport — everywhere. In the back of my mind, I think that the guy was a spy. Nice guy but he always had that camera!

The captains in the Fall River Line were real marines. One or two of them lived in Fall River and the rest stayed on the boat as deck hands. To be a captain you had to be quartermaster, then bow watchman, and second and first pilot. These captains weren't trusted with these boats unless they were full-fledged licensed captains. They were all captains . . . captains of their ship.

Of all the fleets that sailed the Sound, there was never any quite like the Fall River Line. Songs were written about it:

On the old Fall River Line;
On the old Fall River Line;
I fell for Suzie's line of talk;
And Suzie fell for mine.
Then we fell in with a parson;
and he tied us, tied us fine.
Oh, I wish,
Oh, I wish, Oh Lord, I fell
overboard;
On the old Fall River Line!

They would play that song at all the Durfee basketball games.

Most of the boats were destroyed by fires or scrapped for metal. One of the boats was used in Europe as a hospital ship; another one went to California for Government use. It was a shame to see the boats go. We would carry a freight of cloths, cotton, and fish from Fall River, New Bedford, and other places. We'd load up in Fall River then we would go to Newport. Twice a week we would take about 700 to 800 barrels of fish from Newport to other places like New York. We would transport it, balance it, and do everything. That was a lot of work and we would get a dollar and ten cents for each barrel.

Then the trucks started taking over, and taking the freight directly from the mills and ports instead of the boats. Around 1932 the Fall River Line started its downfall because the passengers alone weren't enough money to keep the boats going. We lost most of our freights to progress: trucks, airplanes, etc. As a dining room in a hotel doesn't make money without liquor, the Fall River Line didn't make money without the freights. So when the freights went, so did the Line.

The Fall River Line was owned by the New Haven Railroad Company. When the freights started going, some organizers tried to put together a union — the C.I.O. The union was an excuse to the company to say, "we're losing money and we don't need any unions or anything!" In 1937 the Fall River Line closed. What a disappointment that was.

Everrett Coggeshall

by David W. Allen

I always smoked cigars since I was fourteen. I used to buy a thousand at a time. My father and I smoked them. The man that raised the tobacco and made the cigars came right here. He'd take my order for twenty boxes and ship them to me. Maybe there'd be four of five extra boxes for a bonus. And when the cigars were gone, he'd be back for another order.

Ninety-seven years. I don't know — I've had a different life from most of the boys. I wasn't brought up with a silver spoon in my mouth. I worked from the time I was big enough to do anything at all to the present time. Now the boys go to school until they're thirty years old. I worked for fifty cents a day, nine hours a day. Riding horse, digging potatoes, driving teams, cutting ice, any goddamn kind of a job. When I was twenty-five years old I could run a farm with a hundred acres.

Of course there was plenty of help. My father would say, "Sonny, hitch up the horse and go over to Little Compton and see Bill. Tell him you want fifteen men tomorrow morning, seven o'clock." I'd hitch up the horse and go over there after dinner. Old Bill had five sons, all big enough to work. There'd be men from Sakonnet Point too. None of them had any horses. They had to walk ten miles. They'd be over here at seven in the morning and work until five at night and walk home. Then they'd have to be here the next morning — all for a dollar a day.

I worked for several years before I quit school, riding horse. I cultivated for other farmers on horseback with no saddle. Goddamn old razor-backed horses would cut you in half. I'd get on the horse in the morning and stay on him until noontime when I could get off and eat my dinner. Then I'd be put back on the horse and cultivate the rest of the day. I worked days and weeks for fifty cents a day, nine hours.

When I was eleven years old I was all through school. There was no high school in Westport. I got as far as I could go. My last term in school there were twenty-five kids and I was in a class by myself. The teacher brought me high school papers and things —

# of Westport

contemporary photographs by David W. Allen
old photographs courtesy of the Westport Public Library
and Everrett Coggeshall

square root and cube root. But I was all alone and I wasn't getting anywhere, so I quit it and went to work.

Nobody went to school when they were older. The boys around here on what farms there were would only go the winter term. The girls would go, but the boys had to stay home and work on the farms. These kids going to school today, they don't know anything. When I was going to school I was hiring ten to fifteen men a day to work on different things for my father — keeping the time, taking bills over to the town hall because my father was appointed Road Surveyor for the town.

They had a system in the town on work. You had to itemize your own personal property you used for a job. You got so much for a pair of horses, for the wagon, for the plow. So much for a shovel or a pick ax. Instead of charging up four dollars for eight hours work, you'd have to write all those goddamn things in every day you used them. Then I'd carry an itemized bill over to the town hall to get the money. That was one of my jobs when

I was going to school. I was keeping books, working nine hours a day myself, and trying to learn something at the same tine.

We was the boss of everything from Adamsville down to the Harbor. All you had to do was mention my father's name. They'd give us jobs without us looking for them. We, like damn fools, would take them. People would look to my father for everything. If they wanted a cellar dug, they come to us. If they wanted a stone wall built around the land, we built it. If they wanted the ground graded, we did that. We done all the mowing, all the plowing, all the teaming and everything around here for everybody. Even the roads. We built the roads and repaired them in the spring, summer, and fall. My father didn't have any education, but he was progressive. He could do anything.

Everything that grew in God's creation, he could grow. He was mostly a farmer, a number one thorough farmer. We'd raise five or six hundred bushels of onions, potatoes, and corn. There was two

Far left: Everrett Coggeshall, photographed in 1981 in his 97th year, peers all-knowingly into author David Allen's camera. At this time, Mr. Coggeshall was serving as town constable — the oldest and longest serving policeman in the United States. He died in August 1982. *Above:* Brightman's Grist and Saw Mill of North Westport was typical of dozens of mills in the town around 1900. Among the products milled here was corn used in the making of johnnycakes. Courtesy of the Westport Public Library.

"We was the boss of everything from Adamsville down to the Harbor. All you had to do was mention my father's name. They'd give us jobs without us looking for them."

"What built up Westport Harbor was when they started building the mills in Fall River. Them mill men was rolling in money because they made money to beat hell."

crops we had to have every year, one was Rhode Island corn for Johnny Cakes, the other was a field of oats. You couldn't buy a bushel of meal or corn; you raised it. They weren't shipping it in from the west. We took the corn to the grist mills and had it ground for the cattle. There were mills everywhere there was a brook.

My mother started a vegetable business in 1891. We raised everything you could think of. There were eight houses and we kept them in vegetables all summer. Nobody bought milk, nobody sold milk, so she started that business, too. The vegetable business only lasted from the middle of June to Labor Day because the summer people left and moved back to the city. My mother was a hard working woman. She never lost a minute. When they was building up the place here, she took boarders. The most she ever had at once was twenty-one boarders. There was about six or eight of us in the family what with the hired men. My father, myself, my sister, and her, and maybe a couple of girls working for her. All this and a house full of boarders. She worked like a slave.

Before the 1938 Hurricane, Horseneck Beach was sentinneled by the stately cottages pictured in this circa 1910 photograph. An exclusive resort, gentrified by the likes of Fall River's wealthy mill owners, these houses were entirely wiped out by the unkindly hurricane. Courtesy of the Westport Public Library.

Back in 1890 there were only eight houses and they built it up to one hundred and ten houses before the 1938 Hurricane came. What built up Westport Harbor was when they started building the mills in Fall River. Them mill men was rolling in money because they made money to beat hell. They all came down here. All one family. You couldn't get in if you weren't a cousin, an uncle, or a relative of theirs. They wouldn't let a stranger come in.

A Captain Soule owned it all and he'd sell a house lot to different ones. But the Society, the Westport Harbor Improvement Society it was called,

would check whoever was buying it. See whether they wanted them or not. If they didn't want them, he couldn't sell a lot to them. If he insisted, the Society bought them up. They owned the whole goddamn business. Then when the '38 Hurricane came, it all changed. Houses was floating up from the Harbor — four miles up the river from where they were put. Great big houses fetched up against the wall up to Adamsville where the Mill Pond is. Goddamn, I tore down houses and collected stuff for weeks. The people couldn't come back but to use their lots. The town never allowed them to rebuild any of them again. It killed the Harbor.

I had a fruit and vegetable business down in the Harbor. When the '38 Hurricane came, I was doing about nine hundred dollars a week. I sold an average of two tons a day to one hundred and ten customers. Just vegetables. I also handled milk. One hundred and fifty quarts a day. Milk was five cents a quart and cream was forty. Everything they have in the bloody stores today for fruit and vegetables I sold. I was running to New Bedford, Fall River, and Providence every night. I stopped and bought in Fall River. The fruit and stuff I couldn't get there, then I go to Providence. New Bedford had a Greek who handled only fruit. He had damn

Everrett Coggeshall stands along side his trusty produce wagon from which he spent the better part of his summer life upon in the early decades of this century. The cart is a converted 1913 Model T. Ford. Courtesy of Bertha Hart.

"It got so we'd peddle from eight o'clock in the morning until eleven o'clock at night . . . I never went to bed from the middle of June to after Labor Day."

good stuff. Of course when I first started, there was nothing coming from California or Florida. They hadn't started shipping; but as time grew on, they started — carload after carload.

The wholesalers didn't buy it. The companies shipped it in and it was sold on commission. They'd load a car with fruit and put the name E.L. Fisher, Fall River on it. The railroad would deliver it to the salesman. He'd make the prices on it and sell it. Then he'd send them the money. If Fisher didn't want to take it, he turned it down. The railroad had a spur track out next to a road. They'd put a man

in it from the railroad and he'd sell it. Just to get the freight. That's all he cared about, nothing about the man who owned the stuff.

It got so we'd peddle from eight o'clock in the morning until eleven o'clock at night or somewhere after. I'd be all out of most stuff and I'd have to go back the next morning to the rest of the customers. I'd leave here some mornings one o'clock to go to the Farmer's Market in Fall River. If they didn't have all I needed, I had to wait until five o'clock for the wholesalers to open. I slept on the road from here to New Bedford, Fall River, and Providence. I'd get so

goddamn tired I couldn't stay in the road. Pull over on the side and have a sleep for an hour before I could go any further. It was all right until that sun come up over the goddamn woods. The sun would get me. I never went to bed from the middle of June to after Labor Day.

Beside the fruit and vegetable business, I was in the plumbing business and bottle gas. I had twenty-seven men working for me: twenty laborers, five plumbers, a steam fitter and myself. That isn't including the farm work, peddling, road work and things like that — only the plumbing work. We had to dig miles of trenches

four feet deep for the water pipes. Dig all the cesspools, connect them to the houses. Build the brickwork. All that stuff went with the plumbing business then.

I growed up with the plumbing business from the start. You had to sign up with a company them days. I signed a contract to learn the business with John F. Johnson of Fall River and I stayed four years, from 1897 to 1900. It was a big firm. They had a hundred men: ten plumbers and helpers, forty or fifty steam fitters and gas fitters, and tin smiths. Johnson took work all over Massachusetts and Rhode Island. There'd be men down to Hyannis,

Buzzard's Bay, and Monument Beach. I'd go down to Monument Beach in April with a couple of other men until the middle of June, doing summer houses for people. He'd board us down there so I didn't have to pay board all that time. I got five dollars a week, and when I lived in Fall River I had to pay four dollars for board.

The plumber I was working with and I were coming home one night from a job at Stevens Mill. I had only served for two and a half years. He says, "They're having a plumber's examination in a couple of weeks and I'm going to put your name in. You know more about the goddamn plumbing business than all of them put together." So he put my name in. I didn't go, he went and put it in.

They had the examination in Fall River. Every year they had it in a different place and people would come from all over Massachusetts to be examined. The inspectors came from Boston and they had the examination in the aldermen's chamber. It was a damn big room, probably hold a hundred people. Well, they scattered us all around so you couldn't talk with anybody. The ones that were giving the examination sat up on a platform. They gave us each a paper with questions on it. I had ninety-five questions on one sheet and another sheet equal. They watched you like a cat watches a mouse. You couldn't ask any questions, just answer them. They'd twist the questions up just like a bloody lawyer when you're on the stand. Try to trap you.

Then the next day I had to go to someone's plumbing shop. You had to wipe joints and things like that while

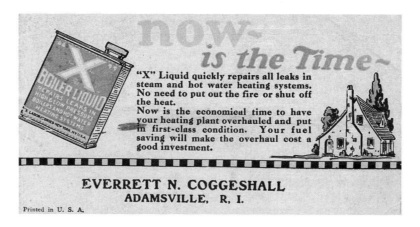

EVERRETT N. COGGESHALL
ADAMSVILLE, R. I.

Printed in U. S. A.

"X" Liquid quickly repairs all leaks in steam and hot water heating systems. No need to put out the fire or shut off the heat.
Now is the economical time to have your heating plant overhauled and put in first-class condition. Your fuel saving will make the overhaul cost a good investment.

A popular place for advertising one's goods and services is on the ever-useful inkblotter, such as these shown here. Leaky boiler? Need a toilet seat? Everrett N. Coggeshall will take care of you. Courtesy of Bertha Hart.

This CHURCH Regal Toilet Seat *will make a wonderful improvement in your bathroom.. Attach it yourself or we will install at slight charge..* Write or Phone
E. N. COGGESHALL
Plumbing, Contracting & Jobbing
Post Office Address, Adamsville, R. I.
ACOAXET, MASS.

Tel. Little Compton 13-13

they stood around and watched you, timing you. You got so much percent for being perfect. Only two of us out of fifteen passed with flying colors. The other guy's father was an alderman from Fall River, so he had pull with the crowd. He passed the examination, but not honest. The boss Johnson, he says to me the next day, "Everett, you'll have to go with him now and do all the wiping because he can't do it."

They wouldn't tell me if I passed or didn't pass the examination. They didn't give me the license. Goddamnit, they worked, me, the bastards. I kept after the plumbing inspector. I said, "What in the hell is the matter with you people? You won't tell me if I passed or didn't pass or anything." He says, "Oh, don't worry about it, Everett." But the boss was putting me right on a new job and I was the boss. I smelled rat that I had passed. They was working me, using me. I was getting five dollars a week and the plumbers was getting nineteen and a half. They were using me for a licensed master plumber and they wouldn't tell me I had the license.

Two years after I took the examination, along toward 1900, I found out I had passed. But I had done a good many houses in that time. The minute my four years was up, I quit and got twenty-seven dollars and a half. I done all right, I done all right ever since — I got no kick coming.

After working for Johnson, I worked all over the country. New York, Attleboro, Worcester, and around the surrounding country. But when the Depression came on they shut everything down. Where I was working in Worcester, prices dropped out of everything. We had plenty of work in the shop. I don't know how many three-deckered houses we had to do, but they just floored the cellars over and put tar paper on. Covered them for the winter. They couldn't get no money to go ahead an build them. I couldn't even get five dollars out of my bank account. You had to give them thirty days notice to draw out your own money. Days and days I never earned a penny. Even though I was number one in the plumbing shop, I'd go to the shop every morning and sit on my tool box all day. Well, I had to pay my board to the hotel, seven dollars a week. I exhausted all of my money so I come home.

"Westport is twenty-seven miles long and seven and a half miles wide, so if something happened up in the north end of town you could be to California and back again before I got the word."

But back in Westport there wasn't any plumbing jobs. There weren't no toilets, just privies outdoors. There was nothing in the house but an iron sink. So I started in business for myself soldering pans, coffee pots, and lead pipes. Fixing hand pumps and selling people new pumps. We called ouselves "tinkers." I take the horse and team, put my stock in it and start out in the morning. I'd go house to house and see if they had anything they wanted me to do. If they did, I done it. I got fifty cents an hour, four dollars a day.

I'm in my seventy-seventh year of being a police officer for this town. The oldest police officer in the United States. I never asked for the job, nor tried to get the job. I didn't even know anything about the job. I got a notice by word of mouth from the selectmen to come to the town hall. I went into the selectmen's office and they asked me to put up my hand. They swore me in as a police officer, number one in the Town of Westport.

I didn't go to work anywhere unless somebody got word to me of some trouble. I wasn't on duty all day. But if there was trouble in the town, the selectmen or town clerk would get word to me through the grapevine. They didn't have telephones. Sometimes I didn't know about any trouble for two or three days after it happened. Westport is twenty-seven miles long and seven and a half miles wide, so if something happened up in the north end of town you could be to California and back again before I got the word. There were no macadam roads and I only had a horse and buggy. Back then I did have a deputy sheriff in the other end of town, and if I needed help I would get word to him some way.

The Head of Westport has been a commercial center in the town since the early 1800s. When paths, worn down by the passage of feet and wagons, needed to be made more accommodating for man and his automobile, Steve Chase was there with his steamroller. Courtesy of the Westport Public Library.

Anything that wasn't right I had to take care of. Stealing, trespassing or anything that was against the law. Boston kept me informed all the time. I had all the new laws from the Legislature. Even had a rogue's gallery with the pictures of all the goddamn punks from here to California that they wanted. The same as you see in the post office.

I used to have to work with the FBI and the federal revenue men during Prohibition. Rum running and all that goddamn business. I didn't give a damn for any of them. I'd arrest the whole town if I had to. But seemed everybody was against me. Even the other constables who were appointed. I'd call them down to help me because there'd be two or three boats down to Charleton's wharf unloading liquor. They'd go any place but where you told them. If you told them to come down to the Harbor, they'd go to Horseneck, or somewhere else looking for me. To kill time. Or they'd go right in there and drive all the people away that didn't belong around there and help the fellas unload. Instead of doing what I wanted them to do, they helped them. They'd get twenty-five or thirty dollars a night for helping to unload. I never took a goddamn penny from none of the bastards.

They was scared to death of me. Christ, they'd be up in the towers, in the windmills and the water tanks, with flash lights. I'd be traveling around with the lights out on the car and I'd see a flashlight here and one there, signaling to different ones. I had houses that had cupolas on the top, widow's walks. I go down to the harbor and hide the truck and go up in one of them. They couldn't see me but

I could see all around the place. I would get a line on them. But hell, I couldn't do anything. You couldn't touch anything because your federal man had to come from New Bedford. When rum running first started, I could get all the dope but I had to call a federal man and he took charge.

I was breaking up stills all over Westport. I'd travel the woods. Take my dog and shot gun and go rabbit hunting, looking for stills. I'd find a place in the woods beside a brook. The tops of birches would be pulled down to hide the spot. There would be a few barrels of mash and their oil stoves. Well, I'd just take and smash the oil stove and still all up and then go on about my business. You'd rarely find anybody, because they could hear you coming. They'd get out of the way. Sometimes they would come out with shot guns and want to shoot me. "Well, go ahead. I got a shot gun, too!" Nothing would happen. I would get out of the way after I'd done my business and leave them alone. I had customers from the plumbing business whose houses I closed up for the winter. I had to move bags of liquor to get at the plumbing. Hell, we fought all the time.

One case I had was a Polish fella making moonshine. They had a fight and had tried to carve one another up. I spent two days and two nights with a Fall River cop trying to find them. If anybody got away from Westport and went to Fall River or New Bedford I had to have a city cop go with me. Them days some people worked two shifts. They'd work in one mill under one name and then they'd work in another mill under another name. You'd have to chase through the mills.

We didn't know who they were but we found out. One night about ten o'clock we found them all playing cards. One of them had a damn knife about eight inches long. He was going to carve us up. They got into a Model T Ford but we ran it into the brook. And tipped it over. Five of them in it. Well, they got a year in jail apiece, so it was alright.

I had to attend all of the town meetings, all the voting and ballot boxes. Anything going on in town, I had charge of, especially, the traffic on the road. This was before macadam roads. Thousands of people would come to the Westport Fair. They'd come from Fall River and New Bedford to Lincoln Park. From there jitneys would bring passengers down to the fair grounds. Acres and acres of land would be filled with cars. Some days I couldn't even stop and have dinner, and my dinner wasn't thirty yards away. I got ten hours every day for a whole week. I was pretty well pooped by the end of it, doing traffic with thousands of cars.

They only had the fair three years. The first year it was nice. The second year it rained a couple of days. The last one, they had rainy days five out of seven. They took out insurance for the rain. They had a cup on top of a building in the fair grounds. I could see it from the road where I was doing traffic duty. They kept the insurance man right there to see that nobody cheated and put water in the cup. But they didn't get enough rain to collect the insurance even though it rained all that time. So they quit and haven't had a fair since.

When I first came to Westport in 1890, there wasn't much ice used, because there weren't many summer people here. I helped build ice houses all around in Adamsville. They had a string of ice houses next to the road alongside of Adamsville Pond. If they didn't get the ice by the first of January they was sweating blood they weren't going to get any. They wanted ice twelve inches thick. It got so there wasn't any ice until maybe February

and it'd be six inches thick at the most. They didn't like that, but that's all they could get.

We sawed the ice with a horse and hand saws. The ice would be marked about five feet long and maybe two feet wide or better, the size of a big cake. A horse with sharp shoes would be put out on the ice, and he'd pull the ice plow. They'd set the saw so it'd go down about eight inches. That would leave a couple of inches so it'd hold up the horse and plow. Then men with great big hand saws would saw them out and float them to the ice house.

The ice houses were just wooden buildings, some two stories high. Inside they were sheathed all the way up and the sides was filled with sawdust. As you built the ice up, you put sawdust between the boards that were nailed to the sides. This was done until the ice house was filled clear up to the top. When they had the ice packed in solid, they covered the ice over with straw. At the last end

maybe two or three loads of straw several feet deep would be packed way up in the peak to keep the ice from melting in the summer. Towards the last end of the season the ice would be getting short, but there was schooner loads coming down from Maine all the time to Fall River. They had ice wagons going around with two men on them filling the ice boxes every day or every other day. They were like prairie wagons with a top over them so the sun wouldn't melt the ice.

But most of the people in the country, like here, didn't have ice. For years and years they used to hang their

food in wells. You'd go to a well somewhere and look in and see five or six ropes going down in there. Pails and things were tied on to them with stuff in them. Trying to keep the food. Sometimes they'd get away from them. The string would break and the food would fall down into the well and ruin the hell out of the water. Then we'd have to bail the wells out as best as we could and take the stuff out of them. I've seen a perfect ham that weighed ten pounds or better be just perfect after it'd been down in the well two or three years. Other times I've seen butter, dish and all, right down in the well. I'd dig it out of the dirt, clean it

up and it'd look like it was just made. But a lot of people died from that. Christ, every once in a while they'd have a disease, dyptheria or something like that and the doctors would condemn the well. We had six in Adamsville at one time. We didn't lack doctors.

I used to test wells. People would come to me and say, "Everett, something's the matter with my water." The women folk used to have a bluing ball, little round balls of bluing they used to put in the water to make the clothes white. I'd go put a handful of them in and wait a day or

Above: View of the East Branch of the Westport River, looking west, around 1895. The old Hix Bridge was destroyed by the 1938 Hurricane. Courtesy of Eleanor Tripp. *Far right:* Everrett Coggeshall. Photograph by David Allen.

two and see where the hell it went. It'd show up in somebody's well somewhere. We'd know there was a water course going through. The doctors would try to find out what the cause was. The wells had been alright for years, but it was all due to people hanging stuff in their wells, spoiling the water.

Water don't stay in a well. It's going through it all the time. If there's two feet of water in a well, the water is changed every half hour. It's not the same water that was there an hour ago. If you've got ten feet of water in the well, it's just the same way. I've seen the damn fools around here, farmers, when their well goes dry in the summer. They'd go up to Adamsville to a pond and fill up twenty milk cans — a whole team load. They'd take the water and throw it in the well. In an hour there wouldn't be any water in it. They'd say, "What the hell's wrong here?" Well, I'd say, "You goddamn fool, the water doesn't stay in a well. It goes right through all the time."

I had summer people here that'd built houses and drilled wells. Of course, they'd go home in September but when they came back in June they'd say, "Everett, pump out my well. I don't want that water. It's been there all winter." If the truth was known, that water hadn't been there an hour. You couldn't make them believe it. I'd have to go down with a pump and pump the bloody well out. Bother to go down and clean it out with a shovel and a pail. They wouldn't believe me but they had to after a while. They'd say, "That damn fool don't know what he's talking about." In the end, though, they'd have

"They depended on me for everything. And they still come to me now if they want anything done."

to admit I was right. Then no matter what you told them, you was right! Had to educate people.

I've always tried to help everybody, do everything I could to help them. I had fellas work for me four or five years that I had sent up to jail for a year. Worked for me after they got out. I never made no enemies. You can't find anybody that will give me a black name. I don't give a damn where you go. Anybody I ever worked for since the first job, I could go back and work again if they was living. Never been fired. Every job I finished, I quit on my own. I'd be asked to come back at a certain time and never go. I worked in Attleboro for two and a half years, before it was a city. Worked doing plumbing in all them damn jewelry shops. When work got slack and we didn't have any jobs in the winter, I

still had to pay board. I'd stand it for a few weeks and not earn my board. But then I had to move; I couldn't afford it.

Back when everything was antique, you had to make do. I was a farmer, fisherman, stable hand — any goddamn thing I could make an honest dollar at. I learned plumbing, the produce business and the farming business. I sold gas stoves, gas heaters, and furnaces. I had houses to look after when my customers would leave after Labor Day. I had to watch them all winter. If the wind blew a blind through a window, I'd have a carpenter fix it and send the bill to the people. I never charged them anything for looking after their property in the winter. they depended on me for everything. And they still come to me now if they want anything done.

181

The Last Woven Yard

Shutdown of the Berkshire/Hathaway

The Call for Capital   *by Dan Georgianna*

Dan Georgianna, professor of economics at Southeastern Massachusetts University, was invited by Spinner to examine the closing of New Bedford's Berkshire/Hathaway textile mill. He traces the flow of money from whaling to textiles, and finally to pure finance, following the call of higher rates of return.

Money not only talks, it listens. Money, or more correctly anyone who owns it, listens for a higher rate of return; people with large amounts are especially attentive. This is the nature of capital: there are only two alternatives: more or less, and more is better than less.

In the decade before the Revolutionary War, Joseph Rotch moved his whaling business from Nantucket to New Bedford. There was more room to grow in New Bedford and better transport connections to markets. Money grew through whaling. Profits though risky were high, many of the ships paying for themselves on their first trip. Furthermore, almost all of the work was done on board during the long voyages. The whales were killed, their blubber rendered into oil and stored in barrels, and the spermacetti oil and whalebone were prepared for market. The merchants only had to sell the product and transport it out of New Bedford.

Since the crewmen on the New Bedford ships were at sea for long periods, few had families in port. Thus the merchants needn't provide them with housing or other community services. The unemployed made few demands on the city but were directed to the wharves where, like it or not, they shipped out for the long years. Also, the crew on a whaling vessel were paid in shares of value of the catch; food, clothing, and the cost of most tools were deducted from their share. Wages didn't have to be paid out before a profit was made, and most of the crewmen's share went back to the merchant, who doubled as outfitters selling clothes and supplies to the crew at outrageous prices.

The merchants grew rich. According to Everett Allen in *Children of the Light,* yearly income from whaling increased from $300,000 per year in 1800 to $12,000,000 in 1854. Because most of the low paid workers lived at sea, New Bedford was probably the richest city per capita in the world in the decade before the Civil War.

However, after the Civil War, profits in whaling fell and became riskier. Natural gas and petroleum began to replace whale oil for light and lubrication. Also, whales became harder to find. The time it took to fill a ship with whale oil and bone stretched out to four and five years.

This loss in yearly profit in whaling led the merchants to lower the seamen's shares and to direct their boats to the Arctic, where whales were still prevalent. But this had its risks also. In 1871, the entire Arctic fleet was trapped and lost when the ice floe returned to land earlier than expected. Two thirds of the vessels were from New Bedford. Again in 1876, the ice took the fleet.

This increase in risk came at a time when the chances for profit on land were increasing. The rapid growth in industrialization begun during the Civil War continued afterwards. The safe, high return on investment from textiles especially called out for more capital. Demand for cotton cloth, bandages, and uniforms surged during the war. Afterwards, the ready-made men's clothing industry boomed based on the sizing system developed during the war.

Thus the New Bedford whaling merchants became wary of the uncertainties of whaling and began to heed the call of more certain profits from textiles. As usual they made the decision together; they decided to specialize in fine cotton cloth following the pioneering cotton firm in New Bedford, the Wamsutta Company.

"Wamsutta Mills," oil painting by William A. Wall, 1853. Built in 1848, Wamsutta brought New Bedford into the industrial age. Nathaniel Willis, son-in-law of founder Joseph Grinnell, wrote that this was "the creation of an industry of which the families of sailors and mechanics could avail themselves, independent of the precarious yield of the sea." Young sailors' daughters might now "earn four dollars a week by independent and undegrading labor." From *William Allen Wall*, by Richard Kugler. Courtesy of the New Bedford Whaling Museum.

King Cotton

Cotton textiles was the industry that had transformed the newly formed United States from an agricultural to an industrial nation. The ageless process of spinning fiber into yarn and then weaving yarn into cloth, had been done by women on the farms of colonial America. Almost immediately after the Revolutionary War, merchants in Rhode Island and Boston set up small mills which quickly replaced the home production.

In 1789, Moses Brown, after using part of the capital gained from the trade in slaves and other goods to found the university bearing his name, built the first textile mill in America based on the skill of a runaway apprentice from England named Samuel Slater. The Rhode Island mills were small affairs usually employing about 20 children under the age of ten and one or two adults in the process of spinning yarn. Wages were very low and usually paid in yarn or script, redeemable at the company store.

Using the joint stock method of ownership, the Boston merchants financed much larger mills in Waltham and quickly spread to Lowell, the first company town in the U.S. These mills were much larger than the Rhode Island mills, employing thousands of highly skilled young women from throughout rural New England, whose tasks on the farm were being replaced by the manufacture of cloth. The women did both spinning and weaving, lived in company boarding houses, and sent their wages home to pay farm debts and send their brothers West or to college.

The cotton textile industry soon dominated the cities and towns of New England. By the Civil War, there were over 900 cotton textile mills throughout New England.

The whaling merchants in New Bedford weren't easily won over to King Cotton. True, in 1848 several of the whaling merchants took stock in the Wamsutta Mills, the first successful cotton mill in the city. But only $160,000 in capital could be raised, about equal in value to the sum of two or three of the four or five hundred whale ships in the New Bedford fleet. The Wamsutta grew steadily, aided by the Civil War. In its first 25 years, capital increased to $2,000,000 and the company was producing some 20,000,000 yards of cloth per year and paying a steady eight to ten percent return, about double the interest rate at the time.

But no other mill followed until in 1871, the same year as the loss of the Arctic fleet, the Potomska Mill was built. After hesitating for another ten years and enduring another Arctic catastrophe, 14 new textile companies were incorporated in the next 15 years as the whaling merchants scurried to move their money from high risk, low profit whaling to the safe eight per cent from textiles.

In 1888, the Hathaway Manufacturing Company was incorporated with Horatio Hathaway its founder as President, Joseph Knowles as Treasurer and Manager, and Jonathan Bourne, William W. Crapo, and Thomas Brayton among its Board of Directors.

With the change from whaling to textiles, the same merchant families controlled the finance and commerce of the city. They continued the joint stock ownership of the mills that they had used in the ownership of the whaling vessels to mediate against competition and to provide insurance against loss. The major changes in New Bedford were the numerous factories in the city and the large increase in population as workers lived in town rather than on the whaling ships and were paid wages rather than a share of sales.

Workers in the spinning room of an old New Bedford textile mill, circa 1900. Courtesy of Mrs. John Vertente.

Growth of Textiles in New Bedford

Capital heeded the call of King Cotton and prospered in New Bedford. From 1881 to the beginning of the First World War, 32 cotton manufacturing companies were incorporated. Almost $100,000,000 of capital was invested in textiles in the city (90 percent of all capital invested in manufacturing), employing 30,000 people. New Bedford was a one-industry town.

World War I was a great boom for capital in the textile industry in New Bedford. According to Wolfbein in *The Decline of a Cotton Textile City,* "Capital invested in the industry doubled in the 7 years, 1914 to 1920 . . . Earnings of the cotton textile mills increased six-fold during the period; in one year (1920), the mills earned 34 percent on invested capital." Two factors account for this growth in capital: increasing demand for tire yarn resulting from the boom in autos and the demand for war materials, especially airplane cloth, bandage material, and uniforms. None of these products were typically produced in New Bedford which had continued to specialize in finely woven cloth. However, the profits were too high to ignore. Also, even though tire yarn and airplane cloth were coarsely woven material, both required combing the yarn for strength, a process which New Bedford mills had perfected in making finely woven cloth.

This decision to switch from fine cloth to war-time production of coarse cloth was an important decision. The industry in New Bedford exposed itself to direct competition with the South, an uneven match. The strategy was to make the most profit from the existing machinery.

There was little investment in new equipment after the war. In 1928, almost 80 percent of all equipment in the mills was over ten years old and most of it was over 20 years old. "Much of the machinery (in the Grinnell mill) was of almost historical value . . . Henry Ford found in the plant some specimens that he thought were of sufficient interest to purchase for his museum." (Wolfbein).

During the war years and for a decade after, making cloth could still produce profits. But capital never sleeps; it always listens and the South was calling for textile capital.

The Call of the South

Industrialization has proceeded the same way throughout history, beginning in England in the 18th century and continuing in Latin America and Southeast Asia today. Small landowning and tenant farmers are ruined by low prices for the produce, usually as a result of national policy or competition from more fertile areas elsewhere. Factory or cottage work is the only alternative. Increased production lowers the price of commodities, ruining craft and home production, thus providing more labor for factories. At the same time women working long hours in factories have no time for self-sufficient production and are forced to buy the commodities they used to make at home.

There was a large increase in tenant farming after the Civil War. At first slowly and then rapidly after Federal troops were pulled out in 1877, the former slaves were forced to work the land for shares, in many cases for the same master. By the late 1870's falling prices of cotton ruined the poor tenant farmers of the Piedmont area. Capital investors gave whites an alternative to slow starvation on the farm; they built cotton mills. By 1880, there were almost 200 textile mills, mostly small affairs in company towns in North Carolina and Georgia. Conditions were fertile for capital in the cotton textile industry in the South. The number of spindles doubled every five years until 1910.

The major advantages to capital in the South were lower wages, newer plants and equipment, less social legislation, and government antipathy to labor unions. Wages were 30 to 50 percent less in the South than in the North and there were no unions. According to Mary Heaton Vorse in an article for *Harper's* Magazine in 1929, trade journals advertised, "Avoid labor troubles! Come South! Plenty of American Cheap labor!"

While the social legislation in the North was far from enlightened, there were virtually no laws against child labor, hours of work, and health conditions in the South. Over 25 percent of Southern textile workers were children, while less than ten percent in the North were. The U.S., China, and India were the only countries in the world to allow women and children to work at night.

The Southern mills also had an advantage in machinery, especially more modern looms, since new technical advances were being made at the same time they were building mills.

The Southern mill owners had the same relationship to their white workers that the plantation owners had to their slaves before the Civil War and to their mostly black tenants after it. They owned the mills, the houses, the water supply, the stores, and the churches. They also owned the state governments and the courts. If their "hands" were desperate enough to strike, the state militia was immediately called in and set up machine gun lines separating workers from their homes and stores, in some cases not allowing workers to receive mail.

The Southern mills quickly dominated in the production of coarse cloth. By 1890 the South was producing as much coarse cloth as New England; by 1929 the South was producing eight times as much as New England. They took longer to catch up in the production of fine cloth. In 1890 the South wasn't producing any fine cloth; by 1919, they were producing as much as New England.

Decline of Textiles in New Bedford

Until 1920, the New Bedford textile industry prospered while the industry in the rest of New England waned under the competition from the South. In 1921 there was a steep though short recession. A recovery followed in the early 1920's. However, beginning in 1925 New Bedford began to suffer the effects first of competition from the South and then of the Great Depression. In 1925 there were 35 companies producing textiles in New Bedford; in 1940 there were 12 left. Twenty-one thousand jobs were lost.

Capital in New Bedford textiles didn't suffer in the 1920's. Dividends were high averaging eight to ten percent, with virtually no reinvestment in plant and equipment. Money was being taken out. While it is very difficult to follow individual pools of capital, most of it probably went to the investment banks in Boston, which were putting money in the newly discovered oil fields in East Texas.

Money fled New Bedford in the 1930's. City officials, businessmen, newspapers, clergy, and labor leaders tried to staunch the flow. The Board of Commerce led campaigns "Help New Bedford Plan," "New Bedford Forward," and "A New Dawn — Help New Bedford Smile Again." Taxes were cut, loans were made, free space was given to new enterprises, and wages were cut.

Beside the general wage cuts of about 30 percent, workers at some of the mills were asked to contribute more to keep capital in New Bedford. In 1937, workers at the Neild mill, which had paid investors cash dividend of 12 percent throughout the 1920's and 40 percent in 1922, were asked by management and union leaders to accept an additional ten percent cut in wages to help pay the outstanding debts of the mill. A group of workers opposed the plan arguing that this was merely a payment to investors and wouldn't save the mill since no one else was willing to lend money. Despite this opposition, the plan was adopted by the overwhelming majority of workers. The mill closed three months later.

While the tax cuts and other subsidies helped bring some low-paying garment shops to New Bedford, none of these attractions were sufficient to keep capital in textiles in New Bedford. The attractions were greater elsewhere, and textiles simply didn't return enough profit. As the current owner of Berkshire/Hathaway, Warren Buffett, said years later when he permanently closed the mill. "When a management with a reputation for brilliance tackles a business with a reputation for poor fundamental economics, it is the reputation of the business that remains intact."

Survival of the Berkshire/Hathaway

During the 1930's economic fundamentals pointed to rayon. People have to wear something. The rich wore silk during the Depression; those copying them wore rayon. The production of rayon more than tripled in New Bedford during the Depression, and the leader in rayon was the Hathaway Manufacturing Company.

The company had been reasonably profitable during the 1920's paying out six to eight percent dividends every year. The owners were well-established New Bedford whaling merchant families: Hathaway, Knowles, and in 1909 James Stanton assumed control. Like most of the surviving mills, the Hathaway grew during the 1930's, adding three mills in 1933. When James Stanton became ill in 1934, control passed to his sons, Otis and Seabury, who ran the company until 1965. Thus, the company had only four chief executives over its first 80 years, the last three being succeeding generations of the Stanton family.

The Hathaway's fortunes followed the ascendancy of rayon. During World War II, the company specialized in the production of parachute cloth; following

that, Hathaway became the largest producer of men's rayon suit linings in the world. After the destruction of one of its mills and serious damage to its largest building complex from the hurricane of 1954, Hathaway was merged with Berkshire Fine Spinning.

Berkshire itself was a product of consolidation of several mills in Rhode Island and Western Massachusetts, under the direction of Malcolm Chace, whose ancestors had learned to build mills from Samuel Slater. The company operated 13 mills in Rhode Island and Massachusetts, employing 10,000 workers, but most importantly, the company had $37 million in cash. Some of this money was used to modernize the Hathaway Mills, while the less efficient mills were closed, at the rate of about one plant per year. In 1962, the Berkshire/Hathaway Company operated seven plants, employed 6,000 people, annually produced one-quarter of a billion yards of material, that sold for more than $60 million, but most importantly had money in the bank. The company, and especially the money in the bank, caught the eye of Warren Buffett, an up-and-coming stock market wizard from Omaha, Nebraska.

The Sage of Omaha

Warren Buffett, the son of a U.S. Congressman and stockbroker, grew up in Omaha, Nebraska and Washington, D.C., was educated at the Wharton School, the University of Nebraska, and Columbia University, and from an early age exhibited extraordinary powers for making money.

Before entering Woodrow Wilson High School in Washington, Buffett had retrieved and sold golf balls at a local country club, had worked in the boardroom of his father's brokerage office in Omaha, sold magazine subscriptions, published a horse racing tip sheet, and operated several paper routes selling 500 copies a day of the Washington Post, of which he is now a major owner. In high school he started the Wilson Coin-operated Machine Company, placing pin-ball machines in barber shops. The operation was a great success. Finishing high school in the late 1940's, Buffett had made $10,000 and purchased a farm in northern Nebraska.

In college, Buffett mainly studied the stock market having discovered that the big money was in finance. He read Ben Graham's *Intellegent Investor,* still the stock analysts' Bible and was greatly impressed. After years of studying charting and other forms of numerology to predict future stock prices, experiencing the book for Buffett was like Saul's conversion on the road to Damascus. "Reading it was like seeing the light," said Buffett.

The system is fairly simple. Because many judgements in the market are based on emotion rather than analysis, some companies' stock will be out of favor and selling at a price less than liquidation value. For those companies, the plant, equipment, inventory, and other physical assets are free for the taking. If the company is undervalued enough, the probability of losing money buying the stock is quite small.

In 1950, Buffett came East to study at Columbia under Graham. Upon receiving his M.B.A. in 1951 and after Graham rejected Buffett's offer to work without pay at his investment company, Buffett returned to Omaha to work at his father's brokerage firm. Buffett kept in contact with Graham and when Graham asked him to join his firm three years later, Buffett returned to New York and worked there for two years as a securities analyst. Finally, Buffett returned to Omaha in 1956, bought a modest house (probably undervalued), and has stayed there ever since.

With his own money and some from his family, Buffett started a limited partnership. The rules were simple: Buffett would get 25% of all profits in excess of six percent per year and he would make all decisions. A few local people and some who knew him from New York put money into the fund. They were well rewarded. The return to stockholders averaged over 30% per year from 1956 to 1969. When the partnership ended, stockholders had received an increase of 30 times; $10,000 invested in 1956 was worth $260,000 in 1969. Buffett's take was $25 million, an increase of 25,000 percent on his initial investment of $100,000.

Buffett ended the partnership in 1969 because he was tired of the pressure of being the league leader in mutual funds, he thought that the stock market was overvalued, and the number of partners had grown to where he would have to register as an investment company, subject to government regulations. Most importantly, he no longer needed other people's money to play the game. The assets from the fund were distributed to the partners, Buffett keeping most of his in Berkshire/Hathaway, a company he had bought in 1965.

The Closing of the Mill

The Hathaway Manufacturing Company was a sleepy textile company under the family management of the Stantons. The decision to merge with Berkshire was a difficult one and split the family. Seabury Stanton was in favor of the merger but his brother Otis was in favor of borrowing from the banks. Seabury won, but a power struggle began with Malcolm Chace, owner of Berkshire Fine Spinning. Ironically, Otis began to side with Chace.

When the stock price dropped to below the book value and even the cash in the bank, Buffett began buying. Buffett didn't know textiles, but he knew money and the benefits of "doing business with someone who operates on nonsensical reasons." Seabury Stanton wasn't in the same league. Like many second and third generation mill owners, he was more interested in his social and business status than in making money. Stanton even bragged about having $1 million in a checking account, a frivolous waste of money according to Buffett.

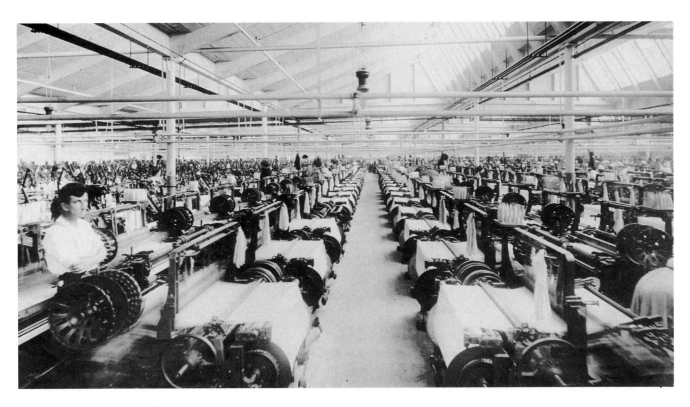

Weave shed of the Nashawena Mill, circa 1925. At the time of this photograph, Nashawena Mills boasted having the largest weave shed in the world, over 500,000 square feet of floor space. In 1928, the mill had 5,385 looms, all of them automatic. Most other New Bedford mills in 1928 were using looms that were over 20 years old. For this reason, Nashawena was able to operate until 1952, when the company liquidated.

The Berkshire/Hathaway is nestled between a neighborhood of three-decker tenement houses and a once thriving commercial district that included South Water St. (behind the mill). In the distance (left) can be seen the twin spires of Mt. Carmel Church, the largest Portuguese parish in the U.S. Photograph by Joseph D. Thomas, 1985.

In 1965, with the help of Chace and Otis Stanton, Buffett bought control of the company; Seabury Stanton, President, and his son, Jack, Treasurer and heir apparent, were out. With the sale of the Berkshire/Hathaway to a stock market speculator, the company was following the road, trodden by many other old line manufacturing companies: from merchant trading in primary commodities, to investment in manufacturing, and finally, to pure finance. The company's main product became money for speculation. After 80 years in the textile business, the Berkshire/Hathaway became a conglomerate with a textile division, and the textile division wasn't doing very well.

Buffett's stocks, on the other hand, were doing extremely well. He had progressed beyond the simple rules of Graham; in fact he had too much money to concentrate on buying a few shares in an undervalued company, but he still had rules. If a company is very undervalued, buy; if a company with market power is undervalued, buy; if owned and still undervalued but with little market power, keep but don't invest money in it; and if fully valued, sell.

The results were spectacular. For example, in 1971 Buffett bought several million shares of the Washington Post at an average price of $6 per share.

Newspaper stocks were then out of fashion, but Buffett realized that a major newspaper has a local monopoly on printed advertising; they can charge whatever they like. "It's like buying a tollgate on a major highway," said Buffett. the stock is now worth $225 per share.

Textiles didn't fit into any of Buffett's rules. Securing market power was very difficult and the other millmen were more interested in making cloth than in making money. Consequently, in the textile business, any attempt to introduce newer, more profitable products or to invest in cost-saving machinery is almost immediately followed by competitors, quickly eliminating any higher profits.

Berkshire's textile division lost money throughout the recession of the early 1980's. There was a modest recovery in 1983, but in 1984 losses totalled $2 million. The cycle was repeating. As Buffett explained the decision to close the mill to stockholders in the 1985 Annual Report, "I won't close down businesses . . . merely to add a fraction of a point to our corporate rate of return. However, I also feel it inappropriate for even an exceptionally profitable company to fund an operation once it appears to have unending losses in prospect."

Late in 1984, Gary Morrison, President of the Textile Division, sent a detailed plan to Buffett, asking for a small investment in new machinery. Without it, he said, the mill couldn't be profitable. When Buffett didn't respond, he knew the end was near. On May 1, 1985, Morrison told local management that the mill was closing. The employees weren't told in order to keep up their morale, while they ran out the mill. On August 12, the workers were informed and shut-down began by departments. Just before Christmas, the mill ceased operations, having used up all raw materials, satisfied all orders, and sold or salvaged the equipment.

On that day, Berkshire/Hathaway stock stood at $2600 per share, up from $11, the average price Buffett had paid 20 years before.

Conclusion: Buy Berkshire/Hathaway

It's easy to blame Warren Buffett and corporate greed for the closing of the Hathaway mill, especially when walking through the dying mill talking to the few last workers, many of whom had worked there for 20 and 30 years. A place of work is like a home, and a plant closing is a form of eviction for the people who work there. Furthermore, it is very difficult to find a new job, probably in a new industry, at 50 or 60 years old. Also, since the mill closed before they were eligible, many people lost pension rights.

Warren Buffett is currently worth about $2 billion, and could have kept the mill open at the same rate of loss for 1,000 years. In fact, the greatest loss in a single year, $2 million in 1984, is less than one percent of Buffett's yearly income.

But it's not that simple. A textile mill is not a charity. Clearly, money yields higher returns outside of textiles. Most of Buffett's investments did exceptionally well; the average return on all Berkshire/Hathaway's holdings was about 25 percent per year. According to Bill Betts, Financial Vice President of the Textile Division, when it wasn't losing money, the mill only averaged about five percent return.

Furthermore, as everyone in textiles says, Buffett had kept the mill open for 20 years longer than expected. Most of the credit is due to the resourceful managers and hard-working people, mostly immigrants, who produced high quality cloth efficiently at relatively low wages.

The union can't be blamed for either closing the mill or for not working harder to keep it open. As Buffett says in his Annual Report to stockholders, if the union had made unreasonable demands for wages or work rules, he would have closed the mill sooner and avoided the losses of the last few years. As for the union fighting harder to keep the mill open, it would have been very difficult. Buffett is not as susceptible to public pressure as Gulf & Western was in the successful struggle to keep Morse Cutting Tools open. Political action probably wouldn't have helped either. The textile industry is dead in New England; too many mills have closed in too many cities.

When the Hathaway mill did close, there were no buyers. It was even difficult to sell the machinery. Most was sold for scrap. Machinery costing a total of $13 million, sold for less than $200,000. According to Kim Baker, Vice President of Manufacturing, modern new machinery was broken up for scrap because no one would buy it at any price.

As he says, Buffett probably did keep the mill open because it was a major employer in a high unemployment area, and labor was cooperative. As long as losses were not larger than others in the industry, Buffett said he would keep the mill open. Perhaps. Real estate values are currently very high in New Bedford, having risen sharply over the past few years. The most undervalued part of the mill was the 2,000,000 square feet of space; Buffett didn't sell that. It is currently being rented for $2 to $5 per square foot and is now about 80% occupied. The mill will yield a higher return in real estate than it ever did in textiles.

The city of New Bedford perhaps could have helped. The only profitable part of the textile operation was spinning yarn. The Hathaway mill had continued New Bedford's reputation for producing the finest combed yarn. Kim Baker says that the market was there and the spinning frames and workers were competitive. All that was necessary was a small investment in new winders. Perhaps the city could have financed low interest loans or cheap space as it did in the 1930s. But Baker says that he wasn't interested, and its obvious from the lack of buyers for the spinning frames, that no one else was either.

Everyone has an alibi, but for me, the most complicating issue is not Buffett's greed; it is my own. Reading about Buffett, I became more interested in buying Berkshire/Hathaway stock than in the closing of the mill. I should have; it was a good buy. In the three months that I worked on this article, Berkshire/Hathaway's stock price increased 30 percent.

Buffett is clearly a genius at making money. His method makes sense and he has been spectacularly successful; he is the best. As his Vice President for Finance asked us "If you can make 20% on your money or five percent, which would you choose?" The vast majority of us would choose the higher return, if we knew what it was. Buffett is simply better at knowing than the rest of us.

The way that a market system is supposed to work is as follows: production and sales should go to the most efficient producer, the one with the lowest costs. This lowers the price. If people are thrown out of work because of this, they will find other employment in more efficient operations or ones that have some kind of cost advantage. There may be some disturbances and some people may lose out, but the majority of us will be better off.

Luckily the mill closed when New Bedford was entering a boom; unemployment in New Bedford is the lowest in ten years. Most probably found some work, though service industries (the booming sector) don't often hire older workers.

What bothers me is that the process is undemocratic. The people who worked at the mill up to the top management of the division had no say in the decision to close. Many had spent their working lives there, but were still the servants of a stock market speculator living 1500 miles away. If we follow the logic of the market, Buffett didn't have much say either. Money ruled.

Workplace in Exile   *by Robert A. Henry*

Mobility vs. Roots

The decision to close the Berkshire/Hathaway was one based on more than economics. It was a decision rooted in the historical process, tracing back to the settling of America with its focus on youth, independence and mobility; a process bent on developing the land and accumulating wealth while preventing workers and their families from establishing roots and a stable community.

In the turbulent social, political and religious climate of Europe in the 16th and 17th centuries, the settling of the New World was seen by many as a God-provided opportunity to begin a new life and create a perfect society. With equal parts effort and Providential prodding, the harsh realities of the new land had to be overcome and the frontiers expanded.

The Native Americans were the first group to test the crusading sword. In 1620, William Bradford, future governor of the Plymouth colony, wrote: "They were only savage and brutish men, little otherwise than wild beasts." In 1765, John Adams entered the following in his diary: "I always consider the settlement of America with reverence and wonder, as the opening of a grand scheme and design in Providence for the illumination of the ignorant and emancipation of the slavish sort of mankind all over the earth."

Following the Revolutionary War and the War of 1812, America established herself in the world of nations. Growth would follow as a matter of course. Huge tracts of land to the Southwest and West, spoils of the Mexican War in 1847, established new borders for the United States. From the Civil War on, wealth and industrial power merged and came into the hands of a few people. Millions of dollars a day had been spent on the war effort, giving rise to new factories. Soldiers who had been born farmers returned from the battlefields seeking employment as itinerant laborers. Money and people were beginning to move.

The Great Migration toward the cities held the promise of prosperity while reference to a "chosen nation" became common. Through a character in his novel, *White Jacket,* Herman Melville expressed a common sentiment of the time:

God has predestined, mankind expects, great things from our race, and great things we feel in our souls. The rest of the nations must soon be in our rear. We are the pioneers of the world; and the advance-guard, sent on through the wilderness of untried things to break a path in the New World that is ours. In our youth is our strength . . . The political Messiah . . . has come in us, if we would but give utterance to his Promptings.

By the mid-19th century, the owners of capital had assumed the roles of explorer, settler and nationalist. Meanwhile, labor became the untapped watershed; resource to be expended. Only the rise of union activity toward the century's end offered a counter-thrust.

When financial growth is the American purpose, permanent human relationships in the community are dissolved — old age and the transmission of traditional values are looked down upon. A system that cultivates transiency erodes a sense of community. The closing of Berkshire/Hathaway was a continuation of the process of erosion.

Labor Struggle in an Immigrant City

The Hathaway Manufacturing Company opened its doors in 1888, at the height of New England's pre-eminence in textile manufacturing. In New Bedford, those who had made their fortunes in the local whaling industry invested feverishly in cotton manufacturing in the decades between 1880 and 1910. All that was needed was a vast pool of human resource to operate the mills. This need was answered by immigrants who arrived by the tens of thousands, hoping to establish roots in the new homeland.

New Bedford's mill workers came from English, Scottish, Irish, French-Canadian, Portuguese, Cape Verdean, Polish and other stocks. This diversity of ethnic people thrust into such a highly structured working situation made solidarity among workers difficult.

During the strike of 1898, which gained national attention, division along ethnic, trade union and political lines added to the problem of worker disunity. Many ethnic groups were denied participation in the unions. Those of English descent, suckled on union activity in their home country, dominated the labor leadership in the New Bedford mills, particularly the powerful weavers' and spinners' unions.

Politics also created divisions. The Socialist groups in New Bedford were accused of instigating trouble within the striking community by Samuel Gompers, the conservative head of the A.F.L., who made an appearance in the city at the height of the commotion. Suddenly, workers who took to the picket lines for economic survival were being forced to make choices on ideological grounds.

Mulespinning in a New Bedford mill (possibly Whitman Mills), around 1905. New Bedford earned the reputation of being the number one producer of fine cotton goods in the world. This process was perfected here, in part, through the manufacture of finely combed cotton and fine yarns spun on mulespinning frames. Courtesy of Mrs. John Vertente.

While the strike of 1898 brought no lasting social or economic gains, it managed to lower public esteem of the mill owners and rallied public support behind the workers. This gave many workers a sense of achievement and perhaps set the stage for a more united front in future confrontations.

Following the strike, capital was available to establish 12 new corporations; the city expanded from a population of 45,000 in 1895 to 75,000 in 1905. Meanwhile, labor conditions deteriorated alarmingly. In 1902, T.M. Young, employed by the *Manchester Guardian* of England to investigate the reason for American dominance of the textile industry, made the following comments on the Chace Mill of Fall River.

The weaving rooms were very ill-ventilated; there appeared to be no fans to introduce a proper supply of fresh air, it was intensely hot, gas-jets were burning in the middle of the room, volumes of steam were spouting up like geysers from the floor, and the condensed moisture was pouring down the closed windows. The faces of the weavers looked pinched and sallow, and the arms of many of them were pitifully thin. I do not care how many dollars a week those people may have been earning; they were badly off.

According to Young, the average pay for male operatives in 1900 was $8.00 per week. Female operatives received, on the average, 50% less.

The New Bedford mills continued to prosper throughout the war years and until 1925. By 1928, New Bedford had grown to a population of 130,000. A continued surge of immigration, mostly Portuguese, began to change the face of the unions. Though the average wage of textile workers had more than doubled between 1914 and 1920, a series of wage cuts during the twenties led to the volatile strike of 1928. With 30,000 textile workers on strike, organized labor

Workers at the Hathaway Mill, around 1910. The woman, second from left, is Mary Jeffrey at about age 15.
Courtesy of Mrs. Joseph A. Jeffrey.

competed aggressively for the workers' support, particularly those of ethnic background who had been ignored in the labor struggle 30 years earlier.

Though the strike lasted over seven months, the workers still lacked a unified front. Leadership was splintered. In a letter to the editor of *The Times* in 1928, mill worker Thomas Corrigan wrote:

> Who are they . . . who have allowed conditions in the mill to go from bad to worse . . . who have made no efforts to organize the workers efficiently? When leaders are being congratulated by the enemy, it is time for the rank and file to watch out. They stressed the fact of conditions being "deplorable" before the wage cut. Will conditions not remain deplorable even if the manufacturers take down the notices and still nothing is being done to alleviate these conditions?

On the other hand, a letter of solidarity from mill owners expressed their determination to stand together;

> Rumors are constantly being circulated to the effect that some of the manufacturers are not in sympathy with the reduction of wages . . . To put an end to this rumor, the undersigned mills emphatically declare that they have been and are unanimous in their actions concerning the present reduction in wages. [Twenty-six mills signed, including the Hathaway. The Dartmouth Mill did not sign.]

The 1928 strike ended with the workers accepting a wage reduction. But this did not save the mills. With the Depression at hand, New Bedford would lose most of its textile corporations in the next 12 years. (For a history of the 1928 textile strike, read "Here We Come, Thousands Strong," by Dan Georgianna in *Spinner, Volume II.*)

The Takeover

On September 13, 1951, Seabury Stanton, Chief Executive Officer of Berkshire/Hathaway, addressed the 97th Annual Meeting of the National Association of Cotton Manufacturers and reiterated the industrialist's lament:

> For many years the textile industry has been fighting for its existence in the face of higher wages and lower work assignments than those prevailing in other areas. Such a condition . . . is within control of the people of the area.

> Employees, their union representatives and general public at large, must be made to realize that New England mills, representing only 22% of the industry, cannot continue to operate indefinitely in an area where, as a result of higher wages and lower productivity per worker, labor costs are substantially greater than those of 80% of the industry located in other areas.

> I believe, and I am sure you will agree with me, that the textile workers here in New England are the best in the world, but we must find ways to convince them that they should give us their best willingly and cheerfully, in the protection of their own jobs.

The labor cost for the 70,000 employees of the cotton and rayon mills in 1950 was approximately $35 million a year higher in the Northeast than in the non-unionized mills in the South. In comparison with North and South Carolina, a typical plant in Massachusetts was paying 227% more in unemployment taxes, 207% more in income and excise taxes, and 113% more in workmen's compensation costs.

Some workers were sympathetic to the manufacturer's predicament:

> Let me ask the mill workers one question: Whose word would you rather take — that of a union leader, or the word of a fine, well-educated man who gave us work for many years? Now that Mr. Stanton's business is not doing so well because of cheap labor abroad, we, the mill workers, should turn our indignation not against him but against the people who are buying Japanese and other foreign textiles instead of ours. [T.B. in *The Standard-Times,* May 9, 1951.]

And those who disagreed:

> The mill owners demand increased production from the workers so why shouldn't the worker demand a fair contract? Let's face the facts. The mill owners have increased the work-loads, and, not satisfied with that, they now want to cut wages. I think the workers have bent over backwards to get along with the owners, but enough is enough. The cost of living has steadily increased, and the mill workers are supposed to sit back and accept cuts which would affect theirs and their children's welfare. [F.R.H. in *The Standard-Times,* May 9, 1955.]

The name of Stanton had been synonymous with Berkshire/Hathaway since its inception as the Hathaway Manufacturing company in 1888. For the workers, the physical presence of the Stantons in the mill denoted stability. Even though their splendid offices were insulated from mill activity, at least the offices were within the mill. The alienation of the workforce, including management, often begins with absentee ownership. The notion that "the owner was also the superintendent, foreman, and the best worker among them," had been dispelled with corporate growth. With the takeover of Berkshire/Hathaway, the owner was totally removed from the workplace.

Seabury Stanton. Courtesy of Berkshire/Hathaway Co.

The headline of *The Standard-Times* on May 10, 1965, confirmed what many suspected: SEABURY STANTON RESIGNS AT BERKSHIRE/HATHAWAY. Said Stanton,

I had previously planned to retire at the time of the stockholders' meeting in December of this year, but I have hastened my retirement due to a disagreement with regard to policy with certain outside interests, which have purchased sufficient stock to control the company.

I am leaving the company in sound financial condition, with all the bank loans paid off, inventories at a minimum, and with a substantial unfilled order position, which should insure profitable operations for the balance of the year, based on present conditions.

The resignation warranted an editorial comment the next day:

To the dynamic period of change, [Stanton] brought dedication, a dominant and persuasive personality, plus the contagious conviction that there was a way around virtually every stumbling block. In a New England that lost 14 million cotton spindles in a 25 year period, in which 150 plants providing 100,000 jobs were liquidated, the name Stanton came to signify to the business world watching with curiosity and admiration, the symbol of refusal to surrender to economic adversity.

Charles Perperas, Cloth Room Supervisor, said:

Years ago you could walk in here and eat off the floor. We had maintenance crews that did nothing but sand floors and varnish them all day long! Every nook and corner was clean. The owners just don't put money back in the plants now.

Detractors of Stanton charged mismanagement, an ivory tower attitude and a showy lifestyle. "The Stantons basically diluted their ownership and they lost control," remarked William D. Betts, Executive Vice-President of the Textile Division, in an interview in 1985. "Building those luxurious offices within the mill complex is not a particularly good use of stockholders' money."

It was generally accepted that the outside interest Seabury Stanton referred to was Buffet Partnership, Ltd. of Omaha, Nebraska. Seabury Stanton was quite suddenly cast out because he stood in the way. There was no emotion involved in the ouster. Warren Buffet was simply looking for a good return on an investment. When the mill made money, the return was generally around one or two percent. Five percent is considered an excellent return in the industry. Buffet was known for demanding a fifteen percent return on all his investments. The possibility that he would divest when the time was right was ever-present.

So in the end, the corporate expansionism which Seabury Stanton and his family had worked to perpetuate, became his undoing. Stanton was victimized by his fiscal immobility. He was not "quick" enough.

With the owner removed from the plant, even building maintainance was at stake. Charles Curran, Maintenance Supervisor at Berkshire/Hathaway, recalled that Stanton period in an interview in 1985:

When the Stantons had the plant, in the afternoon you'd see one of them walking around and they'd get to know the workers. They were very open-type people. They could meet anybody and talk to anybody regardless of what type of job — a floor-sweeper, a weaver, a trainee — regardless, they could talk to that person. When they left, that was one of the turning-points in the people's feeling toward the company itself.

Perspectives on a Mill Closing

At eight o'clock in the morning of August 12, 1985, William D. Betts, Executive Vice-President of Berkshire/Hathaway, Inc., notified union officials that the plant would be shutting down operations. The mill was the last of the major textile corporations in Southeastern Massachusetts that incorporated all aspects of production (such as weaving, spinning and carding) under one roof.

A letter dated that same day and addressed to "ALL EMPLOYEES" was posted on the bulletin boards throughout the plant. The unsigned letter stated:

We regret to inform you that the Textile Operations of Berkshire Hathaway Inc. will be phased out in late 1985. Production will completely cease by late December 1985. The operation is no longer competitive due to depressed fabric prices and record levels of imports.

Your Department Head will give you information in the months ahead as to when your particular department will cease operations.

Manuel Lopes (center) and Napoleon Gladu repair a missing end on the warp by replacing it with an end taken from the salvage. Napoleon is a loomfixer and Manuel, a changeover, in Room Seven South at the Berkshire/Hathaway. Photograph by Joseph D. Thomas, 1985.

During the closing months of the Berkshire/Hathaway, I interviewed many workers who would soon be out of a job. The majority of the workers were immigrants. Many were over forty years old. They had no say in the economic decisions being made around them and their skills as textile workers would now be of little use in the workplace.

The lot of mill manager and mill worker were cast together when Berkshire/Hathaway went from a family-owned business to a conglomerate with its new owner in Nebraska. The managers, many of whom had risen through the ranks, were a trustworthy presence for the workers, but they now had to establish integrity with two parties who were fundamentally opposed — the workers and the owners. Nevertheless, they kept the operation intact until 1985.

Kim Baker, Vice-President of Textile Operations

I know my workers' birthdays, where they live, their wives' first names, how many kids they have, and most of the time I know the kids' first names and the grades they're in in school. I make it my business to know that. It's good management because I am interested in them and they realize it. It has worked out fine for us.

Buffet does his homework, his investigating. But he does it so nobody knows until it's too late. In other words, he had Berkshire/Hathaway in his pocket before the Stantons realized what was going on. I spent a whole day with him in 1965 when he took over the company. He and Mr. Chace came to the Warren plant where I was General Manager at the time. He walked through the mill. He understood it. But he was mainly interested in sitting there and having me go through the performance records and the quality — the seconds, the labor, the financial part of it. Buffet is not a textile man. His priority is singular — investment. He's not wrong for Mr. Buffet.

If you start off with ownership that is not singularly interested in textiles, then every way he can find to make money — another reason, another place — he will jump at that opportunity. What he did, in effect, was to take that money and invest it in the largest return. From his point of view, as an investor, that makes perfect sense. You can't argue with it. From the point of view of social ramifications, or from the textile mill point of view, these were devastating decisions.

If the mills come back, they're going to be very small or they're going into specialties. You won't see the big mills. You won't see the textile operation you're sitting here watching today.

Eventually, the technical knowledge will disappear. There are new techniques, new technology, coming in. I was reading a magazine article about the brand new rubber-covering machines. They're so sophisticated, people who work with them won't even be able to recognize what they are. And that type of thing will come down the road. But in my career, you gathered the knowledge and then you used it on the machines.

Helen Medeiros, 84, works on drawing-in on a harness at Satkin Mills. She is doing it the old-fashioned way, by hand. Each reed, dropwire and heddle has to be threaded, demanding keen eyesight, a steady hand and patience. Fred Satkin says she works as fast as any machine (which also requires at least two people) and she works full time. Photograph by Rachel Barnet, 1988.

People like us, we're going to be out of a job. Down South, they're closing sixty, seventy mills. There are so many people out of work with all that technical knowledge. These buildings here, I'm sure will remain, but not for textiles. When you go down South, you see the change in the textile plants. Any modern mill today is a one-floor business and it's all automated. You don't have pickers like I have. You go to a modern mill and they chute-feed cards. A chute goes right in the back of the card and the cards are doffed automatically. They all have auto-levels and the evenness is controlled. You don't need a yarn lab. It's controlled at the machine.

In my opinion, the industry isn't going to be what it is. It's not going to be what it was in the thirties, and ten years from now it won't be like it is today. I've seen, just in the last ten years, looms that come on line, and in five years they are obsolete. The looms don't have shuttles anymore. It's an entirely different process, and they run three, five, ten times faster than the ones with shuttles.

If you don't readapt to it, then you're going to lose it. That's been part of our problem. We don't respond as quickly as we should to changing technology and higher productivity. That's one of the reasons we lost the competitive edge. But if you want a growth story, there's Satkin over there. He bought the old Schwartz lumberyard. They have 120 water-jet looms over there. Now that's growth in textiles in New Bedford.

To me, the writing had been on the wall at Berkshire/Hathaway for a good five years. In my position, I had to sit here and convince everybody that it wasn't over. I said, "We're trying. We're going to get new winders. We're going to get new looms." I always had hope though.

We tried different marketing approaches. We tried to get into different niches. We felt, if we could get into specialty markets, we could hang in longer and make a profit. Last year I ordered a loom for evaluation and before it arrived, I was told we'd be closing. I asked Mr. Morrison (President of Berkshire/Hathaway), "Should we cancel the evaluation of the loom?" and he said, "that's a thought. What do you think, Kim?" I said, "No, I don't want to." Even though I knew we were going to close, I knew I'd have to keep the hopes up and the attitudes up so this place wouldn't go to pot. So we spent the money and the loom was brought in. We had the filters here. We ran the trials and, yes, everybody was saying, "Oh boy, this is the loom. This is the way we're going to stay in business."

In my own heart, I have to keep face, just like now, with everybody out there. I say, "We have to have a sense of humor. We have to keep our heart. Don't let it get you down or eat you up!" But there are people out there getting sick about it. I can't portray that. Even though I feel it when I go home, I can't let that happen in my position. I've got to keep these people doing the best job they can 'til the end. I can't let them down.

Fred Satkin, President, Satkin Mills

When someone owns a business, he is looking for what he can do better than anyone else. And he understands that we may have a bad year this year and the next, but the following two years will be great and we'll make more. But when you have outside investment, you must show a return of investment on an immediate basis, which is a dangerous type of decision-making process.

I began by studying the business. With conventional looms, you had both a high capital cost and a high labor cost. I was willing to be one or the other, but I wasn't willing to be both. I had gone to the American machinery manufacturers, like Draper, and they virtually told me they were making more money on used parts than they were selling new machines. Therefore, they had no intention of doing research and development in the area of loom modernization.

Those looms had changed very little since the early 1900's. Motors were put on them instead of big belts so they could run individually. They could run a little faster, but speed and quality were limited by the basic motion of throwing the shuttle across, also by the yarn and the strength it takes to weave. So I could only increase in very small increments from that point. Something totally different had to be conceived.

If I could become capital-intensive only, with machinery, then I could afford to pay my people a lot of money. And if I could pay them a lot of money, then they could produce a better cloth because there is more incentive for them. Now I had to find the machine to do it. That was to be the Japanese Nissan loom, which I was one of the first to buy.

On a conventional loom, as one part wears, you don't change the part that wore, you compensate by adjusting another part. So, it's the theory of compensation. That's an art. On these new looms everything is geared and precise. As a part wears, you take that part out and replace it with a new part. Therefore, it's a skill.

Such a skill can be taught fairly rapidly. Right away, I felt that was the major benefit. I could not conceive of why the theory of the water-jet principle wouldn't work.

The real problem in textiles started way back. After World War II a lot of the owners found that their equipment was worth so much on an export market. So as the looms and equipment got older, the owners proceeded to liquidate as a large amount of money could be made.

Berkshire/Hathaway was different. They stayed on because it was a family-owned business. When things started to deteriorate, Buffet came in. He was looking at it as creation of capital, so he liquidated. Virtually all the Berkshire/Hathaway plants were in Fall River, and when I first came here in 1964, those plants had just been closed. Thousands of looms were still there. Someone could have pushed a button and run them. The reason we gave technology away (overseas) was because we were not considering it as competition, but as additional sales at a cheaper price.

An American practice started to come into being at that time. By the time a person becomes president of a major corporation in the United States, he is in his late fifties or early sixties and he knows he can only be president for a relatively short period of time. His bonuses are dependent upon the return of his investing in the short run. So he's not going to put out large capital costs in research and development. He wants the return on his tenure and, therefore, he is personally going to get the best reward. As a result, everybody started to think in terms of the short-term. You're talking about executives in major corporations.

What killed Berkshire/Hathaway in the end was that its real estate value was so much greater than its operating value. At that point there was no point in continuing. Of course, someone analyzed the company and said, "In order for this company to be competitive, we have to make an investment." And investment means a minimum of four million bucks. And Buffet said to him, "What's the return on four million bucks?" And that's the end of the company.

William D. Betts, Executive Vice-President, Berkshire/Hathaway Manufacturing Company

When the company was worth fifty million dollars they should've closed it right down and taken the fifty million of stockholders' money and put it somewhere else. If you want to buy new equipment, you could save this operation. However, in buying state-of-the-art equipment, the textile company buys it and they put it on the floor brand new. It's now a third of what you just paid for it, and the return is very small.

It's simply this way: would you put your money in a savings bank at 3% or 4%, or would you put it in a certificate of deposit at 7%, or treasury notes at 8%? If you have a choice, where would you put your money? If we were averaging a 20% return in other businesses, why would we put it into a business where there is no return? Some years you get a return, some years you don't. But, overall, you tie up a million dollars, say, for ten years and make money for one year, lose money the next, make money . . . But the net of those ten years, you have no return.

My father lived to be 103. He died just a few years ago. I'm sad that he died, but he sure had a good life. And there was no sense putting him on life-support systems. Around here, we were looking for alternatives for four or five years, trying to keep the thing going. In the long term, why buy machinery that takes you thirty years to earn the money to pay it back? And in between you've got imports and all sorts of things like that. Why do it?

The Berkshire/Hathaway Mill was the last of the large mills, and it lasted a good twenty to twenty-five years beyond the others. Basically, it was a well-kept mill and a well-managed mill. Because of that, it probably lived twenty to twenty-five years beyond its normal life.

John Delgado, Weave Room Supervisor

A few of us talked about renting off from the company, running it ourselves. They didn't want to rent one portion [of the mill]. I was a little perturbed.

Weavers are considered semi-skilled workers. Ninety-five percent are Portuguese immigrants. We hire them on a more or less referral service, you know, someone has a brother who does good work. I'm talking from my experience as a supervisor. When I started here in 1968, they had a lot of English and French. During the seventies they started to retire. There was a volcano in the Azores and a lot of immigrants came over then. There was a five-year waiting period. Most of these people don't bother to vote. They don't get involved in politics. If they bothered with it, this city would be a lot better off.

We have 1,200 looms altogether. I'm using a Model-T and [the competition] are using a Cadillac, you know. Some are twenty, forty, or fifty years old. There were 2,500 looms when I started. I don't think they will sell one of these looms. Forty to one hundred thousand dollars for each loom. You would need six to seven hundred of them to match what we do now. These are all written off. Just junks of iron, that's all. A loom is a loom. I've never cried for them. It's the people.

Various Quotes From Management and Workers

Everybody appreciates a pair of shoes, but ten to fifteen years from now, we'll be walking around bare-assed because we'll have to ration textiles. We were efficient and had good quality. If we were bad, I could understand it.

John Delgado, a supervisor, does loomfixing when necessary. Here, he's putting in a salvage end to replace a broken warp end. Photograph by Joseph D. Thomas, 1985.

A lot of these guys are highly skilled. Maybe they don't have the education. Maybe they don't speak English, but they can talk to those machines anyway. They can fix anything.

I would like to send a letter to Reagan to tell him that his grandchildren will have to run around bare-assed.

Cloth Splitter

Sometimes you get up and you feel sick. You come in anyway, because just coming in here and talking to your friends is better for you than staying home.

Alfred Barboza, Weaver/Union Rep

The union here isn't working for us to get what we deserve. This involves two million dollars. The union is always on our side until it involves putting out money. They make it seem like the mill is refusing to give it. We're going to lose out. I wouldn't care if we lost half the money we are due, as long as the union doesn't get it.

They tell us there is no slavery, but it still exists. "Thank you for the good job you did for us," and that's it.

Slasher Tender

Overview of the Spooling
Department, a few days before
Leo Larue (left center) ran out
the last spools by hand.
Photograph by Joseph D. Thomas,
1985.

I've never seen Mr. Buffet. I think he really doesn't know what it's like. Also, that's probably why he's very business-like in his decisions. There's no emotion involved, because he's not here to see it. If you're around people all the time you get attached, right? Some people can be around people and not get attached, but I think that's a minor amount that would do that. Obviously, by not being here there are no attachments for him, so it becomes much easier . . . ownership inabsentia. He sits in Omaha, Nebraska.

Slashing Department Supervisor

Well, it's actually like a family, because you're with people eight hours a day, and you get along with the people. I always get along with everybody, you know. But I see a lot of people in the world, nothing but cutthroats. I'd say it's like a family here, really.

I don't like to move around. If I go to something, I stay there. Like I stayed here. I liked the job.

William Dubois, Loomfixer

Before my time as manager, if a worker was asked to clean up the dust over there today, he'd say, "No, no, that's not my job." Since I took over, everybody's doing everything. If the painters have a lot of work today and the electricians and carpenters don't have too much work, everybody paints.

You treat a person the way you would want him to treat you, and that's the only way you're going to get by in this world. And if a manager thinks he's going to belittle the worker, the worker is going to get him in the end because he has the upper hand. He's out there working with the product. But you have to keep one thing in mind as the manager: You are working for the company and the company has to make money. If the manager doesn't make money for the company, somebody's going to be replaced. You have to use your workers as tools; as a pair of pliers, as a screwdriver, as a saw. But you have to treat them like people.

I have only five guys out there now. I go out there in the morning, if we're going to start a new job, and I sit down with them to talk. I don't pay attention to the clock because . . . I'm explaining a job, the purpose of doing it, and how we want the end result . . . that's valuable time to me. I'm not going to tell them how to do it. If I can suggest ways to make it easier, I'll do that. I always tell them what to expect in the end, and I tell them, "If you guys need anything, let me know." That's the way I operate.

Charles Curran,
Maintenance Supervisor

The attitude you bring to the job, that you come with to work, is what is important . . . like loyalty. So many people are just interested in the paycheck. How they get it, they don't care. Others will do the job to the best of their ability.

We're the people who fell in through the cracks. The plant is closing the 31st, and my birthday is on January 21st. I'm missing getting my separation pay by three weeks. If the company was responsible, I would go talk to them. But the company is not responsible. I think that even Stanton, he would have run into the same problem.

I've never been ashamed of this kind of work. I come from pioneer stock. I've enjoyed working here, since I had to work. We're like a family. But I'm not tied to the machine. I could have left it at any time. And I'm looking forward to stopping after thirty years of working.

Mary Correia, Cutter

EPILOGUE

From the fourth floor of Building Four, in the Spooling Room with my back to the window, I can feel the sunlight which has quietly climbed in through the window, and rests now on my shoulders. In front of me the image remains of the bustle of productivity which had filled this room only a few months earlier.

I am standing between a hope and a reality. The hope, symbolized by the warmth of the sunlight from behind, was the promise given in the early years of the nineteenth century that the sordid plight of the textile mills in England would be purified by the noble nature of this freshly formed nation. The reality is of people, compartmentalized and standardized within a rigid system of efficiency and behavioral control.

Standing here on the oil-stained floor of Berkshire/Hathaway, in a room of slumped, dark shapes amid the echoes, a stark reality is before me. I listen and remember the image of one man looking another man in the eye, a man he has known for thirty-five years, and saying, "I'm sorry, George, but this will be your last day." George is no longer useful as a worker in this system, which does not distinguish between the worker and the man with a family to support.

The shutting down of textile mills is the story of the Georges of this country, workers mostly from foreign backgrounds. It is about the people who break the news to them, the managers, who increasingly shoulder this burden as ownership distances itself in a conglomerate. It is also about the decision-makers, people who determine workers' lives and the American way.

I found Leo Larue alone in the spooling room. As I approached from the far end of the room, hearing the echoing thud of each of my footsteps, he turned to face me, addressing me by name. "Well, these are the last three. The last three spools ever in this mill. After this, there are no more. I decided to run them out myself by hand."

It is a disquieting, yet riveting moment. How many times has this mechanized movement been performed at this machine in this mill? For one hundred years, there has been no difference in the motion; the only difference is that human beings bring meaning to the work. I tried to look at this final act as merely another in a long line of acts. No use, the human being got in the way.

Leo's voice broke the stillness.

"I loved this job. I'm inquisitive by nature, always looking for something else, something better, a better way to do it. Even when I started in the card room, I was inquisitive, looking for a way to improve myself."

Running Out the Mill

text and photographs by Joseph D. Thomas

Information provided by William Isherwood's unpublished manuscript, "Cotton Processing From Bale To Cloth," and from Kim Baker and Leo Larue.

In the yarn mill at the Berkshire/Hathaway, the entire process of making yarn takes place. This process includes picking, carding, drawing, roving, spinning, spooling and a few steps in between. The yarn mill is a four-story structure and is supervised by Leo Larue, a native of Fall River. Leo is as dedicated and knowledgeable as he is hard-working. He took us through the entire yarn mill, introduced us to people, explained the process, and shared his thoughts along the way.

"Did just about every job at the King Philip Mill," he tells us. "Moved up from card room to picker boss to third hand on second shift to assistant overseer. In 1959 I became overseer of carding in Plant E. I'm a mill man. I was born and brought up in the mill. Never got a degree. I started as a scourer in the card room. That's about the lowest, dirtiest job. When you're a scourer, they will pull you off your job anytime and put you on bale-breakers, pickers, drawing frames and roving frames. I learned how to fix machinery in the card room — line and level."

The making of the yarn in this mill begins with the arrival of 700 pound bales of polyester. The bales are taken apart and the fiber is thrown into blenders which weigh and blend the stock to the required specifications. From the blender the stock is put into the picker which produces a roll about 18″ in diameter and 40″ long, called a lap. From here, the lap will undergo "carding," a process which combs and straightens the fibers. The carding machine, employing oscillating combs, flacks and a doffer, will render the lap into a transparent web, pass it through an orifice, and produce a tubular, rope-

The Card Room

Bottom Right: Card Room worker takes the raw stock from the bale and feeds it into the picker hopper (blender). *Top:* The stock is transformed into a lap by the picker, where Tony, card room boss grinder, doffs it, puts it on a truck, and brings it to the card.

like strand called a "sliver" (pronounced sly'ver). For each yard of lap fed into the machine, one hundred yards of sliver will be produced. The carding process is critical in determining the end quality of the yarn.

"Take college men into the card room and they've lost it," scoffs Leo Larue. "I've read the books. Go in there and spend the hours and you do it. That's how you learn. You listen to people. Even the janitors, they'll tell you something. If you shut the door, you're not going to get anything. You can't close the doors.

"Some people look down on mill workers. I have never had that feeling. Most of the people here are proud."

Following carding, the sliver is brought to the drawing frames, doubled and drafted, and refined further by taking eight cans of sliver and turning it into one can. Drawing will add evenness and strength to the stock. From the drawing frame, the

sliver must be refined into a form of yarn. This is done on a fly frame through a process called "roving." By roller drafting the sliver and giving it a slight amount of twist, roving makes the yarn finer. In the end, the can of sliver is transformed into a bobbin of yarn called roving.

"All the machines are different," contends Leo. "There are eight rovamatics over there and they're all individuals. Years ago, we had an old man running twelve cotton combers — a Portuguese man — he was very devoted to his job. Every morning, he would arrive early and say good-morning to each rover. He had a name for each one and prayed to God he'd have a good day and the machine would run good. If the machine ran exceptionally well, he praised the machine, complimented it. If he had one running bad, he'd plead with it to run better — it caused him so much misery."

Opp. page left: Card tender clears the waste from the "scavenger roll" on the front of the card. The card sliver can be seen coming off the rollers at the bottom front of the carding machine. Opp. page right; On the back of the card, the picker laps are being run through the machine. There were 58 cards running in this room with two tenders. Left: Sliver is fed from the cans into the backside of the rovematics for roving. Bottom left: Drawing-frame tender straightens out the sliver coming off the frame and into the cans. Bottom right: Rover tender tends to keeping a clean product.

The final step in manufacturing yarn is to transfer the roving to the spinning frames, where the product will be twisted and refined into a thread-like yarn. The Berkshire/Hathaway used the "ring spinning" process, which employs a ring and a "traveler" in winding and twisting the yarn. The traveler is a fine wire loop that travels around the rim of a finely polished steel ring. The yarn is run through the traveler to the bobbin.

The difference in speed of the spinning bobbin and that of the yarn being delivered from the front drafting rolls (with the traveler taking up the difference) is what determines the amount of twist in the yarn and its strength and density. When the yarn leaves the spinning frames, it is on bobbins.

"The yarn mill is competitive," says Leo. "Years ago we made a survey. Even with antiquated equipment, we

make a yarn cheaper than we can purchase. Thought had been given to further developing this yarn mill by buying new comb-winders. We would have produced a seven pound cone versus a three pound cheese (referring to the type of spool the yarn is on when received by the loom). The large cone lasts longer in the weave room. Cuts on doffing time. To convince Buffet, we had to go through Morrison. They said no to new comb-winders. We tried for ten years. Buffet couldn't get his money back fast enough. He wants a 15% return on his investment. Instead, they made some moves that didn't pan out.

"We have a yarn here we sell to J.P. Stevens, fiber 40, that they've been trying to duplicate for years. Our machines may be old, but they make a yarn people want and no one else can make."

John Simoes, Division Manager, Synthetic Preparation, gave us his theory. "Leo makes a yarn over there, it's called slub yarn or nub yarn. Those are yarns with built-in imperfections,

Spinning

done on purpose to add effect to a particular fabric. They used to try not to produce those, but now you can design and put them in. They have attachments to electronically produce the slubs on the spinning frame. Anyway, Leo was making a perfect nub yarn that J.P. Stevens had been trying to make but couldn't. So when they found out we were closing, they asked if they could see how we do it. It's just something peculiar about that spinning frame and the attachment that allowed it. Maybe it's because his spinning frames are old. It just now hit me! I wouldn't have thought that was why, but Stevens would've had much newer spinning frames and maybe that was why. I don't know."

"Part of our heritage is going down the tubes," Leo laments. "A lot of people have grown up and prospered because of textiles. People were in tears these past weeks as I said good-bye. I try to say good-bye to each one of them. I've had some sad times the last few weeks."

shop in a couple of years in New Bedford somewhere, definitely. Probably with my sister. If you have your own business, it's good. But working for someone else is no good.

"I used to go much faster at this. But not anymore. Nobody cares now (because of plant closing). I would get a lot more done and the spools'd be a little bigger."

"I get a 20 minute break but only take five minutes to eat my sandwich. Then I go the the women's room to have a smoke. I don't usually let them

After leaving the spinning department on the second floor, Leo brought us up to the fourth floor to the spooling department. (The third floor, formerly the winding department, was now being rented to a shoe distributor.) While Leo attended to his supervising chores, we found a friendly Grace Rosario doffing on the spooling frames and making starters. It takes her about five minutes to change and start 60 spindles on the winder.

"You have to wait about five minutes till the spool gets about ½" to ¾" thick," says Grace as she doffs the spindles into a small truck. The large

spools are broken down on the winder to make starters, then go back to the spooler. There, the yarn is wound from the spinning bobbins onto "cheeses" that fit the creels on the warper. Only one row of cheeses is running today with several bobbins running also.

"Can't wait to get out of here. Everybody's gone now. There's no one to talk to. My sister (a twin) and mother have gone two weeks now. My sister's collecting. Mother's home relaxing.

"When you work in a mill all your life, what do you get out of it? You just get old. I'm going to open a dress yell at me. Like if I leave a few minutes early now, they say 'Oh, you can't leave at quarter of, you leave at ten of two.' So I say, What's the big deal? In a few days this place is gonna be shut down. But Leo, he says, 'Oh, Mr. Baker's not going to go for that.' You gotta be kidding, look at this place. There's no one here!

"As long as I can beat the machine, that's about it. It's a matter of timing. Knowing how long it takes to make the spindle a certain size. I used to keep a sheet of paper over there and write down all the doffs I'd do. I was supposed to do 40 doffs an hour but I was doing 60. So they said don't bother writing it down. You're doing plenty.

"Leo's watching now, just let me work. I'll talk to you after.

"I used to train people here and they'd only last a couple of weeks, complain about a bad back and say, 'how do you do that so fast?' But I just did it. I guess I'm good at it."

Spooling

Opp. page left: A spooler winds broken ends (waste) around her hands as she ties in the cheese. *Opp. page right:* Detail shows the spooler, after finding the end on the bobbin, placing the bobbin in the spooler pocket with her left hand, and putting the end in the thread holder with her right hand. The "traveler" will automatically tie the end to the cheese. When the cheese is full, it will be replaced with a starter (a small cheese started on another frame). *Bottom left:* Grace Rosario makes starters and doffs them, throwing them over her shoulder into the truck bins behind her. *Bottom right:* Leo Larue, Yarn Mill Supervisor, poses with Clementina, a spooler tender, shortly before informing her that this would be her last week.

Following the spooling operation, we left the yarn mill (and the domain of Leo Larue) and were escorted to the border, via the second floor, where we ended up on the third floor of Plant B in the synthetic preparation department supervised by John Simoes. Here, the next step, preparing the yarn for weaving, begins with warping. This set-up consists of creels (large metal carriages which hold the cheeses) and a warper head (the machine). The object is to load the creel with up to 540 cheeses and run the yarn off and onto a warp or section beam (the giant spools which go on the loom). Since this mill produces spun yarn (short, coarse fibers) and purchases its filament yarn (continuous length, fine yarn) from other producers, the creel set up is different for each yarn.

In the Warper Room, attendants Juliata Nunes and Tina Gomes had just prepared a set of eight section beams for slashing. They are tying-in another set, filling each creel with packages of nylon, filament yarn to make four section beams. Two creels, set twice, will make eight beams, each with 653 ends (individual strands of yarn). The yarn is fed to the creel through the teeth in the comb roll, called dents. The yarn, a 210 dernier nylon for coating fabric, will be for outdoor use — either rain gear or tents. When starting from scratch, the creel could take a couple of days to fill with two people tying-in to ends from a former beam.

Tina Gomes has been a warper at the Berkshire/Hathaway since arriving in the U.S. 13 years ago. After a couple of months of unemployment she will try to get another job. "Got to have money. No work, no money." She would like to go back to Portugal

but her husband and children would rather stay here. "Some people make $20-$25,000, put it in the bank, and live well in Portugal."

Juliata Nunes says the mill was like a second home to many of the workers, including herself. Her husband is in maintenance and both her parents worked at this mill. Her mother, now 84, worked in the twisting room, her father in the card room.

"This mill contracted with Portuguese workers so their relatives could come over. That's why it's like a big family. It really is! The only choices immigrants have are to work in the mills or clean houses. We came to America to better our lives. That's why we work so hard. A person born here may not care about work as much.

"My son is 17 and at Voke studying electricity and computers. He takes a lot of responsibility for his school work, but not a lot for his part time job. If he feels too tired, he may not go to it. Our generation would never do that.

"We can't change the way teenagers are. The whole idea was to work hard and give my kids an education."

Warping

Left: Juliata Nunes ties-in on the warper creel. These are filament yarn packages not manufactured in this mill.
Bottom: Tina Gomes adjusts the comb on the warper. *Right:* Tina ties-in the warper creel package.

replaced with a lease rod. The lease operation keeps the individual ends separated, preventing their adherence to one another.

In the slashing room we met slasher tender Ernest Bourque and his assistant, Charles Lawrence, working on the filament yarn slasher (continuous length yarn).

Ernest is 46 and has been at Berkshire/Hathaway for 28 years. "The old slasher tenders were all English," he tells us. "They finally let the Irish and French in before letting in the Portuguese around 1940. When the Portuguese came, they said, 'That's the end of this mill.' But this was the only mill that lasted through the 80s and it's 98% Portuguese.

"The slasher room is well organized. The machines are 20 years old but they've been modernized. They didn't modernize enough downstairs, though. They bought old looms.

"I think this closing bothers me less than my friends who know I'm losing my job. I have three sons who work at Varian Corporation and they're all getting laid off. I just grew a 75 pound pumpkin for Halloween. Took some pictures of it with my new granddaughter. I'm not going to worry about unemployment until next Wednesday."

From the warping department, the beams are brought in a "set" to the adjacent "slashing" room. On our visit, the slashers were combining an eight beam set onto one warp beam (or loom beam) with a pre-determined number of ends (5808). The warp would eventually be woven into rayon lining for Hart, Shafter and Martin suits.

In the slashing process, the yarn will be immersed in a sizing solution that will strengthen and prepare it for weaving. John Simoes tells us, "The kind of yarn I run on this side is filament yarn. They are very tender yarns, very fine yarns. Without a protective coating you could never weave them. You could never get them through the heddles or the drop wires. They would just unbraid and fuzz up and break."

Years ago, a horse glue was used for sizing, then potato or corn starch with tallow, now it's a synthetic glue. A lease or string is run through the ends of each warp beam before sizing. After sizing, the lease is removed and

Manuel Gonsalves, 53, is a slasher tender on spun yarn (short fiber yarn, spun in this mill). In the U.S. for 18 years, he has worked at Berkshire/Hathaway for 15 years. In Portugal, he worked in the Coast Guard. "There's no mills in Portugal." He says he loves his job and he can't retire. He must find another job.

"This slasher is better on the eyes than the other ones. You don't have to thread each reed. Some yarns, like the blue, make worse air.

"I can't believe this mill's closing. Few years ago we had six machines going each shift. Maybe it's allright for the young people — they'll find another job — but not for me. My legs are no good. I hurt my arm turning a lever. Something tore like a piece of cloth. Three doctors told me three different stories."

Ted Borges works the second shift on the filament yarn slasher. "I like this job. I've been here since 1957. There were rumors the plant was closing since the day I arrived. We never paid any attention to them."

We met Ted again, one week after his final day at work. He greeted us, glassy-eyed, at the personnel office where he was picking up his last check. He brought his wife with him "I've been here almost 30 years and she's never seen the place. I always wanted to show her where I worked.

Slashing

Top left: Ted Borges pieces-up a broken end by twisting it together with an adjacent end. Each end has its place in the "dent" (tooth) of the reed. *Bottom left:* Manuel Gonsalves tries to straighten out a lap (broken ends which build up on the section beam as the beam rotates) and put the ends back in the warp. *Top right:* Ernie Bourque runs a lease through the warp. *Bottom right:* Ernie looks for a lost end while his helper, Charlie Lawrence, looks on.

From the slashing department, the loom beam will be delivered to the "drawing-in" room where the yarn will be entered through the reed, harness and drop-wires, the final step in preparing the warp for weaving. The harness, together with the reed and dropwires, guide and maneuver the warp. allowing the shuttle to weave a computed design through the warp of the fabric. Until fairly recent times, drawing-in was performed by young girls, whose supple fingers and keen eyesight made them ideal operatives for this highly skilled task. For them, drawing-in involved following a detailed plan laid out by the mill's designers that could require using up to 25 harnesses. Today, a drawing-in machine performs the task of threading each individual end through the reed, harness and dropwires.

After drawing-in, the harness, reed and dropwires are tied together and are placed on a truck, along with the beam, and shipped to the weave room.

The Weave Room

The process of weaving and the mechanics of the loom are subjects too complex to detail in this essay. Simply stated, weaving is an ancient craft which involves the insertion of a weft or filling yarn between two or more strands of warp yarn. The warp, as described previously, is carried on loom (or warp) beams and is a continuous length. The number of threads on the beam makes up the "sley"; and the number of threads intersecting the warp are "picks."

The Berkshire/Hathaway had two basic styles of looms: the Draper power loom, which could weave fabrics between 46" and 72"; and the Sauer looms, weaving fabrics up to 150" wide. Both looms use shuttles to run the weft throught the warp. At one time, Berkshire/Hathaway wove 60% of the menswear lining made in the U.S. At the time of the closing, they were running mostly curtain fabrics, some linings and materials used in women's wear. They worked strictly with synthetic fibers — rayon and polyester blends. Cotton had not been manufactured since 1968.

In the "nuts and bolts" room at the far end of one of the weaving rooms, a group of weavers and loomfixers graced us with conversation. The highest in seniority, they were the last to be laid off and would be working together for two more weeks.

Hilda Albino, weaver: I'm gonna be 62 in August. I was planning on working another year, but, eh . . . maybe take a part time job. Play it by ear. Don't think I can stay home and do nothing. I've been in textiles 41 years in January. Started out as a battery hand. Became a weaver in '71. I feel bad. It's been like a home away from home.

To train to be a weaver, they put you upstairs on a loom for a few weeks. They put me with a weaver, that's how I learned. Some weavers have more pride than others, like right now I do the work the best of my ability. A good weaver is conscientious about calling someone over when the loom stops. If I can take care of it without bothering the fixer or smashpiece, I will.

In my department, I was the only woman weaver. I like it. It's heavy but I like it. Years ago they didn't push for women to work in weaving because women had to have breaks every half-hour. But now, I guess it's because the women who come from the old country, they know as stitchers they can make a lot more money — a lot more than I'm making. I went stitching when I was seventeen and I was too nervous. The boss was always right on top of me. I could've gone to the cloth room but I didn't want to sit down all day.

Opp. page top: Linton Chase, drawing-in attendant, separates the dropwires in search of a lost end. *Opp. page bottom:* Manuel Telheiro, Linton's assistant, repairs a drawn warp. He has to locate the heddle, then bring the end through the proper dent in the reed. *Right:* In the "nuts and bolts room," from left to right, are: Armand Martins, loomfixer; Manny Costa, cloth doffer; Napoleon Gladu, loomfixer; Manuel Lopes, changeover; and Hilda Albino, weaver. *Bottom:* In Department 69, Joe Raposo, weaver, stands by one of his looms.

Napoleon Gladu, loomfixer: I was a weaver for a long time. I've been a fixer for 18 years. You gotta know weaving before you do fixing. A fixer's got to know everything in the room. To be a fixer you gotta go up the ladder. The next job up, in the weave room, is a boss. Years ago they had what they called, third hands. If the fixer got stuck, the third hand was supposed to help them. They done away with that. Third hand would give the changeovers their work. A change is below a fixer. The big jobs, dirty jobs, the changer gets. Changer's supposed to do anything in the room.

Bad weavers worry about the piece work. Some weavers, all they're trying to do is run the loom. They don't care about seconds. All they want is to get paid. That's what they worry about is getting paid at the end of the week.

Manuel Lopes: Most of the people have worked a long time here. The young guys have been laid off already. The ones here now do a good job.

Napoleon: Weavers make over seven dollars an hour. Fixers are the highest paid. $7.60, except for the knotter. There's only one knotter now and he makes about $10.00 an hour. The knotter ties in the warps. Joe Cunha does that. Years ago the fixers made more than them but they went on piece work. In other mills, where there's no piece work the fixer makes more. They used to do about seven or eight warps at one time, now they're up to fourteen with the new machine they got. They can push it now, so they got them on piece work.

Fixers used to make as much as workers at Morse Twist Drill, or even truck drivers! Last 20 years, what happened was we were getting small raises while everyone else was getting big raises. Years ago they were blaming the South for low pay, then the South was paying the same as we were, so they couldn't blame the South no more. Then they started blaming imports.

We got such a good union. Three weeks ago they went up 30 cents. We got four weeks to go and they went up on our dues! And they didn't tell us about it. And we don't see no union. We don't hear nothing. We had a meeting and they didn't even show up for it. People outside waiting for the meeting and they didn't show up! We got a good union, alright!

Manuel: We had three shop-stewards, they were the first ones to leave. They find another job. They run.

Napoleon: When the mill announced the closing, they all ran. Then we got no representation. They were never good but it's worse now. They should come in here and check up on the work once in awhile.

Manuel: We have a union to pay.

Napoleon: They only give us a very small pension. No severance pay. Got to wait till you're 62. I got 38 years and lost severance pay. The people not working are making more than us working. We tried everything. Wrote to the labor board. But we can't get nothing. I gotta look for a job. At 58 it's hard to find a job. They were supposed to do things. Dukakis came down here. They don't do nothing.

Left: Napoleon Gladu, left, and Manuel Lopes, piece-up a broken warp end. They'll do this by taking a strand of yarn, tie a weaver's knot to the warp end, and draw it through the dropwires, heddle and reed.
Right: Joe Weaver at one of his looms.

Hilda: I lose out by eight months.
Napoleon: I got out of the army at 20 and started here. I've been in textiles all my life. That's all I know. Before I went in the army I worked at the Firestone.

We're taking parts off the looms now to run others. They've been selling wrenches, vices, trucks to the workers. Guess they'll junk all the looms. Most of the places have shuttleless looms. That's why this stuff is gone. We'd have to be retrained. At my age, I'm too old to learn something like that. When I started we had 36 looms. They had batteries. Then we went to 60, 80 and 100. We only got 20 looms now. In this room there are 480 looms, there's only sixty something running altogether.

We had a good job. It was a good place to work. Nobody bothered you. I enjoyed myself while I was here. I got no complaints about the company. I had 38 good years here.
Hilda: I'm gonna take it easy for a while. We'll be all done by next Friday.
Manuel: I'm gonna do construction.

Joe Weaver, weaver
I was born August 14, 1925 and lived in Shamokin, Pennsylvania. I went to school 'til I was 15. Had to leave school to go to work. At 17, I went into the Navy and came out at 20 and got married. At 23, I went to work in this mill. Been here ever since. That's my life story.

In Shamokin, I worked in the coal mines. This work here is not as dangerous. You can die down there. It's hotter, tougher, dirtier work. At that time we had bootleg mines. You'd go out and dig your own mine, ya know. Go out, dig your own hole and get the coal out yourself. Me and my brothers did it. Penn Railroad owned

the land. They'd get a royalty on every ton of coal we took out. All you needed was a pick and shovel, dynamite, 55 gallon drum on two by fours, and run it up the slope. We used to have a car up there. We jacked the wheel up, put a drum on the wheel with a cable and that's how we pulled the coal up.

We'd stake claims on the mines and sell the coal to the breakers — the Rozinnis. They're still running breakers today. Breakers had rollers and they'd bring the coal in in trucks. You'd break the coal, run it through

screens, separate it into different sizes, put it on trucks.

My grandfather was picking slate out of the coal when he was nine. My family's been here nine generations. Far back as I know, they all worked in coal mines. They were Pennsylvania Dutch. Ancestors came here in 1760s. They got a family tree back in Shamokin.

I was stationed in Newport for a while. A bunch of sailors used to go over to Lincoln Park. Lots of young girls at Lincoln Park. That's where I

met my wife. She was with a bunch of girls. Outside the merry-go-round, they had the bell with the sledge hammer. Every time you rang the bell, they'd give you a lei. I was winning and giving them away to all the girls. My wife thought I was crazy.

During the war I was in the Pacific. We took the marines off Iwo Jima. I was in Japan the day the war ended.

We settled in New Bedford after the war. When I came here that's about all there was — textile mills. No regrets about settling here. I got in the wrong

business, that's all. When you don't have education, what else can you do. My wife, Irene, got laid off in October. She'd been working here 19 years. She was a unifil-tension cleaner.

I suppose I could've gone to Goodyear or Acushnet Process — that'd be the place to work. That's where they give you your pension. They don't give you the shaft. The union has some contract here where you have to be 62 to get severance.

It was a steady job. The only time I was out of work was in 1955, when we were on strike for 13 weeks.

The weaver was the backbone of the mill. The weaver was more or less steady work — going all the time. Weaver's the guy who made the money for the fixer and the changeover. For instance, you take a weaver making 90%. Then he decides he's gonna dog it — make 80%. So naturally, the cloth isn't coming off

the loom. He's not going to make as much money. Therefore, that's what happened here, beside the imports. The jobs weren't running good, that's some of the things that I think caused the mill to close down. You don't have the weavers or the fixers that you used to have. Years ago, you had fixers who really knew their stuff. There's some people you can put in a mill, whether it be a fixer or a weaver or even a boss. They may never leave the job in

50 years. That's part of it. I don't know what the reason is.

Bosses don't get on people enough. Several years back we had a cloth cutter here. Every time he cut the cloth, he'd waste 10 to 20 yards of cloth. Christ. I was in the office. I told the boss and Mr. Baker. They said, "Oh, we're gonna do something about it." A week later he's doing the same thing. Now that goes on for years — and you're losing money all the time. You're losing that good cloth. It goes to waste or rags. Years ago, weavers used to cut their own cloth — when we had 36 looms. We had a battery hand who took care of the winder. The last several years, they also gave the weaver the winder to take care of. They cut the jobs down. At the same time, they gave the fixer the unifil to take care of. This is something new to the fixer. He had to learn this in a couple of weeks. But this stuff takes years to learn. Same with fixing. He learns things everyday on fixing, things that he never seen before. But now he's got two jobs to take care of.

In my 36 years here, I feel that I've done the best that I could do. When them horses ain't running out there, that's when it's a bad day. When they're running, it's a good day. Those are iron horses.

But they're just machines —nothing special. Like an automobile. You go through a puddle of water, the motor gets wet, and maybe the car skips or stalls. They don't have personalities. They're just machines.

Loomfixing

Bill Dubois, loomfixer at work

Bill Dubois gave me a demonstration of some of the tasks handled by the loomfixer. At right, he's changing the worn-out cover plate on the Saurer loom, which if left unchecked, would chafe the yarn and eventually allow a shuttle to fly out. He also changes the tongue, the leather strip encasing the shuttle, which when worn out, gives the shuttle a "bad flight." He uses wrenches and gauges to set looms; clothespins hold the yarn being pieced-up on the warp. On the Saurer looms, which are much wider than the Draper looms, he uses a 25½" straight-edge along with his 9" straight-edge.

In loomfixing language, I'm told that when changing the tongue, check the "dagger" or shuttle protector. The loom should "bang off" if the shuttle gets stuck. If the "finger" moves in too far, the dagger will shut off the loom. Otherwise the shuttle will tear the shed or break itself. Bill uses gauges to check the reed: "A 90 degree reed to the race." You need a clean "shuttle box to the lay (track)" to make sure the flight is true. The straight-edge lines up against the reed and the shuttle box. It must be true or it will damage the shuttle back.

Bill makes his own tools for leverage and reed hooks. "You can buy reed hooks but most of the people here make their own." He made a tool

to put the picker on the picker stick-lever that throws the shuttle. Other tools in his huge arsenal include: a tool to put the picker on the dobby; a vice which pulls the picker out; easy outs, punchers, chisels, wrenches, drill sets, tap and hexagon die set.

Bill started out as an oil and water runner at the age of 16. He designed a waste can drain system in 1962 which is still used on most of the looms. "The parts cost me 50 cents. I put the idea into the suggestion box. The company paid me $10."

Opp. page: Alfred Frias, weaver, tends the unifil. The unifil holds the yarn packaged in "cheeses" (foreground), which supplies the filling yarn for the warp, via the shuttle. *Below:* Bill Dubois employs his fixing tools. He squares the reed on the Sauer loom *(bottom left)*; replaces a worn picker (which throws the shuttle across the loom); and adjusts the back-binder of the shuttle box. Bill's vice, like his wrenches, is hand-made.

Cloth Room

Charles Perperas, Manager of Product Development and Quality Control

"I went to New Bedford Tech before World War II. It was one of the best technical textile schools in the country. My job here as technical director encompasses the laboratory, quality control and designing.

"My dad was a good Greek — in the restaurant business. He owned Lorraine's in downtown New Bedford. My Godfather was designer at the Hathaway mill for years. As a kid, I used to go with him. He had a power loom in his shop in his basement. He made and sold table runners and bureau scarves on the Cape. His father was a weaver back in Greece. They had several hand looms and spun the yarn themselves. He got his family and neighbors to work. They would bring in fabric from Europe. Americans were always specialized. But Europeans would run many different patterns.

"The designer/quality control person tells the weaver what to do. The weaver has to be familiar with what the designer wants. Once it's set up, you follow the patterns. A top notch weaver is one who can operate dobby equipment as opposed to a plain loom.

"You can make six to eight changes on a plain loom — from twills, oxfords, etc. Once you exceed twill, then you go into dobby. Once you go beyond dobby you're into Jacquard. With the Jacquard, you can do birds, flowers, intricate patterns."

Gloria Prenda, cloth inspector

"Don't forget to seam that together now," directed Gloria, while she and Margarida Silveira went about their job of seaming together 118" wide fabric. They also inspect the cloth on the large tables, cutting out the damaged part, and will work on widths as large as 140". Gloria has been at this mill for 21 years.

"We never had a warning slip! And then what? You're out on your can getting nothing. I feel sad that we're closing. It's like a family here.

"I was adopted by Portuguese parents. My mother worked in the Gosnold Mill. She would run 100 looms at a time and come home sweating. She used to wear a corset, a heavy embroidered Jacquard material. When she came home, it was soaking

wet with sweat. They complained about the heat, but it was their job. They'd say, 'muito quente, muito calor.' Mother said there was three things they used to say, 'caseira, igrejeira, trabalhadeira.' Her life was work, church and house. In my mind, I see my mother at the sink washing her corset every night. I used to say, 'Gee ma, that's all you do.' I can't remember what my father did except that he worked at Revere Copper and Brass.

"At 16, I used to bring all my books home to study, but I didn't study. My mother said, 'If you're not going to study, it's time to go to work.' So I was working there when I was 16.

"My mother always went to church. One time the church newsletter mentioned a group of soldiers who wanted pen pals. I wrote a very plain letter. If you ever got it, you wouldn't answer it. A month passed and I had six letters in my mailbox. All from my pen pal who looked like Glen Miller. He was overseas but he said he liked me already. He liked the way I wrote. I ended up marrying him.

"I cry when I think about this place closing. It's not the same — going to unemployment and standing in line. It's like begging. You feel it's not really your money."

Mary Correia, head grader

Mary started at the Berkshire/Hathaway 30 years ago when she ws 31. She's been here ever since. "This job offers variety. This one occupies my mind as well as my hands. I had intended to retire in January. I have nine children. For now, when I retire, I just want to relax."

At a vacant cloth-inspecting table, a paper heart, crudely cut, is taped to the table with a red rose across it and a cross made of blue tinsel beside it. A sign in pencil reads: "Rest in Peace. Amen. In Memory of Mary Correia's machine. 1955-1985."

Top left: Charlie Perperas and his skeleton crew of cloth room workers during the final days. Left to right, Rubin Macedo, Joao Medeiros, Patricia Alexander, Mary Correia, Charles Perperas, Arnoldo Freitas, Mary Sylvia, Dorothy Almeida, Kevin Brodo, Walter Elias. *Bottom left:* Gloria Prenda (left) and Margarida Silva (in the Sauer loom cloth room) stitch two fabric ends together. *Right:* Mary Correia *(top)* and Louise McGoff *(bottom)* inspect cloth.

Community Sponsors

American Eagle
Motor Coach, Inc.

Medeiros
Bus Company, Inc.

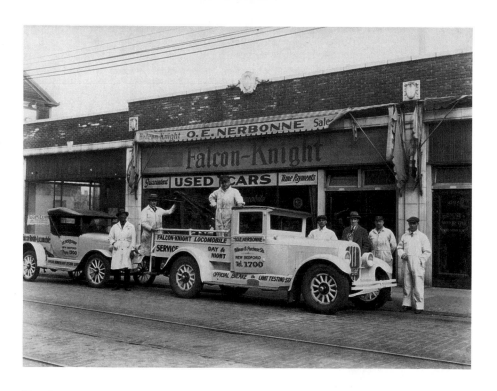

Specializing in charter bus
and luxury coach service.

Thirty years the area's leader
in pupil transportation

The safe and reliable way to travel

72 Sycamore Street
Fairhaven, Massachusetts

Daily Service to Boston

993-5040

The Standard-Times

*Serving Southeastern Massachusetts
Complete News & Information
Daily and Sunday*

226

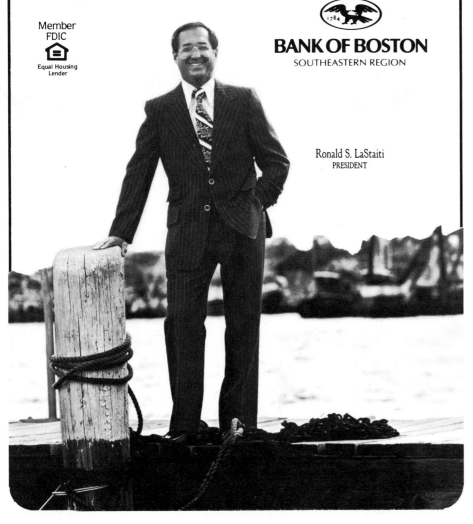

Fine clothing
since 1900

Silverstein's

ROUTE 6
ACROSS FROM BUTTONWOOD PARK
NEW BEDFORD

229

Bibliography

Legacy of the New Deal Sources used by the Federal Writers

A Guide to Island Places and **Folklore, Customs and Legends.**

Attleboro Sun. April 3, 1933.

Banks, Charles E. *History of Martha's Vineyard.* Boston, 1911.

Boston Globe Scrapbook. "Underground Railroad." New Bedford Free Public Library.

Boston News Letter. 1786.

Brereton, John A. and Archer, Gabriel. "A Brief and True Relation." Massachusetts Historical Society Collection, 1843.

Burgess, E.S. *The Old South Road of Gay Head.* 1926.

Emerson, Amelia Forbes. *Early History of Naushon.* 1935.

Hine, C.G. *History of Martha's Vineyard.* New York: Hine Brothers, 1908.

Hough, Henry Beetle. *Martha's Vineyard, A Summer Resort.* 1935.

Speck, Frank G. "Indian Notes and Monographs, 1928." Heye Foundation, 155th St., New York, NY.

Vineyard Gazette. Edgartown. September 1935 and August 1936.

Woods, Annie M., *Nomans Land. Isle of Romance.* 1931.

From These Strains and **Portuguese in New England**

Author Unknown. "Syrians and Arabians in the New World." *American Review of Reviews.* November 1916.

Author unknown. "The Children and I Have Happily Found Liberty." *Literary Digest.* 1919.

Hitti, P.K. *Syrians in America.* New York, 1924.

Kirschbaum, William G. "Serious Epidemics in New Bedford." New Bedford *Evening Standard.*

Local Census Reports. City of Fall River. 1937.

Pease, Zephaniah W. "Recollections of New Bedford." *Morning Mercury.*

Roberts, Peter. "The New Immigration." New York, 1912.

Sources used by *Spinner* Writers

Banks, Ann. *First Person America.* 1980.

Billington, Ray. "Government and The Arts." *American Quarterly.* Winter 1961.

Boss, Judy, and Joseph D. Thomas. *New Bedford: A Pictorial History.* Norfolk, VA: Donning Company, 1983.

Burns, James MacGregor. *Roosevelt: The Lion and the Fox.* 1956.

Davidson, Katherine. "Preliminary Inventory of the Federal Writers' Project." The National Archives. 1953.

Federal Writers' Project of Massachusetts. *Massachusetts: a Guide to its Places and People.* Boston: Houghton Mifflin, 1937.

Hobson, Archie, ed. *Remembering America: A Sampler of the WPA American Guide Series.* Columbia University Press, 1985.

Kugler, Richard C. *William Allen Wall.* New Bedford: Old Dartmouth Historical Society, 1978.

Leuchtenburg, William. *Franklin D. Roosevelt and the New Deal.* 1963.

Library of Congress, Photographs and Prints Division.

Mangione, Jerre. *The Dream and the Deal.* 1972.

Norton, Mary Beth et. al. *A People and a Nation.* Volume II, 1986.

Schlesinger, Arthur, Jr. *The Age of Roosevelt: The Politics of Upheaval.* 1960.

Spinner Publications. *Spinner: People and Culture in Southeastern Massachusetts.* Volumes I, II, III. New Bedford: Spinner Publications, Inc.

Standard-Times. New Bedford: May 10, 1965 and August 12, 1985.

Stett, Bill. *Remembering America.* 1985.

Stryker, Roy E., and Nancy Wood. *In This Proud Land.* New York City, 1973.

Terkel, Studs. *Hard Times: An Oral History of the Great Depression.* 1970.

Wilson, Joan Hoff. *Herbert Hoover: Forgotten Progressive.* 1975.

Wolfbein, Seymour. *The Decline of a Cotton Textile City.* 1944.

The Last Woven Yard: *Shutdown of the Berkshire/Hathaway*

Allen, Everett. *Children of the Light.* Boston: Little Brown, 1973

Anon. "Annual Report of the Berkshire/Hathaway Company." 1965-1987.

Bernstein, Irving. *The Lean Years, 1920-1923.* Boston: Houghton Mifflin, 1972.

Bianco, Anthony. "Why Warren Buffett is Breaking His Own Rules." *Business Week.* April 15, 1985.

Buffett, Warren E. "Early Fears About Index Futures." *Fortune.* Dec. 7, 1987.

Copeland, Melvin. *The Cotton Manufacturing Industry of the United States,* Cambridge: Harvard University Press, 1912.

Dunwell, Steve. *The Run of the Mill.* Boston: David Godine, 1978.

Georgianna, Dan. "Here We Come Thousands Strong." *Spinner: People and Culture in Southeastern Massachusetts.* Vol. II, 1982.

Gutman, Herbert G. *Work, Culture and Society.* New York, 1966.

Hough, Henry B. "The Wamsutta of New Bedford." New Bedford, 1946.

Isherwood, William. "Cotton Processing From Bale to Cloth." Unpublished manuscript, copyright, William Isherwood.

Kanner, Bernice. "Warren Buffett — Meet the Smartest Investor." *New York.* April 22, 1985.

Loomis, Carol. "The Inside Story of Warren Buffett." *Fortune.* April 11, 1988.

Train, John. *The Midas Touch: Strategies that made Warren Buffett America's Pre-eminent Investor.* New York: Harper and Rowe, 1987.

Wolfbein, Seymour. *The Decline of a Cotton Textile City: a study of New Bedford.* New York: AMS Press, 1944.

Young, T. M. *The American Cotton Industry: a study of Work and Workers.* London: Scribner, 1903.

Index

Spinner Membership

Spinner Publications is a non-profit organization which relies on the support of the community and on groups interested in promoting cultural enrichment in Southeastern Massachusetts. In addition to publishing books on our cultural heritage, we present programs in the community such as curriculum development in the schools, photography and art exhibitions, film showings and a lecture series. We have also organized a textile museum and archives which we hope will flourish and serve local residents and scholars.

With public support, we will continue publishing a variety of works and provide working opportunity for area writers and artists.

You can be a part of this effort by becoming a Spinner Member. Spinner Members receive introductory gifts, subscriptions, invitations to all our openings, and discounts on all publications and photographs.

SUSTAINING MEMBER $100.00
- Have your name printed on a special acknowledgement page in the next *Spinner* volume, and receive
- A numbered hard cover edition
- A copy of the oral history magazine *History Spoken Here*
- 20% discount on *Spinner* publications and photographs
- A Lewis Hine archival photograph and forthcoming New England Fisherman Calendar

SUBSCRIBING MEMBER $50.00
- Receive a hard cover edition of the next *Spinner* volume
- A copy of the oral history magazine *History Spoken Here*
- A Lewis Hine archival photograph and forthcoming New England Fisherman Calendar

SUPPORTING MEMBER $25.00
- Receive a soft cover edition of the next *Spinner* volume
- A Lewis Hine archival photograph and forthcoming New England Fisherman Calendar

For more informaton on Spinner Membership and on all our publications, please write.

Other Publications Produced by

Spinner Publications
P.O. Box C-801
New Bedford, MA 02741

☐ **New Bedford: A Pictorial History**
A 240-page illustrated history tracing the city's history from 1602.

☐ **A Picture History of Fairhaven**
A 220-page illustrated history of the town featuring well-known local authors.

☐ **History Spoken Here**
An oral history magazine written by junior high school students.

☐ **The New England Fisherman Calendar Series**
Featuring 13 large photographs depicting the history of New England's harvesters of the sea.

☐ *Spinner: People and Culture in Southeastern Massachusetts, Volume I*
Featuring neighborhood, ethnic history, farming and industry.

☐ *Spinner: People and Culture in Southeastern Massachusetts, Volume II*
Folklore essays, photography, oral history and featuring regional culture and history.

☐ *Spinner: People and Culture in Southeastern Massachusetts, Volume III*
Features Lewis Hine photography, industrial and ethnic history, cranberries and fishing.